What people are saying about …

Come and See

"I love Todd Wagner, his family, and Watermark Church. With people in large numbers giving up on the church, I love that Todd still loves it. So do I. If you want to have hope for Christ's church, dig in to this thoughtful, well-written, and engaging book. Come and see the Jesus who adores his church and can still make her a wonder to behold."

Randy Alcorn, author of *Heaven, If God Is Good*, and *Managing God's Money*

"Todd Wagner is one of the most effective Christian leaders I've ever known. In his new book, *Come and See*, he extends a gospel-centered invitation to the local church to trust Jesus in every aspect of our lives and worship. This book will equip older saints, brand-new believers, veteran pastors, new church members, and really, all of us."

Russell Moore, president of Ethics and Religious Liberty Commission of the Southern Baptist Convention

"Todd Wagner has a prophetic urgency for the church to rise up to its vocation. How many other churches do you know where people get dis-membered and re-membered every year? If it's been a while since you've felt the depth of God's calling on the church—or on your own life—you might want to come and see."

John Ortberg, senior pastor of
Menlo Church, Menlo, CA

"Todd Wagner has this way of delivering truth with a straightforward, no-nonsense clarity and simplicity that leaves you feeling hit between the eyes and loved at the same time. This book is no exception. Todd's love for the Scriptures and, especially, its Author is inspiring and contagious. His trust of the Scriptures and, especially, its Author is downright challenging."

John Stonestreet, president of the Colson
Center for Christian Worldview

"Todd Wagner has a burning passion to see the local church become all that Jesus has called her to be. With clarity and conviction he paints a picture of believers who actually are the church rather than merely going to church. *Come and See* will both challenge and inspire you to do your part to help the church be all she's supposed to be."

Larry Osborne, author and pastor of
North Coast Church, Vista, CA

"In *Come and See* we have a book that makes much of God, His Church, and His mission that is wrapped in both boldness and grace. This is the kind of book both believers and seekers should be reading."

Matt Chandler, teaching pastor of
The Village Church and president of
Acts 29 Church Planting Network

"Helpful. Accessible. Freeing. Our God is an inviter. I'm so grateful for Todd Wagner and the way he shares God's invitational heart and passion to see people come alive in Jesus. *Come and See* is a must-read for anyone, at any point, on their journey to Jesus—from the newborn believer to the seasoned leader looking for a resource to help bring others along. This is a book you'll want to keep close by."

Louie Giglio, pastor of Passion City
Church, founder of Passion Conferences,
and author of *Goliath Must Fall*

come & see

Everything You Ever Wanted in the
One Place You Would Never Look

todd wagner

with john driver

David C Cook®

transforming lives together

COME AND SEE
Published by David C Cook
4050 Lee Vance Drive
Colorado Springs, CO 80918 U.S.A.

David C Cook U.K., Kingsway Communications
Eastbourne, East Sussex BN23 6NT, England

The graphic circle C logo is a registered trademark of David C Cook.

The website addresses recommended throughout this book are offered as a
resource to you. These websites are not intended in any way to be or imply an
endorsement on the part of David C Cook, nor do we vouch for their content.

Details in some stories have been changed to protect
the identities of the persons involved.

Unless otherwise noted, all Scripture quotations are taken from the New American
Standard Bible®, copyright © 1960, 1995 by The Lockman Foundation. Used
by permission. (www.Lockman.org). Scripture quotations marked ESV are taken
from the ESV® Bible (The Holy Bible, English Standard Version®), copyright ©
2001 by Crossway, a publishing ministry of Good News Publishers. Used by
permission. All rights reserved; and NLT are taken from the *Holy Bible*, New Living
Translation, copyright © 1996, 2007 by Tyndale House Foundation. Used by
permission of Tyndale House Publishers, Inc., Carol Stream, Illinois 60188. All
rights reserved. The author has added italics to Scripture quotations for emphasis.

LCCN 2017933743
ISBN 978-0-7814-1488-3
eISBN 978-1-4347-1114-4

Published in association with the literary agency of Wolgemuth & Associates, Inc.

The Team: Tim Peterson, Keith Jones, Amy Konyndyk,
Jack Campbell, Susan Murdock
Cover Design: Nick Lee
Cover Photo: Getty Images

Printed in the United States of America
First Edition 2017

1 2 3 4 5 6 7 8 9 10

071417

*This book is dedicated to the thousands of
friends who, like I do, call Watermark their
spiritual home and who so patiently admonish,
encourage, and help me more fully experience
the Life I have always wanted. You all are
living examples of all that I have written about.
May the Lord multiply your kind all over the
earth. Ultimately however, it is dedicated to
and especially an expression of thanks to the
kind Father who is forever for me, whose Son
was given for me, and whose Spirit provides
everything I need to know and make known all
that is Life indeed. May you alone be glorified in
this work, and may millions more come and see
the goodness and grace that exist only in You.
To the first I am temporally and to the
latter I am eternally thankful.*

Contents

Author's Note

Before you turn to the first "real" pages of this book, let me address a few things about the journey we are about to take together. Years ago, when I was first approached by some publishers about writing a book, I offered to do so *if* they would agree to entitle it *The Book You Should Not Read*. You likely aren't surprised that their marketing department was not wild about the idea.

My pitch was that the book would be about the beauty, sufficiency, perfection, and life-giving goodness of the Word of God. It was a Truth that had taken me a long time to learn, and it is a Truth to which I now gladly commit to respond for the rest of my lifetime. My reasoning was simple: if there is any book you should read through, pray in, live out, and pass around, *that* would be the book I would want to write. And since that book had already been written, I didn't think it to be wise to write a book that did anything but commend you to other one … and the beauty, sufficiency, perfection, and life-giving goodness of the gospel of Jesus that it celebrates from beginning to end. With that little bit of history, it might be easier for you to understand the structure and flow of the book you now find in your hands.

First of all, as the pages begin to pile up to your left, you will notice that more and more footnotes will pile up at the bottom. I know this is not always a common thing to see in a book like this one. But the reason for this is simple: I want you to see where every crazy thing I'm about to say comes from. In other words, I am not offering steps to the life you have always wanted out of my own wisdom; rather, I want to share with you Truth from the ages. Tried. Tested. Trustworthy. Proven. Truth I have experienced and Truth I am experiencing. Know then that the references in these footnotes are not meant to be passed over. Instead, it is my hope that reading *this* book will make you want to read the other.

Secondly, much of what I will say to you—especially in the beginning—may sound completely ridiculous to you, as some un-realistic, high-minded ideology that simply cannot work in "real" life or in communities of real people. I assure you it can, and I would absolutely love for you to come and see this book fleshed out where I live. However, my greatest joy, and what I pray for even more, is that you would pursue these same things with your friends where *you* live so that you would soon come to experience for yourself the life for which you were created. If this book doesn't produce hundreds, if not thousands, of communities who experience what we are experiencing, it will have missed its purpose and the prayers that have accompanied my writing will have fallen short of their intention. What you read are not just my thoughts; instead, the stories and ideas discussed are only a few of the unfathomable modern-day miracles that are happening each and every day in the lives of those who have come and seen what I hope these pages will show you.

If it is happening in them, then why not you, and why not now?

Come and see with me,

Todd Wagner

Chapter 1

Trust Me

Something went terribly wrong.

What was supposed to be a Saturday afternoon adventure initiated by a loving dad soon became a lifelong memory for my entire family. It began with a short bike ride with my two oldest daughters, Ally and Kirby, who were five and three years old, respectively, at the time. I strapped them into the bike trailer, and we were off to a living candy land where they could choose anything their little hearts wanted.

In reality, this "candy land" was only a local convenience store with a large candy section, but to them—and with a little help from Dad's verbal skills—it seemed like Willy Wonka himself had invited them to his factory. Their innocence, coupled with the total confidence that only children can have in their daddy's words, had left them completely captivated. A few turns and a short ride later, we finally found ourselves walking down the largest candy aisle on our side of Dallas.[1]

I had promised them that they could each pick out anything they wanted. I had also assured them that I, in all my decades-old candy-consuming expertise, was there to help. Fullness of joy and pleasures forever … I assured them that all this would be theirs *if* they would only let me help them. "Stick close and trust me," I said. "I know where all the good stuff is." All I wanted to do was bless them. I wanted nothing from them other than the privilege of sharing with them my life, my resources, and my love of all things good.

"Come and see," I promised, "that no good thing is withheld from those who love me."

When we were finally inside and standing before the seemingly endless aisles of options, they were appropriately impressed— M&M's, Spree, Starburst, candy bars of every kind, gummy bears, and buckets of gum surrounded them like water surrounds fish.

There was only one problem: they were both so little that they could only really see the lower shelves, and anyone who has been to a big candy store knows they don't put the best stuff down low. Down low is where the penny candies, single-wrapped Laffy Taffy, and individual Jolly Rancher candies live.

To my three-year-old, this was not a problem. It was an opportunity. She was certain that she knew the way to the good life and

---

1   Clearly this was before the days of Buc-ee's, which is best described as a gas station/convenience store the size of a small mall with candy aisles proving everything is bigger in Texas.

that she needed no further revelation from her "there is no way he can know what is good for me better than I know for myself" father. She immediately fixated on a certain piece of candy conveniently located on her level—the bottom shelf—and then brought it into the clutches of her sweet and ever-so-confident little fingers.

Her choice was seemingly perfect for a three-year-old. It was pleasing to the eye, bright red with yellow designs, round, and impulsively easy to reach. She was also oblivious to the fact that it only cost a few cents and that even though it was pleasing to the eyes, it would not be pleasing to her palate. She couldn't see that her self-confident choice was actually keeping her from the even greater things available if she would just set her mind on the things above and listen to the one who created her.

I honestly had not yet paid much attention to Kirby's choice of candy because Ally, my five-year-old, was engaging me in her selection process and was therefore having a much different experience from her little sister. Ally was not content to pick from the shelves she could see. She knew me better than her little sister because she'd had two more years of relationship with me. She knew I was able to use my strength to lift her up to places she could not otherwise go. And she knew that I *knew* candy.

She knew that anything with her daddy involved was going to be better than going it alone. So instead of reaching out for the easiest choice, she reached out for her daddy's hand. I was always ready to take that hand—and the little person attached to it—into my arms and carry her to better places than she could ever go otherwise.

I lifted her up, and we began perusing the upper shelves where the choices were more plentiful and much, much bigger than the lower shelves offered. She asked me lots of questions, and I shared with her lots of warnings and promises about what each choice would give her. I listened to her describe her confectionery desires, and she listened to me describe the best way to satisfy them. It wasn't long before we chose together a three-and-a-half-pound bag of Skittles.

Meanwhile, I was frequently looking over at Kirby, and I kept assuring her that there was another strong arm willing and eager to scoop her up as well, but it was becoming increasingly obvious that she was passionately committed to her own appetites. She clearly did not understand that "her ways were not my ways" and that my ways were far better … as high as the candy packaged in pounds is over the individually wrapped candy, my ways were better. Each time, she said, "No." She seemed full of self-confidence as she instead showed me the piece of candy she had chosen all by herself.

I tried many times patiently to talk her out of her choice, but it was clear that she had made up her mind. I told her that even though what she had chosen looked good and satisfying, I was certain (as an expert in the field) that it was not what she really wanted. I kept offering to take her up in my arms and help her find something that would be far better—something of greater value—something that would bless her for more than a fleeting moment. But she was resolute … and since I had given her a choice of anything she wanted, that was that. I told her that she was free to make her choice but she was not free to choose her consequences. That bright red candy was hers if she wanted it, but it was also going to be hers to eat.

When we left the store, Ally opened her oversized bag of Skittles and rustled around within looking for a red piece of candy of her own. She had quite a few red pieces, but they were *all* clearly smaller than Kirby's one red piece. Kirby's face beamed with pride as she grew more confident not only that had she chosen the best red candy there was *and* that she had made a better choice than her big sister but also that her choice (despite rejecting her father's offer to help) was going to make her happy.

As Ally quietly chewed on one Skittle and then another, her little mouth experiencing a rainbow of flavors in ever-increasing, sugar-infused bliss, Kirby opened her big red piece of candy and quickly popped her brilliant choice into her mouth. For a few seconds, the world was as it should be. The thin layer of sugar that covered the outside of her candy choice was indeed sweet, and the size of the knot as she hid it in her cheek was much more impressive than Ally's little Skittles, which quickly disappeared within her mouth. With each Skittle that Ally consumed, Kirby's three-year-old self became increasingly confident that her own understanding was better than mine.

At least for about three seconds.

Slowly at first, but then with increasing speed, the confident expression on her face and the satisfaction of her choice began melting away. After a few brief seconds of smug satisfaction, discomfort gave birth to displeasure, which quickly initiated a reflex to discharge the Atomic Fireball from her mouth like a little red cannonball.

Seconds of pleasure had morphed into lingering pain.

Lesson learned.

Hot cinnamon is not kind to a three-year-old tongue, and so three-year-old hearts would be wise to listen to their kind thirty-year-old fathers.

My Father knows where the good stuff is.

My Father wants His children to have the best.

My Father has a higher and better view of things than His children have.

And above all, my Father is someone who can be and should be trusted.

The Cost of Trusting Not

Something has gone terribly wrong.

What was supposed to be a long life full of goodness and pleasures forever has turned into something else altogether. An overconfident world has chosen to embrace a way that seems right to them only to find out things have not gone right at all. A tragedy is happening where triumph should live. Something that was supposed to make the Creator of the universe more famous is instead making many people think He has failed. What is supposed to be *attractive* to us is instead *detracting* from His beauty.

But all is not lost.

In the midst of the burning emptiness that so many of God's children are experiencing, there is an offer to help. There exists a path back into the Father's arms where He wants to lift us up, bring us healing, and remind us of the hope that His divine love is still present and available to us. His strong arms are ready to hold us near to Him. His kind voice waits to remind us that all we are looking for can actually be found by reminding ourselves that a loving Creator is still on the lookout for us.

This book exists to remind you that God is alive and well—and still doing the same amazing things you vaguely remember hearing about in long-ago-told, too-good-to-be-true stories. In fact, what if I told you that just within my small circle of friends in the city where I live, more miracles have occurred in the last few months than in all of the long-ago stories from Jesus's days combined?

Even better, what if I told you that the "miraculous" occurrences often celebrated on obscure TV channels late at night have little to do with what I am talking about? What if you discovered that while miracles are supposed to be awe-inspiring evidences that God is still there and still at work, they were never supposed to be the kind of nonsense being embraced by false teachers who want you to plant a financial "seed of faith" today so you can experience abundant financial blessing tomorrow?[2]

Would you keep reading if I told you that the mundane rituals that define most people's *religious* experience are more a result of us compromising truth instead of living in it? What if I told you

---

2   I am intentionally not yet giving full details here, so if you are a skeptic, don't let me lose you before you let me explain what I mean. And if you are a "God is still in the business of doing first-century miracles" kind of friend, I look forward to being more specific about what I am talking about. I have an entire chapter explaining what Jesus meant when He said "even greater works than these will He do" coming, so stay tuned.

the reason you are not experiencing more of God's kind intention for you and your city is actually something *you* can do something about? And what if the time we are going to spend together in the pages ahead is a key part of you doing that something? Would you be surprised to learn that the reason the miraculous is still happening today is because Jesus *is* who He said He is and He actually meant everything He said? What if I told you God's glory and your good have always been a part of God's plan ... and that His plan for both actually involves both you and the Church?

You would probably roll your eyes.

Not that many years ago, I would have too.

But my reality has changed, and I believe as you read this book and are informed or reminded of the fullness of His truth, yours will be too. In just the last few years, I have personally been a part of a group of friends who have watched bar crawlers, housewives, drug addicts, sex addicts, addicts to self, atheistic philosophers, materialists, driven workaholics, homosexuals, cultural Christians, abortionists, drug dealers, homeless men, impoverished million-aires, promiscuous women, unfaithful husbands, dead religionists, liars, predators, strippers, modern-day Pharisees, pornographers, fallen church leaders, prisoners—and a whole host of others[3]—experience something so completely transformative that they are now living radically different lives full of hope, transparency,

---

3   This is not a made-up list. It is a partial one. There are names I know attached to every one of these labels. Even better, I have been an eye-witness to their sustained transformation from societal destruction and self-destruction to life.

boldness, freedom, and joy. What if I told you that you could be—no, *should* be—a part of something like that?

That, my friend, is the *real* question.

In the pages ahead, I hope to convince you that you should not only want a life like this but also that you actually *can* have a life like this. Even more incredibly, I am going to either inform you or remind you that the way you can be a part of such dramatic life change is by fully investing in something that, for most people, seems full of anything but the life you seek. If the words I write do their job, they will provide you with a compelling picture of the means through which these kinds of occurrences are actually intended to happen—and are happening—every day.

Come and see.

Chapter 2

Sweet Lies

The Atomic Fireball story has lingered in our family lore because it is about so much more than just candy. It is a story about a then-thirty-something father who needed to be reminded—through the blessing of parenting—of his own need to trust his much wiser, "My ways are not your ways ... as far as the heavens are above the earth so are My thoughts higher than your thoughts ... there is a way which seems right to man but in the end it is the way of death ... lean not on your own understanding ... no good thing do I withhold from those who love Me"[1] Father.

As I had time to reflect later that day, I was gently reminded of how *I* am prone to drift into my own moments where I live as if I do not believe my loving, perfect Father really knows and loves the good stuff.[2] I too often think like a three-year-old kid in a candy store, convinced that if God really loves me, He will just let me have what I want. I have constantly reached for that which has thin

---

1   Isaiah 55:8–9; Proverbs 14:12; Proverbs 3:5; Psalm. 84:11.
2   Psalm 16:11.

layers of sugary sweetness (after all, that is what makes temptation so tempting) but which *always* leaves a burning aftertaste. And trust me, I have learned that the older we become, the candy we choose costs us more than a mere three-second sting in the mouth.

In the journey of the pages to come, we will traverse a diversity of paths, but all of them will in some way relate to the basic goodness of the Father and His desire to *bless you*. I am not talking about "your best life now" kind of blessing, as it is commonly portrayed by those who promise health, wealth, and prosperity in ways clearly inconsistent with the Scriptures. I am talking about a richness of life that fills and sustains your soul in even the most difficult times of famine, poverty, and sickness.

I am talking about the life of purpose, hope, strength, and meaning that Jesus Himself describes as "the abundant life."[3] I am going to share stories of how the Father, in His kindness, has allowed me and many others I know to live in the "sense of awe"[4] that always accompanies the divine. I am going to remind you that God wants the same—more, in fact—for you. I am going to make the case that this kind of life for each of us can only be experienced within the right kind of faith community, and I am going to make the case that this life is only available to you when you avail yourself to all of who Jesus is and to all of the means of grace He makes available to you.

But before we go there, we must go *here* first. We must enter the candy store of options in this world and choose to take a long,

---

3   John 10:10.
4   Acts 2:43.

hard look at the way we interact with the One who is offering us top-shelf goodness.

If you're like me, there's a good chance you have struggled—perhaps only *some*times or perhaps at *all* times—to trust God enough to catch a glimpse of what exactly it is He wants you to see from His vantage point. As a leader of people, I often hear others say that (and more often observe people behave like) they just do not or cannot trust God. How could they? Their mouths are still burning from the pain of what they have either invited (or have had shoved) into their mouths. They don't understand how a loving God could allow such circumstances … even if those circumstances are direct results of their rejection of the counsel of a loving Father.

It has been my experience that, in the end, *every* problem we face is directly tied to our questioning of the goodness of God. Show me a person—or a world—whose mouth is burning, and I will show you those who think they know where the best and most fulfilling candy is. I should know—at one time or another, I've chosen my own "sweets." I know, and I am guessing you may also know, that when we buy into the lie that God is not a truly loving, good, powerful, attentive Father who wants nothing more than for it to "go well with you,"[5] we have bought a fireball of trouble.

Kirby did not want my help because somewhere within her psyche, which is simply the Greek word for "soul," she did not really believe I desired the best for her. Her soul did not trust me in that moment; and whether it was because her young age had

---

5   Deuteronomy 4:40.

not afforded her the chance to walk with me long enough to learn to trust me or because innate rebellion and self-confidence haunt every daughter of Eve (and every son of Adam), she was—at her core—a fireball chooser.

The *bottom line* was that she only had *bottom-shelf* trust ... and that, my friends, never works out well for anyone. But what is an expected behavior for a three-year-old should not be the continual habit for healthy adults. Still, the rebellious child inside of each of us seems always to want to doubt God's intentions even as we overestimate the brilliance of our own intuitions.

One wise man said it this way: "For though by this time you ought to be teachers, you have need again for someone to teach you the elementary principles of the oracles of God, and you have come to need milk and not solid food. For everyone who partakes only of milk is not accustomed to the word of righteousness, for he is an infant. But solid food is for the mature, who because of practice have their senses trained to discern good and evil."[6]

If our time in these pages accomplishes what I intend, both of us will be wiser for it. I sincerely desire that the words we share (in *my* writing and in *your* reading) will "mature" you and me to a place where our "senses are trained to discern" that God's ways are always good because *He* is good ... and that our self-reliance is never a good idea because we are not—not self-reliant, that is.

Herein lies the bottom-line truth to the sweet life: *our own bottom-shelf choices lead to our own bitter lives.*

---

6   Hebrews 5:12–14.

One of the greatest college coaches who ever lived said it this way: "There is a choice you have to make in everything you do. So keep in mind that in the end, the choice you make, makes you."[7] Or as Jim Elliot, a man who gave his life in an attempt to share this truth with those who had never heard it, famously said, "God always gives His best to those who leave the choice with Him."

Amazingly, even after years of suffering through sour lives, the same lies that have always pulled us away from God's best are still finding their way into our thinking. The same liar has always used the same lies, and he has done so with largely the same success. Pay attention to the next paragraph, and you will hear a familiar hiss that our Eden-dwelling first parents also heard.

"And he [the serpent] said to the woman, 'Indeed, has God said, "You shall not eat from any tree of the garden"?' The woman said to the serpent, 'From the fruit of the trees of the garden we may eat; but from the fruit of the tree which is in the middle of the garden, God has said, "You shall not eat from it or touch it, or you will die."' The serpent said to the woman, 'You surely will not die! For God knows that in the day you eat from it your eyes will be opened, and you will be like God, knowing good and evil.'"[8]

Take note of his tactics: "Did God really say that?" It's a simple *question*, but its *intention* is to lead Eve—and us—to *question* God's *intentions*. The liar always wants us to doubt God's goodness and to reject God's words of life for us. He tempts us with questions accusing God's character—questions like "What do you mean by

---

7   John Wooden.
8   Genesis 3:1–5.

'no good thing does He withhold from those who love Him'? This fireball-colored fruit pretty much disproves that! Look, here's the deal: God knows something good that you don't know—and He's trying to keep that goodness from you."

"God just cannot be trusted," says the venomous salesman.

This is the first lie: *God is not good. Trusting Him is a mistake.*

And the liar is not finished. In fact, he is just getting started.

He wants to undermine who your Father is because, once you doubt someone's heart, it is a short walk to also reject everything they say. With the groundwork of character assassination already accomplished, the enemy moves his focus to playing word games. Any parent knows that communication is the key not only to keeping our children safe but also to building meaningful relationships with them. Yet the lying one slithers into the picture with age-old doubts about what God has spoken. "God said what? Really? Come on … that's never going to happen! And if you don't believe me, just look here: I have my hands all over this thing you aren't supposed to touch and nothing is happening to me."[9]

This is the second lie: *God's Word is not true.*

The last deception comes in the form of a dare—a culmination of the previous two lies compelling us to act. "Since God does not have your best interests at heart and since you can't believe or trust

---

9   The poor teaching and communication of Adam is what sets up this
    lie. Bad teaching and poor leadership is at the root of *a lot* of problems.
    Contrast what God said to Adam in Genesis 2:17 with what Eve appar-
    ently heard or understood from Adam in Genesis 3:3, and note that God
    did not say they could not touch, only that they could not eat. Adam's
    adding to God's words with the restriction not to touch may have helped
    set Eve up to think God's words should not be trusted.

what He has said, then you should do whatever you want. Don't trust Him; trust yourself. Besides, making your own decisions makes you more like God in the first place. This isn't going to cost you your life … it's going to let you experience it for the first time."

This is the third lie: *disobeying God is not that big of a deal.*

The story did not go so well for Eve because it turns out that taking advice from a serpent who wants to kill you over the advice of a Father who wants to love you is a pretty big deal—like "the fall of man" big. And ever since that moment, we have all taken big falls, because we have all believed these little lies. And every time, there is a little sweetness followed by a lot of pain. And, like Kirby's, that pain may not always be immediate, but you can be sure it is imminent.[10]

The bottom shelf may seem right, and it is certainly easy to see and take hold of, but that doesn't always make it right or worth holding onto. The guilt. The broken relationships. The addictions. The meandering without purpose. The lies on the bottom shelf do not quench our thirst; they only lead us deeper into the desert. "There is a way which seems right to a man, but its end is the way of death."[11]

---

10   One of the cruelest things about sin is that sometimes the amount of "sugar" covering the reality is a little thicker than other times, so we "suck" a little harder and longer. But make no mistake—even when the pain of rebuke doesn't hit us quickly, the problem is still there. Solomon observed this long ago when he said, "Because the sentence against an evil deed is not executed quickly, therefore the hearts of … men among them are given fully to do evil" (Ecclesiastes 8:11). Don't make the mistake of being fooled into fully—or even partially—doing evil. Trust your Father. He is good. He loves you, and disobeying Him always leads to a burning mouth.

11   Proverbs 14:12.

It's Your Choice

I do not necessarily expect you to believe me just because I am saying it, but I do ask that you allow me to plant another thought in the recesses of your mind—a truth to savor so you won't be seduced by savory lies. If you spend any amount of time with me, you will hear these words spill out of my mouth.

God is not looking to rip you off … He is looking to set you free.

This is my way of saying that God is good and that He can be trusted. It is my way of not walking in the counsel of the wicked, standing in the path of sinners, nor sitting in the seat of scoffers, but delighting myself in the law of the Lord. It is my way of seeking to meditate on it day and night.[12] It is my simple reply to the steady lies that continue to come my way.

Yes, I know what you've heard. Yes, I know what you've felt. Yes, I know how you've hurt. Perhaps you've even wondered what kind of loving God would even provide such a choice that would allow people to choose so much pain.

My daughter Ally once asked me the same question. I told her to consider what life would be like if she just lived with the dolls in her room. She could spend the rest of her life in that little space with her plastic and plush friends having tea parties and exchanging pleasantries. She could make them play with her. They would never hurt her and never leave her. They would always say yes to any idea she wanted to offer. They would offer no moodiness, no betrayal, no disappointment.

12　Psalm 1:1–2.

No disappointment, that is, unless you're disappointed that there is also no love. Why? Because conscious love only comes from conscious choices.

Her friend down the street, on the other hand, would cause her trouble. She would be able to reject her, make fun of her, abandon her for "better" best friends, speak poorly of her, and even hate her. But her friend also had the ability to do what dolls—or a preprogrammed humanity—could never do. She could love her.

Even a five-year-old realized it was worth the risk of getting hurt in order to be loved. She told me so back then and has since walked that path well into her twenties—even to the extent that she was willing to walk down an aisle and risk having someone break her heart like no heart ever deserves to be broken. All of this risk and reward exists for her—and for us—because we are made to love and be loved. We are made in the image of the perfect lover.[13]

That is why the Father has given us these choices. Yes, we have all chosen to hurt Him, but we can also all choose to love Him. God is not making us love Him—we get to choose which shelf we will pick from, His shelf or ours: goodness and mercy[14] or danger and destruction.[15] The Father never intended for us to die. He has always wanted His children to live. There is an enemy who is a liar—and he is the one who has come to steal, kill, and destroy.[16] But you don't have to let his lies deceive you. Your Father

---

13   1 John 4:7–8.
14   Psalms 23:6; 25:10.
15   Proverbs 2:22; 6:27–28; 7:24–27; 9:13–18.
16   John 10:10.

has stooped down[17] to show you just how much He would love to pick you up.

Once, a man named Philip found something so absolutely life-changing and potentially earth-shattering that he just had to share it with his brother, Nathanael. He looked for Nathanael, and when he finally found him, he simply said, "Come and see."[18]

I can imagine Nathanael must have been more than a little skeptical when he heard that his brother's excitement was focused on a "Rabbi," even as I can imagine you might be feeling the same. If you are prone to think that the last place you would ever look for life is in something called "church," you wouldn't be alone. But Philip was certain Nathanael's response was rooted in the fact that he had never met "God's kind of Rabbi," even as I am certain any lack of confidence you might have in what I am describing can only be attributed to your lack of personally experiencing God's kind of church.

Having trusted in a perfect Father's way allows me as "an older sibling" to compel you to allow yourself to be lifted up into a higher set of arms and to gaze into something you simply cannot see from a lower vantage point. We all make choices every day, but these choices—who we are going to follow, who we are going to trust, what we are going to think about our heavenly Father—these are the most important choices any of us will ever make. I live to tell you, as I tell others, that what the Father has for you on the top

---

17   Philippians 2:5–8.
18   John 1:45–46.

shelf is goodness. He is rich in mercy. His way satisfies. *His way is what you have been looking for your whole life.*

Think of a movie you've seen that you know one of your friends will love, but he's skeptical. He's been bored and "hurt" before, having wasted $10.50 and two hours on the last five movies he's seen and walking away feeling disappointed and stupid because he has been swindled again and again by epic movie trailers' manipulated highlights that grossly overpromise and underdeliver on the actual experience.

We've all bought *that* ticket.

Though what if there's a *Braveheart*[19] waiting for you out there, but your past bad movie experiences are keeping you from going to see it … and you need a friend—one who's been there and experienced the best of all that movies promise to deliver—to buy your ticket and inspire and encourage you to come and see what is about to become your favorite movie of all time?

Come and see.

---

19 According to IMDB (www.imdb.com/list/ls000054490/) and my female friends, I need to put *The Notebook* here as another example. And according to my wife, I still need to see it.

Chapter 3

Not a Chance

So is there really a "movie" like this that a Divine Director has made for you not just to see but actually to live out in real life? I certainly didn't believe so and there was no way you could have convinced me to buy that ticket, especially if the word "church" would have been found anywhere on the marquee.

In fact, if you had told me when I was younger that someday I would attend church regularly, I would have denied it. If you had told me that I would someday be a pastor, I would have taken a swing at you. If you had told me that I would someday write a book even remotely related to the topic of what the Church is supposed to be (and that you would be reading it), I would have told you to get some help—significant help—no matter how expensive.

Yet here we are. I'm writing, and you're reading. The Bible calls the Church the bride of Christ. Honestly, it is quite the responsibility to write about someone else's bride—and probably a good way to get punched yourself if you don't do it well. And if that is the case when writing about anyone's bride, how much more true is it when you are writing about the apple of the King of the universe's eye?

When you think about the love of your life, I am guessing it would be fair to speculate that your mind does not immediately run to "church." Mine certainly did not. Yet in the pages ahead, I'm going to make the case that it should.

Everyone wonders if there is a perfect love for them. We want to know who they are, where they are, and what we need to do to find them. This book will answer those questions. I am going to invite you to "come and see" that the One who created you is more anxious for you to find that love than you will ever be to seek it. The God who made you—the *only One* who can truly meet the deepest longings of your restless heart—loves the Church and longs for you to love it … not because He needs you to validate His opinion, but because He knows it will give you *life* if you do.

He's not looking to rip you off … He's looking to set you free.

Perhaps you're reading this and you seldom think about church because when you do, you get bored, bothered, or even downright angry. Maybe your thoughts about it make you want to use words your mom told you never to use, especially in church. Or maybe you think about the church all the time because you are passionately dreaming about what it could be—what you know it should be. Regardless, I know that at some point, you have dreamed about the girl or guy of your dreams. I mean, who hasn't longed for someone who cherishes us, honors and respects us, and brings us intense pleasure? We dream about someone by whom we are highly valued.

These ideas are core to our beings. We tend to consider the possibilities of such things happening only when we meet a certain *person*. Yet most people would never consider such things occurring when we become Jesus's bride. To our great detriment, we do not associate such lofty and intimate ideas with this "thing" called church. Nonetheless, the bride of your dreams is Jesus's bride … and the Guy of your dreams is the Church's groom. You are the bride. He is the groom.[1]

Yet so many who are "the bride" never experience the fullness—the incredible life—that this relationship offers. Why? Surely part of the reason is because we cannot believe it could be true. We know our own brokenness so well that it is hard to imagine someone could love us this deeply—especially Someone who has "searched us and known us"[2] and who is "intimately acquainted with all our ways."[3] It does not require false humility for us to surmise that we would be the last "person" on earth who would be chosen by an all-knowing, all-powerful, beautiful, divine Lover.

But such is amazing grace and the story of rescue and redemption scribbled from the beginning to the end of Scripture. God's Word is not full of God's rules; it is full of His love and plan to rescue, redeem, and reengage with us. History is His story of pursuing us and making us His prize—a prize that is both beautiful and admired by a watching world.

---

1   The very idea of taking a bride or being a groom on earth—what most of us think of as the happiest day of our lives—is a type of the ultimate love only fully found in Jesus's love for His people. See Ephesians 5:25–32.
2   Psalm 139:1.
3   Psalm 139:3b.

But herein lies the rub: the world sees us as we are—prone to wander and prone to leave (or never *really* get to know) the One we love. The world wonders what in the *heaven* God is doing loving us ... and even choosing us to begin with. Additionally, the world is confused when it sees the bride looking like anything but what she should if she is really in love with Him. The unfaithfulness of the bride of Christ is no small problem in this world.

But in spite of all this, the Church—as God intends—is actually the hope of the world. She is beautiful. Life-giving. Stunning. A glory to behold, which is why this book is all about a correct view of her and your part in the picture. God wants to woo your heart and use your relationship with Him to show His goodness and love to others.

It is time we diligently seek to know and understand God's intentions for us. He is ready to tell us. The question is this: Are we ready to listen? God is not One to hide His desire for us. His will is not tucked away somewhere high in the Himalayan Mountains where only a yak and a Sherpa can take us. It is right here. We will never desire to know God's will more than He is willing to reveal it to us. If it is a buried treasure, God has given us the map and shown us the image of what we desire.

So let's dig.

Never Alone

So many books focus on a singular, burning issue within the soul of humankind that plays out in several different questions. *How can I make my life count? How do I get my "best life now"? How do I find the love, purpose, and meaning my soul longs for?*

The answers are *not* found by simply gaining everything we want for ourselves. Instead, they are found in understanding what God wants for us—and in trusting that what He wants for us is to be reconciled to Him so we can also be reconciled to one another. Our Father doesn't just want *my* life to count; He wants *our* lives to count. He wants us to experience a tangible expression of His love from one another.

As hard as it is to get your own life to work, it's even more difficult to get multiple lives to work together, mainly because we can really annoy one another. Making anything plural generally makes everything more complicated. But it also makes everything more fulfilling. Can you name one thing in your life—something healthy, mind you—that is better because you have isolated it from others and hidden it from everyone's view? I can't think of anything, and apparently Solomon couldn't either. He said, "He who separates himself seeks his own desire, he quarrels against all sound wisdom."[4]

We all know good food tastes better and is more enjoyable when shared with good friends. Moments of joy are multiplied when there are others with whom we can laugh and celebrate them. Work is made easier when shared. Sorrows are lighter to carry and burdens easier to bear when others are in the pain with us. And that is why God wants you to know the beauty of His bride.

---

4   Proverbs 18:1.

There are movements afoot today touting a spiritual viewpoint that is completely unsupported by and not celebrated in Scripture. Today, maybe because they have been turned off by their interaction with the "bride," people love to say they don't need the Church. They say that just "me and Jesus" is more than enough. And while it sounds very spiritual, the truth is that it is very heretical.

If that seems too strong a statement, take it up with Jesus—it was His idea. As we're going to discover, His design and intention for the Church are that His people become part of a true community—a true body that is closely connected to one another. Does adding the plural to our singular lives complicate things? Yes. Is that supposed to keep us from pursuing it? No … unless you want less than the life He has promised to give to you.

I know, I know. You've probably heard all this "community, body, connection, blah blah" before. But stay with me. Through the imagery of these paragraphs, I want to help you visualize both the ancient and the modern Church as God Himself intended it to be. If the thought of the Church doesn't thrill your soul, the only conclusion is that the church experience you know is a counterfeit, because the real deal is drop-dead gorgeous. Welcoming. Inspiring. Courageous. Life giving. Awe inspiring. Mesmerizingly beautiful bride. So beautiful that anyone who sees and knows her will be compelled to encourage everyone they know and love to *come and see.*

I know I have my work cut out for me to bring you along so you can see this viewpoint, but that is why I am writing this book and why I am praying for you as I do so. I'm asking you to listen to what God says He wants for you and not to be limited by what you may have only been exposed to yourself.

A great church is not a particular size, nor is she shepherded by a particular kind of human leader. Her greatness is not defined by what kind of physical structure she lives in. Bigger is not always better. A large church functioning outside of the intentions Jesus has for His bride is a bigger mess than a smaller messed-up church.

A great church is beautiful for a very specific set of reasons—and they are probably not the reasons you might expect.

How Would You Describe It?

Luke 15 reveals several stories of how lost things not only matter to God but are also worthy of an all-out search party. It also reveals how found things are worthy of an all-out celebration.

At Watermark, the church I pastor in Dallas, we purpose to take the "mattering," "searching for," and "celebrating" seriously. We know Jesus came to seek and save what is lost,[5] so if we are His disciples, we ought to make it a priority to do the same. We also know the angels rejoice in heaven when even one sinner repents,[6] so we figure it makes some sense to throw a little party ourselves when lost sons and daughters come home.[7]

---

5   Luke 19:10.
6   Luke 15:10.
7   Luke 15:24.

In our community, each of the elementary schools in the area host "carnivals" to help raise extra funding for their schools. Bounce houses. Games. Cotton candy. The works. A friend of mine was driving by one of these fund-raising carnivals when her little girl, who had grown up watching our community of faith celebrate like the angels do in Luke 15 (assuming the angels have bounce houses and like cotton candy … and why wouldn't they?), looked out the car window and exclaimed, "Look, Mom! A church is having a baptism!"

What a different impression of church my little friend Avery had than most of us. The truth is, many people are probably more likely to drive past a funeral home and see a somber family gathered to mourn and say, "Look, Mom! A church!" I am not suggesting that every time we get together we should fill our gatherings with gimmicks and flash so that we will appear relevant and alive. That tactic has been tried and needs to be abandoned. Jesus's bride is not attractive because she is covered in anything cosmetic.

I am talking about true beauty. In Avery's case, what she recognized was a culture of real joy and celebration because, from the beginning of her communal life, she had seen these things in the way God's people gathered and cared for one another.

It's pretty safe to say that if a first-century child riding by on the back of his mom's donkey saw a man stooped over playing with kids, drawing a crowd, filled with laughter, and making "all the little ones feel welcome"—that he might say, "Look, Mom! There's Jesus!" When the world sees these same things today, their first response *should* be, "Look, there's another gathering of those Jesus people!"

Yes, I know we have work to do, and that is why I am writing these words to you.

Too many younger generations have only experienced excitement about what God is doing in the Church when they load buses to ride to environments *away* from their church. We have all observed kids and students who go to camps or conferences and come home thrilled about what they experienced *there*. But once they return *here*, a tragic return to "normal" returns with them. Why? Because *here* looks nothing like *there*. Over time, every impression—good or bad—that they develop about *the* Church is forged and reinforced to them by *their* church. It is no wonder that across the nation, most of them leave *the* Church and *their* churches the moment they graduate from high school.[8]

But I believe that every Spirit-led, biblically informed church should want their kids (and guests and parents and singles—everyone) to see that a biblical, grace-filled, passionate, full, joyful, life-infused, transforming, life-changing, awe-inspiring God is at work *everywhere* His people are—not just *there* at camps and conferences, but also *here* as well. In their homes. In the Church gathered. In the Church scattered about their daily lives.

God wants *their* church—every place His bride is gathered—to be the place where real lives experience real life and real change because they are properly introduced to the living God who is

---

8   Daniel Burke, "Millennials Leaving Church in Droves, Study Finds," CNN, May 14, 2015, www.cnn.com/2015/05/12/living/pew-religion-study/.

still in the business of making Himself known and remaking His people. Church—the people of God—should always be the place where others can come and see what Philip wanted Nathanael to see: a Person (and a people) in which there is no deceit.[9] Paul made it clear that when others really know Christ, they will see love from a pure heart, a good conscience, and a sincere faith.[10]

But this is *not* what church is for many, and it is why too many people have seen all they want. They came, they saw … and they left.

This is not overly insightful—just honest observation. I regularly hear from visiting friends who have never before seen or experienced in *their* church the kind of things I have been describing. They say they are more familiar with either superficial activity or uninspiring ritual. Compromise. Mediocrity. A lack of accountability. Holding to forms of godliness that deny God's power.[11] These are rampant in churches all across America and Europe.

There is no perfect picture of the bride of Christ on earth. Watermark certainly isn't. But I can say that we are a place where you will recognize what God intends for His Church and a place that I joyfully get to invite others to "come and see." I think of my Watermark family like Peter—struggling to keep our eyes on Jesus instead of on the waves.[12] But like Peter, we have also been radically changed through becoming intimately acquainted with Jesus. Like Peter, we have the sense to cry, "Lord, save me!" And

---

9   John 1:47.
10 1 Timothy 1:5.
11 2 Timothy 3:5.
12 Matthew 14:28–31.

not only is He saving us from ourselves, He is also willing to use us as His servants to be a part of His process of saving others.

This book is not about Watermark. It is not about any other one church or denomination either. This is not about *us* at all. That is the point. Our church—and many others out there—are simply experiencing glimpses of what God intends for everyone to *come and see*. What is happening in our midst is what should be happening anywhere God's people gather, because things should be alive and working anywhere God is living and at work.

Full devotion is normal for a believer; being full of faith and power is what should be normal for the Church.

There is a definite disconnect here. People in the culture feel it. People in church leadership feel it. People in the pulpits feel it, as do people in the pews. It is a chasm between what is and what should be. Why do we see such vast differences of culture and Christlike power between people who all claim to believe the same message? Why are some parts of the body full of life and too many others suffering from anemia? It is *not* because God is done with the Church. It is not because the bride of Christ is supposed to be average. It might be because you have never truly met her.

Words mean something—and the words people use to describe their churches or even the concept of church are telling. Too often, when others are asked to describe what their church experience is like, you hear words like "boring," "irrelevant," "hypocritical," and "judgmental." Sometimes they will respond with the name of a certain denomination. An address. A facility. They might even name a personality. A well-known preacher, worship leader, or author.

Why are these the terms associated with church? Because in most cases, these are the only impressions of church we are allowing people to see. I am on a mission to change that—it is not a mission I came up with; it's God's—the "Divine Director's." I'd like to show you *exactly* what He has in mind for this mission … and for your role in it.

Chapter 4

First Church of Ever

When we begin to connect with new people at Watermark, we always start by looking at the first time the bride was introduced to the public.

"They were continually devoting themselves to the apostles' teaching and to fellowship, to the breaking of bread and to prayer. Everyone kept feeling a sense of awe; and many wonders and signs were taking place through the apostles. And all those who had believed were together and had all things in common; and they began selling their property and possessions and were sharing them with all, as anyone might have need. Day by day continuing with one mind in the temple, and breaking bread from house to house, they were taking their meals together with gladness and sincerity of heart, praising God and having favor with all the people. And the Lord was adding to their number day by day those who were being saved."[1]

---

1   Acts 2:42–47.

If the world is looking for a solid description of the Church, here it is. But instead of just listening to the description, I ask my new friends to try *seeing* it instead. I ask them to imagine they are on assignment as a beat writer for the *Jerusalem Times* with the task of observing and reporting about this new community of people who are beginning to create significant buzz around the city. Three thousand people have come to faith in one day,[2] and more are being added daily.[3] People are meeting every single day—not just one day a week—in the temple and in their homes. They are selling their stuff and sharing the profits.

These people are shaking things up and rocking the status quo.

Now imagine you have a friend who is a part of this new community. You ask him to meet you in the local café (the hummus is terrific there) just to get the scoop. After catching up on small talk and niceties, you get right to it.

"What in the world has happened to you?"

"Well, I'm hanging out with a new group of friends."

"Where?"

"Anywhere really. It is not really a place but a group of people."

"What is not a place?"

"The church. Isn't that what you're asking me about?"

"Church? What's *church*? I've never heard of that before."

"Well, it's a community of people who, by God's kindness, have seen Jesus and gather together to love one another and follow in His steps."

---

2   Acts 2:41.
3   Acts 2:47.

"Jesus? Isn't He the guy whom everyone loved but the religious establishment hated? And isn't He dead? Look, I got sent over here to interview you because word on the street is that something very different—very alive—is happening with you people. And again, what is a church?"

At this point, your friend's explanation will not include any mention of a denomination, since those do not even exist yet. "Well, I guess you could say it's called the First Church of ... Ever?" It is also doubtful he will offer up a specific address or location. After all, everyone knows where the southern steps of the temple are and beyond that, the Church is meeting all over the community. *"Walk down any street in Jerusalem, take a left, and then turn ... well, anywhere."* And though Peter did stand up to do the talking on the Day of Pentecost, your friend will not mention a specific individual as the leader. There is broad leadership in the movement led by eleven men, original followers of this said-to-be-dead Jesus guy. That's a whole mess of chiefs, except that they are all letting the personality focus fall on one Chief—Christ Himself.

Their church *then* would not be described using the same adjectives as most people who attend churches *today*. You ask your friend to describe what is going on, and based on what we know was happening from the passage we just read, we can imagine he would say something like this:

"We are alive." Makes sense—their whole way of living had changed. "There are awe-inspiring things happening in our midst." Since signs and wonders were being done through the apostles, that seems like a fair description. "We are attractive." God was drawing many new people to their community—and they were actually coming. "We are aligned." They were steadfast under leadership and in service, gathered with one mind in the temple and in homes. "We are acts-oriented." It's hard to accuse them of being lazy or passive.

"Okay, that's pretty impressive," you say, feeling confident that you have more than enough to submit your article by the deadline. But before you can express your gratitude for his help, he interrupts and keeps going—and in rapid-fire succession this time.

"And we are biblical, blessed, bonded, caring, Christ-exalting, committed, compassionate, connected, consistent, and creative, dedicated, devoted, discerning, disciplined, driven, effective, encouraging, energized, evangelists, exciting, engaging, faithful, focused, friendly, fun, fired up, generous, godly, growing ..."

"Uh, I think that's plenty. And besides, I'm kind of running out of papyrus sheets, so ..."

But he doesn't catch your drift or miss a beat. "We are humble, hungry, hospitable, intentional, inspiring, intimate, intense, joyful, like-minded, loving, magnetic, miraculous, motivated, neighborly, obedient, ordained, others-minded, passionate, powerful, praising, prayerful, proactive, productive, progressive, pure, purposeful, redeeming, radical, real, relationally minded, relevant, respected, sacrificial, safe, scary, selfless, Scripture-loving, servant-hearted, single-minded, sold out, Spirit-filled, sincere, submissive, tenacious, teachable, transformed, trustworthy, thankful, unified, unselfish, unspoiled, unwavering, wholehearted, and wise. We are a people full of wonder who worship God—you should come and join us!"

By this point, the hummus is long gone—and you know you've obliterated your editor's word count. But be honest: If the Church were really all these things—as Scripture says it is—you would definitely be checking it out, wouldn't you?

How could you not?

Picture This

So what happened? Something has gone terribly wrong; *that's* what happened. The description of the first church is supposed to be the description of them all because the Leader of the first church is supposed to be the Leader of them all. The problem isn't that God has stopped being in the business of changing the world by changing lives. The problem is that we have gotten into the business of doing *His* business *our* way, not being "people of *the* Way."[4]

If church, as you think of it today, were truly a reflection of the adjectives we just used to describe it in Acts 2:42–47, my bet is that you would feel differently about it. *A lot* differently. You wouldn't be alone. You might be thinking, *That is the exact kind of community of people I have been looking for. That is the purposeful life I really want to live, but I didn't know it actually existed. What you are describing is what I have been searching for my whole life. In relationships. Clubs. Teams. Work. You name it. So don't mess with*

---

4   Acts 9:2 shows us that early Christians were being referred to as those "of the Way."

me—just tell me: Where does something like this exist? Even though I'm not sure I can believe, just out of curiosity, I'm going to come check it out.

That is exactly what God had in mind—that in this lost, dark, broken world where there are only shadows of hope, a light would enter in. That people would begin to live in real relationships with a real God. That they would be that alive, awe-inspiring, authentic … a worshipful kingdom-of-God-on-earth community.

The Church is supposed to provide others a picture of God's kingdom—a glimpse of heaven on earth. It is not a place you are supposed to *go*; it is a people who are supposed to *be* … and you can still experience what God intends His Church to be. When you see life change, grace, compassion, mercy, sharing, provision, warmth, and hope—with a diligence to preserve the unity of the Spirit in a bond of peace[5]—aren't these at least small descriptions of heaven? Yes, they are. And instead of growing dimmer over the years, the Church is supposed to be growing brighter day by day as we yield more and more to the Spirit's grace, power, and direction. Less of us; more of Him.

From the very beginning, this is what God intended church to be. My goal is to let you be reminded in these pages of what God, who loves you, wants you to experience: a community that is alive, awe-inspiring, attractive, aligned … well, you can go back and reread the rest. God created you for this. Your heart longs for it—even if you have only seen a glimpse of it from a distance. I know that once you begin to experience this kind of

---

5   Ephesians 4:3.

community, you will want to do far more than *attend* at a church building—you will want to find others who are committed to joining you in *being* the Church that Jesus has always wanted to build.

Do any exist? Is that possible? Yes, they do, and yes, it is.

It is my pleasure to awaken your heart to *come and see.*

Chapter 5

Gather 'Round

Don't "Start" a Church

Several years ago, a small group of friends asked me to spend some time with them as they sought counsel about how they might go about "starting" a church. They had met while in college and had become passionate about God's kingdom because they witnessed so many of their friends throwing their faith away in exchange for the lower-shelf fireballs so abundantly available on college campuses.

They wanted something more, so they began to meet with one another to share life together. They counseled each other, prayed for each other, and taught one another the Scriptures. They told more and more people about Jesus and saw many people join them in their pursuit of Christ. They discipled these new believers and continued to gather with them. Then together, they all began reaching out to even more people who did not yet know the depths of the grace Jesus was offering to them.

It didn't take long before between forty and sixty of them were meeting together on a regular basis to encourage and equip one another. Some of them were humbly leading and shepherding others in the group, and they were asking me, "What's next?" They had just graduated, and they wanted to be intentional about making sure the momentum they had experienced during college did not wane as they transitioned into their next season of life.

After hearing their story, I said, "It sounds to me like you already are faithfully being the Church. What do you mean you want to 'start one'?"

Seemingly confused, they replied, "No, we mean we want to know what it would take for us to be ready to meet on Sunday mornings." *Now* I understood what they wanted from me. They thought the last step to legitimizing their group as a church required a change in time and place—specifically to gather on Sunday mornings.

It is true that from the beginning, the first disciples gathered together *not* on Saturday, the traditional Hebrew Sabbath, but rather on Sunday, the first day of the week. This was an early distinctive of *the Way* (as Christians were often called during the first century).[1] They started their week together on Sunday as a way of saying to themselves and to those around them that everything had changed because of the world-altering event that had happened on another Sunday: Christ's resurrection.[2]

---

1   Acts 9:2.
2   Acts 20:7.

Sunday was their day to gather and to collectively remind themselves of God's kindness in giving His Son. They wanted to remember that they didn't have to work to attain His favor but could rest in the hope of the Messiah who had delivered them from the oppression of sin and self—and the destruction that followed. It is finished, so they celebrated that they could know God intimately and not just as some vague idea because, as John said, "we have beheld His glory."[3] He walked in their flesh and paid their debt.[4] He was raised from the dead, so they were no longer dead in their transgressions but were alive in Christ.[5] Sin had lost its sting, and death had lost its victory.[6]

You see,[7] reminding ourselves and encouraging one another with these life-changing realities of grace is the real job of the Church "gathered."

As pastorally as I could, I told these passionate young men, "Don't you dare tell your people that you're going to 'start' a church." The look of continuing and increasing perplexity on their faces asked me the inaudible question of their hearts: *But why?*

So I answered without hearing their question. "Don't reinforce an idea that is causing the Church of Jesus Christ to be useless in this generation. Don't say you are 'starting a church' just because

---

3   John 1:14.
4   Romans 4:25; 1 Peter 3:18.
5   Ephesians 2:5.
6   1 Corinthians 15:55–57.
7   I say "you see" because I hope you will indeed be able to see that from all the previous Scripture references that these were the sentiments of the early disciples. More on this in chapter 6.

you are changing when or where you gather. Based off of what you have told me, you already *are* a church."[8]

Jesus told the woman at the well that the time is coming and is now here when the true worshippers of God will not base their worship experience on certain locations, rituals, or times of gathering.[9] We weren't at a well, but my goal was the same. I did my best to explain to them what I will now do my best to explain to you—the real reasons why the Church should gather.

Let's begin by examining the wrong reasons.

A Deal You Don't Want to Make

I recently shared a meal with several friends who, like me, happened to be pastors in the Dallas area. One of them proposed a gathering—a solemn assembly, if you will—where we would call other pastors and church leaders from across the nation to join us in challenging people to deepen their spiritual walks by moving forward beyond mere membership and into true discipleship. Now I know these labels and terms mean many different things to many different people, but from my understanding of Scripture and

---

8   To be a church, all that is needed is to have a group of people who are committed to Christ, His Word, and one another under godly authority. You need to take care not to forsake your own assembling together, but you also don't need a regular Sunday-morning place to assemble. You need to care for and disciple children in your midst, but you don't need a children's ministry. You need to worship God in Spirit and Truth, but you don't need a guy with a guitar, a V-neck T-shirt, and skinny jeans.

9   John 4:21–24.

what the Bible clearly calls all believers to be, I had to speak up because I saw two big problems.

First of all, they were not addressing the fact that too many churches are simply allowing "believers" to *attend* Sunday services without being *attentive* to the call of Christ on their lives every hour of their week. This has become commonplace and normal. Secondly, they were implying that many churches— maybe even theirs—had "members" who were not actually disciples. I told them that moving most "churched" people from membership to discipleship was avoiding the bigger problem with the American Church throughout our history: the constant consuming of religious services without responding to Christ's call on one's life.[10]

What most people in church really need—and I mean people who think of themselves as believers, not guests or those exploring the faith—is not a move from *membership* to *discipleship*, but rather a drastic move from *attendance* to *membership*.

From God's standpoint, *membership* (connection to His body) is supposed to be synonymous with *discipleship* (connection to Him).

In both the Old Testament and the New Testament, some of the strongest admonitions and warnings in Scripture are given to those who hold "to a form of godliness, although they have denied its power."[11] Don't just take my word for it; listen to what Amos and Isaiah have to say about it.

---

10 Matthew 15:8; 2 Timothy 3:5.
11 2 Timothy 3:5.

"I hate, I reject your festivals, nor do I delight in your solemn assemblies. Even though you offer up to Me burnt offerings and your grain offerings, I will not accept them.... Take away from Me the noise of your songs; I will not even listen to the sound of your harps. But let justice roll down like waters and righteousness like an ever-flowing stream."[12] "'What are your multiplied sacrifices to Me?' says the LORD. 'I have had enough of burnt offerings of rams.... When you come to appear before Me, who requires of you this trampling of My courts? Bring your worthless offerings no longer.... I cannot endure iniquity and the solemn assembly.... They have become a burden to Me; I am weary of bearing them.'"[13]

And if Isaiah and Amos aren't enough, just listen to Jesus. "You hypocrites! Isaiah was right when he prophesied about you, for he wrote, 'These people honor me with their lips, but their hearts are far from me. Their worship is a farce, for they teach man-made ideas as commands from God.' For you ignore God's law and substitute your own tradition.... You skillfully sidestep God's law in order to hold on to your own tradition."[14]

What kind of worship would Jesus consider to be in vain or even a farce? It begins with what I call "The Deal." The Deal is the mostly unspoken arrangement that many modern church leaders have made with modern church "members" (and remember, I am using the term "members" loosely).

---

12   Amos 5:21–24.
13   Isaiah 1:11–16.
14   Mark 7:6–9 NLT.

Basically, The Deal goes like this: members agree to validate pastors and leaders by showing up fairly regularly and agreeing to pay enough offerings to keep the lights on and keep the weekly activity of the church operational. In return, "pastors" agree to preach civil, encouraging, self-help life messages, never asking too much of those attending.

And they both tell each other that they are doing what God wants them to do.

I say all this not to sound judgmental or to indict any church in particular. In fact, if your first inclination is to think of someone else in your life who seemingly lives under The Deal, I challenge you to put them out of your mind, at least for now. In this moment, I want to ask you to examine someone much closer to the subject: yourself.

Whether pastor or attender, are *you* cutting that deal?

What is the unspoken (or spoken) arrangement *you* have with church? Do you think the way you view "church" is in alignment with the way God views His bride as described in Scripture? There is no condemnation here—I promise that by God's grace, these are questions I am always asking myself … and you should absolutely be asking yourself, too, for within the answers lie more than models of various church systems or questions of relevance in style or delivery. The most important reason you should ask these questions *about* the Church is that you are actually supposed to *be* the Church.

So what exactly does "being the Church" mean?

Do You Think?

The answer begins with examining the way we presently view the Church, and I don't mean just philosophically or on the basis of whether or not we are able to use biblical terms when we answer. We may know that the Church is the body[15] and bride[16] of Christ. We may even venture as far as to say that the Church is the light of the world, a city on a hill that cannot be hidden.[17] Some of us may even say with confidence that the Church is so powerful that "the gates of hell shall not prevail against it."[18]

You should say those things ... but you should also be living examples of them.

What we "know" about the Church is only helpful if our knowing turns into our doing. People say what they think, but they do what they believe. The problem most of us run into today is we are around or are a part of a church full of thinkers instead of believers.

People may *say* what they think, but they *do* what they believe.

Your six-year-old child may know that Lucky Charms and chocolate milk are not staples of a healthy diet, but if you leave her alone in the kitchen, this is exactly what she will eat all day every day. If you have a teenager, they may know Whataburger[19] and Dr Pepper aren't the best for them, but follow them around

---

15   1 Corinthians 12:27.
16   2 Corinthians 11:2.
17   Matthew 5:14.
18   Matthew 16:18 (ESV).
19   That's Texan for cheeseburger.

when they have a little extra cash and see what they are eating. You want to get personal? This author knows better than to live on Peanut M&M's, pizza, and Blue Bell ice cream, but don't ask for my food receipts.

What you *do* is more important than what you *know*—whether you know it or not.

One piece of evidence displaying what most people really *think* (not believe) about the Church is found in two commonly used words: "regular attender." It is not a good thing that we have *accepted*—and perhaps also tragically made it *acceptable*—to think that there is such a biblical thing as a "regular attender" in the Church.

Hear me out here. Or better yet, hear Jesus out here. In the words of these pages and every time I speak, all I desire to be is a servant of Christ and a steward of the mysteries of God.[20] I don't want to come to you with superiority of speech or of wisdom; I only want to proclaim to you the testimony of God,[21] so that your faith will not rest in the wisdom of man, but in the power of God.[22]

This means that I love you enough to tell you what God says. What if I suggested that "regular attenders"—*if* they are defined as "believers" who attend church services and events without being attentive to the call of Christ on their lives every other hour of their week—should more accurately be called "irregular believers"?

---

20   1 Corinthians 4:1.
21   1 Corinthians 2:1.
22   1 Corinthians 2:5.

Pause for a moment here. You may be reading this as someone who doesn't know what the Church should look like—so maybe you don't really care what I call these people. Why does it matter? It matters because it affects the beauty and integrity of the bride of Christ whom God wants you to come and see. Trust me—it matters more than you *think*.

Or maybe my suggestion that you are an "irregular believer" stings a bit? Maybe you fall into this culturally acceptable category and you have no idea what would be different if you were a "regular believer." You might be asking yourself: *Now what am I supposed to do? Is this Wagner guy trying to get me to do a lot more stuff? I'm barely holding it together as it is, and now he's telling me that it's not enough?*

My goal is neither to make you feel condemned nor to obligate you to a lifestyle of increased busyness and activity. But I would ask this: If you are barely holding it together now as a "regular attender," do you really think you are experiencing what Jesus has in mind when He calls the Church His beautiful bride,[23] from which He withholds no good thing,[24] who will experience the abundant life,[25] so that she may proclaim the excellencies of Him who has called her out of darkness into His marvelous light,[26] and so that the Church can communicate His boundless grace and liberating truth to the entire world,[27] including *your* family and friends? In other words, church attender or not, does the life you are currently

---

23   Revelation 19:7.
24   Psalm 84:11.
25   John 10:10.
26   1 Peter 2:9.
27   John 8:32.

living accurately reflect what God says will bring glory to Him and abundant joy to you?

If you're not sure how to respond to these questions, then keep reading. I intend to bring you to a place where you can. I hope you are encouraged to know God wants to take you away from a place of personal condemnation, overwhelming tasks, and constant wondering about what you're missing so He can lead you instead into a life full of purpose, unashamed honesty, transformed community, and personal fulfillment as you live out the life He has already prepared for you.[28]

Trust me when I tell you that being a "regular attender" is not where you will find everything you've ever wanted. A distant dating relationship does not bring the same depth of joy, fullness of intimacy, or fulfillment of heart as oneness with a lover brings. It is time to stop dating the idea of following Christ and commit to it.

And be sure of this: *God wants you to be more than a regular attender at an average weekly gathering of mostly bored adults.*

With regular attenders making up a greater percentage of the Church than passionately engaged followers, it is no wonder church is the one place most people would never look to find the life they've always wanted. Regular attenders don't typically gather with gladness and sincerity of heart.[29] They don't have favor with all the people.[30] They don't devote themselves to sound teaching or to pursuing relationships with people from house to house.[31] They

---

28 Ephesians 2:10.
29 Acts 2:46.
30 Acts 2:47.
31 Acts 2:42.

don't contribute to or experience the overwhelming goodness of life found in the many adjectives we explored earlier. In general, they miss out on the sense of awe God intends to exist in them and be made evident through them.

The only explanation for you or me not radically running toward God's best intention for us is that we have not yet come to understand Him personally and fully—the God in whose presence there is fullness of joy and at whose right hand are pleasures forevermore.[32] When you taste and see His real goodness, you don't worry that you have to attend to His business, because you *tend* to want more and more of Him. You will want to drink deeply, my friend, because for the first time in your life, you won't see yourself as the most interesting man or woman in the world … you will finally know *Who* really is.

Ask yourself this question: "If 'fullness of joy' is what God calls me to, why would I want anything else?" Answer? Because we don't really believe that *this* is what God really wants for us. We believe again that age-old lie: God is not really good.

But what if He is actually as good as we "know" He is? If so, then we can really "believe" Him, trusting that the life He calls us to experience will not burden us, but rather bless us beyond measure.

The divine call to come and see invites us to engage wholeheartedly in everything God intends—for when we *live* as God intends us to live, we will be as *alive* as God intends us to be. Soon, we will see that Christ is still doing today exactly what He was

---

32 Psalm 16:11.

doing when He physically walked on the earth: creating stories that gather crowds and keep disciples up late at night reveling in the hope and awe that life with a good and loving God provides.

Those young men who were wanting to "start" a church were already living in the midst of great stories. They really didn't need to "start" anything together; they needed to make sure they didn't "stop" being on mission together. They were already being the Church.

What we all really need has already been started ... and we are being invited to come and see what it really means for us.

Chapter 6

Have a Great Week of Worship

The Reverence in Reminding

For many people, the idea of following Christ is completely wrapped up in having reverence for the time they gather each Sunday—and obviously, I have nothing against being reverent in our Sunday services. But is such a reverence for Sunday really the foundation of who we are as disciples? And even more importantly, if we are "over-revering" this particular component of our Christian experience, are there other crucial, biblically based elements we are "under-revering" elsewhere?

Many people attend churches with solid doctrinal statements and an order of service that feels "reverent" and respectful of God—and maybe even is both these things. But just as Jesus said that there is nothing outside a man that can defile him,[1] there is no

---

1   Mark 7:15.

service we can attend or ritual we can be a part of that can make us reverent. Reverence was never intended to be only an hour of our week or a mere portion of our lives.

Reverence is an attitude of the heart, not an order of service.

Too many of us equate reverence more with an order of Sunday service, not the way we order our daily lives. Certainly our corporate gatherings, the content of our songs, and the quality of our speech should be God-centered and God-honoring. They should each help us remember afresh the greatness of our King, who is eternal, immortal, and invisible—the only God to whom honor and glory belongs forever and ever.[2]

Beyond that, though, we should always ask ourselves: "What exactly is holy here?" Surely it is more than what we say or where we gather to say it. What is actually holy is that when we gather together, we speak of God—and not necessarily using the Queen's English, but rather the King's heart. We speak out that He is loving, kind, compassionate, and filled with grace and truth, that He sees us in our rebellion and darkness, our self-centeredness and brokenness, under the weight of sin and death but that He has come and made provision for us.

When we come together, our time should be spent intentionally reminding ourselves and others of these very specific truths. Even if we already know these things, in essence we are saying, "Let us remind ourselves of *who* we are and *what* we are to do in light of *Whose* we are!"[3]

---

2   1 Timothy 1:17.
3   2 Corinthians 5:14–20.

This, my friend, is what we must consider to be "holy." This is why we gather. This is why we sing. This is why we give attention to the public reading of Scripture, exhortation, and teaching.[4] We must pay close attention to these things, for as we do, we ensure salvation both for ourselves and for those who hear us.[5] This is why we welcome each other and embrace each other—to *remind* ourselves of the freedom and purpose found in the fullness of grace and truth in Christ.

The reminding itself is not the reverence; the reminding is what we do so we ourselves will be reverent in our right responses to God.

It is a mistake that some churches look at other churches as if they don't have a real reverence because of the forms they use to remind themselves of the truth rather than evaluating their faithfulness in functioning as people who actually live these things. It is always a mistake to focus more on how someone expresses God's truth than on evaluating the truth itself.

We should take great pains to be reverent with truth. In fact, we should be absorbed in it, not just so our *declarations* may be true, but also that our *doings* may be right responses to truth. As Paul said, "Until I come, give attention to the public reading of Scripture…. Take pains with these things; be absorbed in them, so that your progress will be evident to all."[6]

---

4   1 Timothy 4:13.
5   1 Timothy 4:16.
6   1 Timothy 4:13, 15.

Gathering together is essential.[7] It is biblical. It is historical. However, what happens as a result of our gathering is inseparable in importance from what we do when we gather. This time of gathering is not where the Church is ultimately *equipped*, nor is it where it is ultimately *defined*. No, gathering is where the Church is ultimately *reminded*.

If we come to a reverent room where we arrive on time and hush our kids but walk out of that reverent moment and live irreverent lives, what we did in that room is a mockery, and God disdains it.[8] Jesus quotes Isaiah when He says, "This people honors Me with their lips, but their heart is far away from Me. 'But in vain do they worship Me, teaching as doctrines the precepts of men.'"

The religious practice of the people described in this passage was incredibly reverent, but it was missing one crucial component: their hearts. It's as if God is saying to His Church, "I wish you would quit coming in here, acting reverent for an hour, and then going out and continuing to divorce one another, squander your time, slander one another, and build up wealth for yourselves in storehouses. You have highly reverent meetings, but you are not highly reverent people."

What makes a church a reverent church—or a worshipping church—is not solely what they do in the hour they are gathered; instead, it's defined also by what they do the other six days and twenty-three hours of the week—by the lives they lead when they are *not* gathered in their largest corporate gathering.

---

7   Hebrews 10:24–25.
8   Amos 5:21–24; Malachi 1:6–10; James 1:22; 1 John 3:18.

Time and Equipping

In most churches, this crucial time of reminding ourselves of His greatness and grace lasts about one hour—sixty minutes—3,600 seconds. That is not a lot of time, especially if your expectation is that all the spiritual equipping you need will be accomplished in this one hour. Make it ninety minutes, and you could say the same thing.

What if your local school told you they could completely educate your child in only one hour per week? Your reaction would probably match mine: no matter how amazing a teacher may be, one hour is simply not enough. If you only eat one hour each week, you won't be very well nourished. If you only work out one hour each week, you won't be very strong.

The same principle applies to our time gathered as the Church. Members should not think that a one- or even two-hour gathering can fully equip them to be the fully devoted followers of Christ who experience "all the adjectives" God biblically intends for all believers. This kind of church paradigm will constantly leave you in need of someone to teach you the elementary principles of the oracles of God ... still needing milk and not solid food.[9] In other words, you'll be malnourished and generally ill-equipped.

Gathering on Sundays is not the primary purpose of the body of Christ at all, even though it is where most Christians and churches place their primary energies. No, the principal, biblical task of the Church is to make disciples. It is about

---

9   Hebrews 5:12.

making, not *meeting*. Making disciples is a whole different animal than a one-hour meeting. Making disciples is a process. It's about life together in submission to His Spirit and attentive to His Word. Among many other things, it's about learning, living authentically together, confessing, and being "filled with the knowledge of his will in all spiritual wisdom and understanding, so as to walk in a manner worthy of the Lord, fully pleasing to him: bearing fruit in every good work and increasing in the knowledge of God."[10]

On Watermark's very first Sunday gathering, I spoke about this exact topic, emphasizing that we cannot define worship as the time we gather corporately. Rather, worship should be viewed as a right response to everything we believe about Christ that then compels us to do everything we do with our lives.[11] When we came to the end of our time together, the last words from my mouth as we "scattered" to go live faithfully in our families, communities, schools, workplaces, and travels were these: "Have a great week of worship!" Even though I did not plan to say those words that first Sunday, I have intentionally said them every week since.

The Church gathers *regularly* so that it will scatter *rightly*. We gather to worshipfully remember;[12] we scatter to worshipfully live.[13]

---

10   Colossians 1:9–10 ESV.
11   Romans 12:1.
12   1 Corinthians 11:23–26.
13   Colossians 3:17, 23.

This is not a legalistic benediction that our new liturgy requires but a practical way we, as a body, remind each other that everything we do is "to will and to work for His good pleasure."[14] No church leader should ever give anyone the impression that regularly attending a weekly church service allows them to check the big box on their "God Card" for the week. *Way to go! You're all good and God's all good with you for another week!*

May it never be.

Ephesians 4:11–16 gives us a fuller glimpse of the purpose of the Church: "To equip the saints for the work of ministry, for building up the body of Christ."[15] This full passage reveals that this biblical process of equipping will lead us to "grow up" into "maturity" in Christ. Conforming to the image of Christ as an act of worship and out of love for Him is what we should all be running after.

The Church should desire to mature its people, not just have them meet regularly.

But let me encourage you with something so spectacularly incredible that without firsthand experience, I myself would find it difficult to believe. What God says would happen in this process of living reverent lives in authentic community not only honors Him but also actually *blesses* us. Only a truly good God could orchestrate something so great and seemingly contradictory—that in celebrating and surrendering to Him, we also find the very thing

---

14 Philippians 2:13 ESV.
15 Feel free to read all of Ephesians 4:11–16 ESV, as I will continue to expound upon it as we move forward.

that will make our lives worth celebrating. Worship, the very thing that His perfection demands, leads us to the only thing that will perfectly satisfy us.[16]

I have personally seen God's miraculous work in the lives of believers who commit to being fully devoted disciples ... and I mean messy, addicted, broken, sick, hopeless people. I gladly submit myself as exhibit A.

Lives have been changed. Addictions have been overcome. Marriages have been restored. Insecurity has been abolished. Even appetites have been transformed. Fallen people have formed real, authentic relationships with honest—and sometimes difficult, but always life-giving—commitments to one another. We gather to remember His goodness and remind each other why we should not grow weary in doing good.[17]

We remind each other that worship is what we do 24-7, not just one hour each week. We purposely avoid the exhausting *busyness* of doing church and to stay passionately focused on the Kingdom *business* of making disciples.

For all of us, the results of grace are *exactly* what God said they would be ... and they are worth making a change in the way we think about the Church.

---

16   Psalm 73:25.
17   Galatians 6:9–10.

Chapter 7

Changing Ships

The Adventure Begins

Change begins with moving from "just me and Jesus" to "all of us and Jesus." As I told you before, I never thought I would be excited about the Church, much less become a pastor. Imagine my surprise when my friends and I found ourselves not being able to shake the excitement of investing our days watching Jesus work in the lives of everyone we met who was willing to follow Him with us, and then spending our nights telling the crazy stories of what He had just done—barely able to go to sleep because we were so excited to wake up the next day and do it all over again.

Imagine my delight to be able to tell you that this is exactly what I have been doing for the last two decades of my life.

If Jesus was who He said He was, then He is still alive and ready to do something to bring glory to His name. So just like that bunch of ragtag fishermen and sinners who lived two thousand years ago, we said, "If you're willing, why not do this with us?" We set out and invited anyone who wanted to join us to come along. From the beginning, we envisioned that anyone who truly met Christ would join us and "proclaim Him, admonishing every man and teaching every man with all wisdom, so that we may present every man complete in Christ."[1]

It never crossed our minds that someone would regularly hang around without really being changed—or really even wanting to change.

From the very beginning, Jesus included other people in the process of bringing life to others. His followers were quickly sent out to "go, preach, saying, 'The kingdom of heaven is at hand.' Heal the sick, raise the dead, cleanse the lepers, cast out demons."[2] Jesus has always wanted His friends to join Him in the work of kingdom building.

The idea that people should come and sit never crossed His mind, and it should not cross the minds of those leading His people today. I don't want people to come and watch me do ministry; I want them to do it with me. So we came together as friends to live authentically with one another and to call others to join us in experiencing the grace of Christ that allows us all to live in freedom and devotion to Him. This was the beginning of Watermark Community Church.

And from the beginning, we wanted to change the way people viewed what it meant to be a "member" of Christ's body.

---

1   Colossians 1:28.
2   Matthew 10:7–8.

One of our early videos highlighted this change. This was long before the days of HD video. In fact, the footage came from a VHS tape I received in the mail from one of the major cruise lines.[3] It wasn't the slickest, smoothest, or most impressive media piece we've ever produced, but to this day, I still use it … just not from a VHS. And everyone who has ever joined Watermark has seen it.[4]

The video opens with helicopter footage of a cruise ship—the kind where you take your family to "get away from it all." The sun hangs high in the sky, warming the seas and the skin of the thousands of passengers enjoying their vacations. The waters are crystal blue. The bar is stocked with drinks—and from the looks of the way they are dancing, the passengers seem to be following suit. The people are living it up, having the time of their lives with nary a care in the world.

Then words on the screen make the observation that, all too often, people evaluate a church in much the same way they choose a cruise ship. Whether consciously or otherwise, they ask certain questions that reveal their expectations. *Do I like the music in the ballroom? Do I like the captain and his staff? Do I get good service? Is it pleasant and comfortable? Do I like the experience enough to sail with them again?*

---

3   For all my millennial friends, this was just the year 2000, but it already feels like a century ago. A VHS is a poor-quality video about the size of a small shoebox. You might have watched the original *Lion King* on VHS when you were a newborn.

4   If you would like to see a video like this one, my friends at ignitermedia.com have made a similar version that any church can use at www.ignitermedia.com/products/884-cruise-ship-vs-battleship.

This observation may be all too familiar to you. Especially in the southern United States, there seems to be a church on most every corner. Little churches. Big churches. Traditional churches. Modern churches. Churches with pithy little sayings on their removable lettered marquees. "Free Gift … Inquire Inside!" Or this theological beauty: "Son Screen Prevents Sin Burn." Or this needful warning: "Give Satan an Inch and He Will Soon Become a Ruler."

Our many churches of all varieties are like the many cruises or destinations you can sign up for—and to my surprise, hundreds of thousands of people do so every year. Even more surprising and tragic to me is that so many people float through their "church" experience being largely satisfied with the amenities and personalities instead of being alive and participating in the adventure of Christ's rescue mission and the defeat of evil.

In fact, many regular attenders "upgrade" ships every few years when the service and amenities seem more appealing elsewhere. Generally, their reasons for changing are more about their own preferences than anything substantive. Music is too loud. Music is too traditional. Preacher is too funny. Preacher is too boring. People are too judgmental of me. People are not judgmental enough of the world.

Yes, there are actual reasons you should jump ship from a church, but I haven't mentioned any of them yet. And when they do exist, you should make sure they are based on biblical principles more than personal preferences—things like mission and dogma, not music and dress. But in most cases, the problem is that for too much of modern Christendom, people's relationships with a specific church body is wrapped up more in their own preferences than in kingdom principles.

But I digress … back to the video.

Just as the camera is catching the widest angle of the largest party deck on the cruise ship, the music switches. Steel drums and melodic dance beats are quickly eclipsed by snare drums and a single trumpet blowing a strong, military melody. The seas are the same. The sun is the same. But suddenly, the voyage drastically changes, as an intimidating battleship enters the frame, decked out with an artillery of huge guns, a sharply dressed and uniformed crew, and a fresh coat of an unmistakable haze gray—the visual hallmark of American naval vessels.

The text of the video explains that we believe a more appropriate metaphor for a church is a battleship. And trust me, if this is true, then the whole line of questioning for these warrior-sailors doesn't even resemble the questions of the cruise ship passengers.

Is the ship flying the right flag and fighting for a clear, noble mission?

Does the captain understand that he and his staff serve a higher authority? Do they gladly take their orders from Him? Do the officers create opportunities for all crew members to be prepared to contribute in a significant way to the mission? Is every individual cared for, developed, and honored in their efforts?

Both ships float, but they could not be more different in their culture, mission, and the expectations of the passengers or crew.

Which set of questions are you asking, even if only inadvertently by the way you live—or don't live—in authentic community with other Christ followers? To you, is being a "member" of the body of Christ more about being a consumer or a contributor? Are you a member of the crew or a passenger waving down the waiter for refills on your margarita, spiritually speaking of course?

I asked our team to conclude the video with a specific verse that anyone can consider when they think about what it means to "sail" with us as we live on mission together in Dallas. After all, we have no desire to promote our own idea of what church membership should be—our job is to want what Jesus (our Captain) wants for His Church (His ship). The verse that came to mind sums up Jesus's intentions nicely: "No soldier in active service entangles himself in the affairs of everyday life, so that he may please the one who enlisted him as a soldier."[5]

Trust me, just like my little girl who couldn't see the top shelf of candy in that old market, we're beginning to approach the higher, better stuff … past those lower shelves where bored adults sit in mediocre services. Where "The Deal" is cut, and people are content to show up, shut up, and pay up. Where pastors are going through the motions, people are unmoved, and nonbelievers find nothing to come and see.

It is almost as if Thoreau were talking about the Church when he said, "The mass of men lead lives of quiet desperation."

Even though much of the Church's historical identity has been lost in the fog of postmodernism, trust me when I tell you that

---

5   2 Timothy 2:4.

Jesus is still looking for disciples who want to join Him in the biblically grounded, life-changing mission of serving with Him. What kind of ship are you looking for? Let me invite you to the adventure of Christ's navy, where God's people make war and the serpent's head is crushed. Where hope lives … and where all people are called to be fully devoted and on mission with Him.

Become part of a thriving community with no *regular attenders*, but where all members are *regularly attending* to the King's business.

Turn That Ship Around

If you're reading this, it might be because a friend gave you this book to show you a true picture of what the Church should be. I want you to know that no one is blaming you for *not* interrupting your weekend or investing your life to attend a weekly ritual—something that, as I have said, has far too long defined what the world thinks being a Christian is all about. And I know that, even if you don't yet embrace the deity and glory of Jesus, you still want your life to matter, to have purpose, dignity, and power. And I want to ask your forgiveness if you've never before been invited to a place where you can see true dignity and power at work as God intends.

But I also want you to know that there are places where this exists—places where you can come and see a real, visible image of the invisible God. Not chicanery. Not emotional manipulation. Not empty ritual. Not legalistic adherence. Not uninspired, mechanical obedience. Not performance-driven insecurity. Not modern-day cultural adaptations of ancient traditions that have all the appearances of godliness but deny its power. I want you to avoid such churches as these.[6]

Or maybe you're reading this and the church you've been attending, or even in which you have been in leadership, has drifted off course toward being a cruise ship instead of a battleship. Maybe yours is not really about a church drifting at all because this is all you've ever really known about the concept of church. To you I say, *don't lose heart* ... but *do* consider how we can change the course. It is time to turn that ship around before it collides with the iceberg of compromise and certain judgment. There is hope, and things can change. "'Return to Me,' declares the LORD of hosts, 'that I may return to you.'"[7]

In fact, things can change a lot faster than you might think. For years, I've heard too many pastors and lay leaders compare the process of turning around the culture and mission of their church to turning an aircraft carrier in the ocean. *We have been around a long time. We have a long history of moving this way. We are not a new start-up. It is not like we are able to just turn this thing around ... We are an aircraft carrier of tradition.*

So I decided to find out just how hard it is to turn an aircraft carrier. I had a friend who was an officer on a nuclear sub connect me with his friend who is an F-14 pilot—a lieutenant commander in the United States Navy. Nonchalantly, I emailed him to ask

---

6   2 Timothy 3:5.
7   Zechariah 1:3.

exactly how much time and distance it would take to turn an aircraft carrier completely around.

His first reply was, "Man, I've never officially timed it."

"Come on, just give me an estimate," I answered. "A couple of hours? Ten miles?"

His reply complicated things: "There are lots of variables here. Is the deck empty, that is, are there no airplanes on it? Is the ship light loaded or weighed down with fuel and airplanes on the hangar decks below? Does the ship need to turn just to change course or to launch and land airplanes—because if this is the case, it needs a steady deck positioned into the wind at a certain speed."

Yeah. I had not accounted for all those variables, or for the extreme competency of an F-14 pilot. "How about you just give me worst- and best-case scenarios," I surrendered.

"Well," he replied, "in a non-max-performance scenario, I would say the ship usually takes about ten to fifteen minutes and about five nautical miles to change course and set up for landing and launching. This is under normal ops, non-emergency, and with normal weight and deck loads."

Then came the info that I hope forever sinks the excuses of those who think they have to keep sailing in the wrong direction because they are a big ship. "And I would estimate a 180-degree turn at max performance in *five minutes* or so—and a couple of nautical miles."

Five minutes.

If this is your church we're talking about and you're not sailing in the direction your Commander desires, whatever your scenario, may I suggest you do what you can to start turning as fast as possible because, just like in a war, lives are at stake.

When Irregular Becomes Your New Regular

Even on a cruise ship, when lives are at stake, crew members do not ask what is easy, convenient, or popular among passengers. You do what you have to do, especially when your call is to be a "good [steward] of the manifold grace of God"[8] as though God were making an appeal through you to everyone around you to be reconciled to Him.[9]

For you leaders especially, recognize your calling and privilege to "be on guard for yourselves and for all the flock, among which the Holy Spirit has made you overseers, to shepherd the church of God which He purchased with His own blood."[10] You're the one charged with leading the spiritual body of Christ, the one God wants those who don't yet know Him to come and see. You are God's plan A ... and He has no plan B. I'd again recommend that you assume a max-performance scenario is absolutely necessary.

Unfortunately, the Church (big *C*) is filled with churches (little *c*) that are filled with regular attenders, many of whom have no distinctive differences in their lives from nonbelievers other than the fact that they "attend" church. For the most part, "irregular

---

8   1 Peter 4:10.
9   2 Corinthians 5:20.
10   Acts 20:28.

believers" lead the same "regular lives" as those who don't claim to know Christ at all—except maybe for an uneventful trek to an uneventful service once every week ... or three. Otherwise, they both lead to the same characteristic: lives of quiet desperation.

The marriages of irregular believers are filled with the same suspicion, shadows, and regrets because nothing in their supposedly supernatural experience with Christ actually affects their real relationships. Addictions still abound with no hope of breaking free from the images, substances, or habits that enslave them. Anger breaks out and spreads like wildfire, unabated, unaffected by fruits of the Spirit like patience and gentleness—fruits that are supposed to be present and growing on our branches when we are connected to the Vine.[11]

When what should be "irregular" for those who know Christ has become normal and commonplace, it is time to reconsider what we accept as "regular."

It is simple, really. The real gospel of Christ's grace actually changes people's lives. It changes the way we think. Changes the way we feel. Changes the way we act. Changes the trajectory of our mission. Changes our relationships and our communities. In short, it changes everything.

If you follow the bread crumbs of your faith experience back up the trail to where you started, and if you can't find any transformation in your story along the way, then you should probably stop

---

11   See Galatians 5:17–23 for a longer list of what grows in a life not constantly connected to Christ, as well as the fruits that should be present when we are. John 15 describes this "abiding" process between the vine and branches.

and explore whether or not you have experienced a real understanding of the real gospel in the first place—because when Jesus
is present, so is change.

When He comes near, things that are one thing become something else altogether. When He came near water, it became wine.
Fishermen became fishers of men. Blind guys, deaf guys, and dis-
abled guys became seeing guys, hearing guys, and dancing guys.
Pharisees who had a facade relationship with God became very
uncomfortable.

And when He came near and died on the cross, we became alive.[12]

May we never forget that the real message of Jesus is a message of
real change. This change is not initiated by us. Instead, it is instigated
by the God who sent His Son to be the Change for us and in us.[13]
Many espouse a gospel that says, "Just try harder and everything will
be okay." But the truth is, dead people can't try harder to become
alive.

The change I'm talking about is not initiated by our guilt, our
works, or our religion. This kind of change originates from Christ
Himself, transforming us "from death to life"[14] in such a drastic
way that no human can ever dare claim credit.

The bottom line is that when dead things start living, that is
how you know Jesus—the real Jesus—has come near. But if dead
things remain dead, then one has to ask if the real Jesus has actually
been there or not.

---

12   Ephesians 2:5.
13   2 Corinthians 5:21.
14   Romans 6:13.

It's not my job to determine whether or not you have a "saving faith" or a "said faith." I tell the individuals near my ministry the same thing I am going to tell you. It's not my job to *see through you* to see if you have genuine faith; it is my job to *see you through* to greater faithfulness. I simply want you to come and see what Christ really intends for you in all His fullness. Why? Because if the version of "life in Christ" you are living hasn't transformed you in a radical way, then you have yet to experience fully the absolute joy of what He has planned for you.

The sad truth for too many people is that today's "regular" church is nothing more than a gathering of regular attenders, not a transformative body of devoted disciples who are committed to doing life together—together with Jesus and together with His people. Regular attenders who remain isolated from true commitment to others in the body, people who are not "individually members of one another,"[15] are irregular believers, or even worse, they are potentially nothing more than enlightened orthodox pagans.

The "body" metaphor that Scripture uses for the Church is helpful here. If an appendage becomes detached from the other members of the body, it's going to be a bloody mess. The English language uses the word "dismembered," and it is always the result of a horrific accident or illness ... and it is *always* tragic.

Again, the main problem with the "just me and Jesus" idea is that Jesus Himself never recommends it. He says you need His Church—His body—*if* you are going to thrive as He intends. So while it is true that a relationship with Jesus really is all we need to

---

15   1 Corinthians 12:27; Romans 12:5.

be saved, it is also true that anyone who has a genuine relationship with Him will want to live in relationship with others as His divine will demands.

Otherwise, it's not the real Jesus we really want; it's merely our own distorted version of Him. And then it's not just Christ we're distorting; we're also distorting the body that is irreversibly connected to Him. When we don't see Jesus clearly, we certainly can't clearly see what He truly desires for His Church.

But when the fog dissipates and you see Jesus, then the truth becomes clear: you need the Church—the real Church. The beautiful bride of Christ. Not modern sketches of her that hang crookedly in the galleries of our culture. Not traditional forms of her that focus on the performance of certain rituals but neglect the transformative change that real life together in Christ ultimately brings.

You need more than a supplement—a shot in the arm on Sundays to get you through the week. You need to experience the real transformation that occurs when you submit to His plan and live in grace-filled, accountable community with others who are doing the same. This is not only the life you need, but the life you really want—the one you were designed for.

Everything you ever wanted in the one place you would never look.

Chapter 8

_____

The Trouble with Commandments

So much of the way we process what God says and does comes through the filter of whether or not we trust that He is good, sovereign, and that He loves us. But even when we believe these things about God, our inability to understand the perfection of His ways[1] can still leave us struggling to trust Him.

I liken this to my own children's relationships with me, especially when they were young. Whether they were traveling from place to place in my car with me or living and sleeping daily in the protection of my house, most of the business I was about as their father and the scope of my care for them were well beyond their ability to consider, much less comprehend. Of course, I did not begrudge them for this; instead, I focused on living in such a way before them that they had no reason to question the love and deep

_____

1   Isaiah 55:9; Proverbs 25:2; Deuteronomy 29:29.

concern I had for them. To protect. To comfort. To nourish. To celebrate. To love unconditionally.

In other words, with all they couldn't understand about me, all I desired and all they needed to know was how much I loved them … and that they could trust in this love completely.

It is all too easy to allow the *infinite* mysteries that envelop our heavenly Father—you know, the stuff of omnipresence, created universes, microscopic infinity, and the like—to cause us to miss the *intimate* awareness of us that is also fully His nature. If we are not careful, we can let the transcendence of God cause us to question His nearness. As long as we hold on to the truth that He is too good to be unkind and too wise to be mistaken, we will always be able to trust His heart, even when we cannot trace His hand.[2] His Word certainly teaches us that there is a multiplicity of things only the Father fully understands, but His love, affection, and heart to rescue and bless His children are not intended to be among these mysteries. In fact, the very reason He sent Christ was to reveal the true image[3] of Himself in present grace so we could stop confusing the shrouded mysteries of an Eternal Creator with the now completely illuminated mercies of an Eternal Father.[4]

---

2   Charles Spurgeon first said, "The worldling blesses God while he gives him plenty, but the Christian blesses him when he smites him: he believes him to be too wise to err and too good to be unkind; he trusts him where he cannot trace him, looks up to him in the darkest hour, and believes that all is well."

3   Colossians 1:15.

4   John 1:1–18; Hebrews 1:3; Colossians 2:9.

God knows that you must understand this key attribute of His nature so that you are not vulnerable to the enemy and his lies.[5] If you are firm on any one truth about your Creator and Sustainer, it should be His love and concern for you.[6] "So that Christ may dwell in your hearts through faith; and that you, being rooted and grounded in love, may be able to comprehend with all the saints what is the breadth and length and height and depth, and to know the love of Christ which surpasses knowledge, that you may be filled up to all the fullness of God."[7]

To "comprehend" the literal dimensions of His love? To "know" this love in Christ? To be filled with the "fullness" of God? These are not the words of someone trying to hide something but of someone desperately trying to reveal something fully. Jesus was God's human, living, divine exposé, perfectly written and painstakingly delivered to the world in a human package. And when that package—His body—was torn and ripped open like a Christmas present, the free gift of God's unfailing grace and love for the world was forever revealed—no longer hidden.

So while God still possesses characteristics of His eternal existence that are utterly unknowable to us,[8] the goodness of God—the kindness of His intention toward us[9]—should no longer be one of

---

5   1 Peter 5:8; John 8:44.
6   Romans 8:37–39.
7   Ephesians 3:17–19 (ESV).
8   Deuteronomy 29:29.
9   Ephesians 1:9.

them. He sent Christ to remove the veil[10] over this mystery and forever reveal[11] His grace once and for all.[12]

You will never want to seek or know God's will more than He wants to show and reveal it to you.

But it is all too easy for us to live "in church" as if it's our job to pursue and please God instead of continually remembering that "*He chose us* in Him before the foundation of the world, that we would be holy and blameless before Him. In love He predestined us to adoption as sons through Jesus Christ to Himself, according to the kind intention of His will, to the praise of the glory of His grace, which He freely bestowed on us in the Beloved."[13] We make church about *our* work, *our* effort, and *our* performance instead of *His* love—because His ways are too wonderful for our shame-filled, guilt-ridden lives to attain on our own.[14]

But when we *fully* know that Jesus *fully* loves us, only then will we *fully* trust in what He commands us to *fully* do. And only then will we *fully* comprehend the love that God sent Christ to reveal. And only then will we, His Church, reveal the love that Christ intends us to reveal *fully* to the world.

When we understand the Father's nature, we are not compelled by a command; we are compelled by His love.[15] Our actions toward God are not the cause of God's love but the evidence of

---

10 2 Corinthians 3:16.
11 Colossians 1:26.
12 1 Peter 3:18.
13 Ephesians 1:4–6.
14 Acts 13:41.
15 2 Corinthians 5:14.

God's love in our lives. We love because He first loved us.[16] "For this is the love of God, that we keep His commandments; and His commandments *are not* burdensome."[17] As C. S. Lewis said, "The Christian does not think that God will love us because we are good, but that God will make us good because He loves us."

Part of that "making good," as Lewis put it, should be evidenced in the way we become servants, caregivers, and lovers of one another. Jesus even takes it up a notch when He says that our love for one another is evidence that we are His disciples *and* that He is the Father's Son. "A new commandment I give to you, that you love one another, even as I have loved you, that you also love one another. *By this all men will know that you are My disciples*, if you have love for one another[18] ... that they may all be one; even as You, Father, are in Me and I in You, that they also may be in Us, *so that the world may believe that You sent Me.*"[19]

These verses couldn't be any clearer: if we don't love, the world will not know that we're His disciples *and* the world will not believe that Jesus was sent by the Father. Those are two *huge* implications. This love is our mark[20] that we are Christ's *and* that Christ is the Father's—that we are *His* men and Jesus is *the* Man.

This love is a command. We tend instinctively to think of obedience to commands as something we have to do because a

---

16   1 John 4:19.
17   1 John 5:3.
18   John 13:34–35.
19   John 17:21.
20   You can fully read this idea in Francis Schaeffer's classic work *The Mark of a Christian*.

power greater than us is *lording* itself over us instead of being compelled by the power of the love the *Lord* Himself has demonstrated by giving Himself for us. Jesus contrasts the way the world uses power with the way He, in His goodness, uses power. "You know that those who are recognized as rulers of the Gentiles lord it over them; and their great men exercise authority over them. But it is not this way among you, but whoever wishes to become great among you shall be your servant; and whoever wishes to be first among you shall be slave of all. For even the Son of Man did not come to be served, but to serve, and to give His life a ransom for many."[21]

Christ leads by His love.

Napoleon, of all people, observes this truth. "Alexander, Caesar, Charlemagne and I myself have founded great empires; but upon what did these creations of our genius depend? Upon force. Jesus alone founded His empire upon love, and to this very day millions will die for Him ... Christ alone has succeeded in so raising the mind of man toward the unseen, that it becomes insensible to the barriers of time and space."[22]

If you view following God like soldiers followed Napoleon, Alexander, or Charlemagne, you are not paying attention to history. It is the love—the kindness of God—that leads us to repentance[23] ... and it's the goodness of God that makes it easy to follow Him.

---

21   Mark 10:42–45.
22   Quoted in Henry Parry Liddon, *Liddon's Bampton Lectures 1866* (London: Rivingtons, 1869), 148.
23   Romans 2:4.

If you're like me, when I forget the kindness of God, I "bow up" in self-defense instead of "bowing down" in glad surrender. I somehow think my own "kind" way will fill my life with more good than the way of my loving King. But I'm always wrong. There is a way that seems right to man, but in the end, it is the way of death.[24] The result of following "my kindness" is that I often hurt not only myself but also the people I love most, causing pain and confusion in their lives.

Why do I do this? Because I forget that God's commands are part of God's goodness in my life. I separate them as if I trust God's grace up to the point that He commands me to do something, then suddenly, I trust it no more. I fear and rebel. I turn away. I assume the Father does not have my best interests at heart anymore because, to me, commandments mean I'm going to be forced to do what I would otherwise never want to do.

I think that God's trying to rip me off, not set me free.

My guess is that I am not alone in this kind of thinking. I know I see it—or something very much like it—living inside the hearts of many who regularly attend services in buildings we call churches. Somehow, we fall into the trap of thinking that following God's commands will lead to *no good thing* instead of reminding ourselves continually that "*no good thing* does He withhold from those who walk uprightly."[25]

That is why we do not trust His commandment to love one another in the way that leads us to Christ-centered, authentic

---

24 Proverbs 14:12.
25 Psalm 84:11.

community as members of His body: we don't trust the One giving the command.

Get On Board

If you think of yourself as being *drafted* into a war you don't want to fight rather than being *drawn* into a relationship with a Commander-in-Chief who loves you and desires to see you thrive, prosper you, bring you honor, and allow you to be useful, you'll never love the idea of God's community—His Church—the way He intends. But when you really begin to know God and to run with Him instead of just sitting around religious services—when you really begin to believe and behave as if "this is the love of God, that we keep His commandments; and His commandments are not burdensome"[26]—*then* you will fully experience what He is offering you—life—and you will come to know that the life He offers is appropriately described as the "abundant life."[27]

Abundance—of life, of purpose, and of joy—comes when you abandon yourself to His commands. I know this sounds counter-intuitive, but that's only because *it is*. "He who has found his life will lose it, and he who has lost his life for My sake will find it"[28] is not only a radical idea, it also is a hard sell. We are not easily convinced that to be free we have to be subject to something other than ourselves. The offer to be our own gods has never worked out

---

26   1 John 5:3.
27   John 10:10.
28   Matthew 10:39.

well for us, but it is an offer that remains just as tempting to the sons of Adam as it did to Adam himself.

We are easily convinced we are our own best masters—that is, until the chains of sin "so easily entangle us"[29] that we are held "captive by the devil to do his will."[30] Perhaps you know all too well what I am talking about, or perhaps you are still rolling your eyes, oblivious to the fact that sometimes the way that seems right to you is actually leading to death in some part of your life.[31] I was an eye roller too, following the lie of trusting in my own wisdom despite the wisdom offered to me from God.

But there is an alternative to being a slave to sin. God invites us to humble ourselves, listen, and find life. "But he who listens to me shall live securely and will be at ease from the dread of evil."[32] You see, God isn't looking to catch you in your sin; He is looking to free you from the sin that has captured you. Let me reveal again a truth that merits a continual reminder: "His commands are not burdensome."[33]

I can hear you from beyond these pages. *Todd, I am all about the gospel. I have no desire to be a command keeper. Have you ever heard of grace? Don't you know anything about the finished work of the cross and the futility of our works? Why do you want to slap the burden of legalism and the problem of performance on a stressed-out, weary people?*

---

29 Hebrews 12:1.
30 2 Timothy 2:26.
31 Proverbs 14:12.
32 Proverbs 1:33.
33 1 John 5:3.

My answer is, of course I don't. The gospel is wonderful, and our salvation is won by Christ alone through faith alone. Working *for* your salvation is futile,[34] but not working *out* your salvation is foolish.[35] "Performance-based acceptance" is a trap, but "acceptance-based performance" is the only way to respond to Truth.[36] As it has been well said for centuries, "We are saved by faith alone, but the faith which saves is never alone."[37] Legalism is man doing things so he will be loved. Licentiousness is man thinking he can do anything because he is already loved. Loving worship is man doing all he is asked because he is already loved.

This is where too many people in today's modern Church miss the ancient Church's way. From the beginning, the expectation was that full devotion was normal for the believer. It was never to be reserved for the salaried, the seminarian, or the "super saint." Devotion and obedience were the normal expectations of *every* follower. Jesus said, "If you love Me, you will keep My commandments."[38]

---

34 Ephesians 2:8–9, Titus 3:5.

35 Philippians 2:12–16.

36 If you don't believe me, then read a little of Paul. Almost every epistle he writes starts with doctrine (Romans 1–11) and then moves to doing (Romans 12–16). They start with the word of truth (Ephesians 1–3) and then call you to walk in truth (Ephesians 4–6). They start with orthodoxy (Colossians 1–2) and end with orthopraxy (Colossians 3–4).

37 See John Calvin's *Antidote to the Council of Trent* (1547) where he actually uses the word "justifies" instead of "saves." "It is therefore faith alone which justifies, and yet the faith which justifies is not alone: just as it is the heat alone of the sun which warms the earth, and yet in the sun it is not alone, because it is constantly conjoined with light."

38 John 14:15; 1 John 2:3–6.

This means that if we have an obedience problem, we have a heart problem. We don't need to try harder to be obedient to Christ; we need to love Him more. This is what Jesus said to Judas: "If anyone loves Me, he will keep My word."[39]

To reiterate, I am not—and Jesus certainly wasn't—talking about earning your salvation here. That is impossible. But nobody who comes face to face with the love of God and who personally understands the implication of that love remains unmoved—or said another way, is looking to cruise.

Any purpose for a church other than full devotion from every disciple as God has laid out for us in His Word will lead a church away from the fullness of life Christ desires for all of us.[40] When the seemingly unattainable, radical purposes of God are dumbed down to the attainable, dead, religious practicalities of man, all kinds of poisonous counterfeits are produced. When we can't see the "power of God" manifest in the salvation[41] of His people *on earth*, it is reasonable for a watching world to assume there is no God powerfully working *in heaven*.

When the awe-inspiring, life-changing, radical transformation of real lives is not regularly seen, it is only a matter of time before people who gather in God's name begin looking for other reasons to be enthusiastic about their mission. These "churches" and the

---

39 John 14:23.
40 Colossians 1:28–29.
41 And I mean here salvation in its fullest sense, which includes: (1) deliverance from the penalty of sin (justification); (2) deliverance from the power of sin (sanctification); and (3) a hope-filled people living expectantly and full of joy waiting for deliverance from the presence of sin (glorification).

people who attend them will drift toward either increasingly bizarre "evidences" of God's power or an increasingly bizarre infatuation with obscure doctrines and particular theological positions. That is why so many churches are filled with unfulfilled, unchanged, unknowledgeable, "uncompassionate," unmoved people who somehow think that this is what God intends for His bride. *These people remain unchanged and bored—and the world watching them remains unimpressed and bothered.*

If this is the kind of life God intends for those who follow Him, who wants—who would ever want—to come and see it?

"Church membership" should mean that people commit to a God-ordained process of letting Christ's free gift of grace actually lead them forward past a onetime moment of repentance and into real life transformation as they follow the biblical directives to meet, pray, share, confess, serve, and love one another. This is the kind of spiritual body Christ had in mind for His people from the beginning.[42] When you grasp these truths, you can join the many who are still eagerly engaging their friends every day, begging them to "come and see" the same divine love and transforming power that made Andrew compel Peter, Philip compel Nathanael, and me compel you to come and see.

Being a member of the body of Christ—in your local church—was never meant to be a ticket to a cruise ship where the amenities and comforts eclipse the purpose and mission. If you are a disciple,

---

42 For a satirical and tragically familiar description of the alternative, see http://babylonbee.com/news/unrepentant-hedonist-really-banking-sinners-prayer-recited-age-7/.

then you are called into an extreme privilege where every inch of what is dead, enslaved, and worthless in your life is redeemed by the grace of Jesus to become completely alive, free, and fulfilled. And if you are not a disciple, wouldn't you be curious to at least come check out the people who know a King who is bringing healing and hope to their lives, causing everyone who observes Him to say, "Nothing like this has ever been seen in Israel"?[43]

Yes, being a fully devoted disciple who understands that church membership means exponentially more than regular attendance or social acceptance is pretty extreme in today's world. But grace and its results were never supposed to be tame—they have always been extreme, always producing a "sense of awe," always creating "no small disturbance."[44] Jesus never meant for His Church—those supposedly rooted and grounded in the wildest grace imaginable—to be tame. He intends for her—for *you*—to be alive, powerful, authentic, moving, growing, changing, and ultimately, to be a compellingly accurate and attractive reflection of that real grace He died to offer to the world.

Being a member of *a* church is supposed to mean you are a member of *the* Church.

The Church is the awe-inspiring spiritual body of Christ that is just as full of life, integrity, and righteousness as Christ Himself was when He physically walked the earth. We are His body *now* just as much as He was in a body *then*. In the same way that the unrighteous Pharisees only tended to God's business when they

---

43   Matthew 9:33.
44   Acts 19:23.

were going through the motions in the temple, there is a tendency among irregular believers today to go through the motions in whatever religious house they attend.

And, my friend, that cruise ship—full of regular attenders (that is, irregular believers)—has got to sail.

Chapter 9

Build It Right

The 3 Bs

It's always easy to criticize from the couch.

I'm far from the days when I could accomplish anything on the field of play that even remotely resembles elite competition, but that doesn't keep me from watching others and then, in my "the older I get, the better I was" mind-set, go on to critically observe and evaluate the young studs still competing. While I am fully aware of the giftedness, effort, energy, and discipline it takes to be an elite, professional athlete (something I never approached), as a lover of sport, I still make "humble" observations about open receivers, blitz reads, backdoor cuts, open lanes to the hoop, or other "obvious" misses by those competing. These are easy to note when I'm sitting comfortably in front of my large-screen TV *without* a three-hundred-pound defensive tackle closing in on my backside.

The "arrogance of the observer" syndrome doesn't just occur on NFL Sunday afternoons or throughout a grueling NBA season. It is just as prevalent on Sunday mornings and throughout various arenas of ministry.

Anyone with a healthy perspective on what really matters would agree that the leaders of Christ's Church should take the business of leading God's people even more seriously than an athlete takes his effort to play a game.[1]

Like the coach of a beloved team, anyone who has ever tried to provide leadership in God's beloved Church is painfully aware that the observing masses are equally as eager and willing to criticize what they see played out on a church stage as they are a competitive one. They criticize a sermon—though they've never delivered one. They criticize a small group—though they've never led one. They criticize a mission—though they've never sacrificed to accomplish one.

It would do a lot of us some good to remember that "the arrogance of the observer" is an arrogance compounded by a lack of awareness of the difficulty of actually being in the game. We all may not be able to compete at the highest levels in athletic arenas, but we are all called to live our lives in a way that is excellent and honorable in spiritual ones.[2] So while it may be okay (though still not recommended, unless you really want to be "that guy") to grumble at the playmaking ability of your favorite point guard or

---

1   1 Corinthians 9:25–27.
2   Philippians 2:15–16; Ephesians 4:1–3; and Philippians 1:27, among dozens of others.

quarterback, it is not an option to grumble or walk in an attitude of disputing[3] with those who are running point on guarding your soul.[4] *Especially* while you keep watch on your couch.

So if grumbling and disputing are out, what does it look like to get in the actual game and be a disciple? How do you dive in beyond cultural perceptions and "run in such a way that you may win"?[5] What does it mean to be a part (a member) of God's team (body), and is it worth it?

Real, biblical membership in the body of Christ begins by either discovering for ourselves, or reminding ourselves, what the calling for the Church truly is. What is our mission? Why do we exist? If you don't completely understand the mission, then odds are you will never wholeheartedly engage in fully devoted discipleship.

Let me lay it out for you plainly. For everyone from all walks of life, our calling as a local church—and as *the* Church—remains the same: to make fully devoted followers of Christ. Our goal is not conversion, baptisms, to have people gather weekly at appointed times, or to have people give a certain percentage of their income. These may be component parts of the whole, but when we make them our goal, we miss our calling.

Our goal is full devotion.[6]

This goal means we "proclaim Him, admonishing every man and teaching every man with all wisdom, so that we may present

---

3   Philippians 2:14.
4   Hebrews 13:17.
5   1 Corinthians 9:24.
6   Philippians 3:12–15.

every man complete in Christ."[7] We do this "for the equipping of the saints for the work of service, to the building up of the body of Christ; until we all attain to the unity of the faith, and of the knowledge of the Son of God, to a mature man, to the measure of the stature which belongs to the fullness of Christ. As a result, we are no longer to be children, tossed here and there by waves and carried about by every wind of doctrine, by the trickery of men, by craftiness in deceitful scheming; but speaking the truth in love, we are to grow up in all aspects into Him who is the head, even Christ."[8]

Again, we don't want people just to become members of a church as most people define membership; we want to remind, encourage, equip, and ultimately shepherd them into the fullness of God's intention of His people … *that* is the endgame.

And here's the secret now revealed: God's complete intention for His people is fully seen in Jesus. Being like Jesus is the activity of the Church. Properly defined, church activities should mean simply being like Jesus, not being in a building, a baptismal, or a Bible study. Members of the body of Christ are "living stones … being built up as a spiritual house for a holy priesthood, to offer up spiritual sacrifices acceptable to God through Jesus Christ."[9] Members of the body of Christ are constantly dying to themselves so they can be available to the living God.[10] Membership in the

---

7   Colossians 1:28.
8   Ephesians 4:12–15.
9   1 Peter 2:5.
10   Romans 12:1; Galatians 2:20; John 3:30.

body of Christ means you are living in a way that continues the work of Christ on earth.[11]

When every follower of every local church embraces these truths, then everyone who observes the Church will observe what God wants the world to see in His people—and the "world will know that the Father has sent the Son."[12] The body will do as the head desires, and the world can then "come and see" what God really intends for them.[13]

One of the reasons we are so dysfunctional in church today is that many leaders think their job is to build or grow a church. Most pastors and leaders spend enormous amounts of their energy trying to figure out how to accomplish the *3 Bs*: butts in seats, budgets, and buildings. These can become all-consuming to them because we as a society give leaders the moniker of success based on these *3 Bs*. Entire denominations measure and monitor statistics related to these *B*s to evaluate their efforts.

It is worth noting, if you look at the Scriptures, that Jesus doesn't tell shepherds to pursue these things at all. Instead, He says, "Go therefore and make disciples."[14] He also says, "*I* will build my church."[15] Churches today seem to have reversed this

---

11   Colossians 1:24–25.
12   John 17:23.
13   It is worth noting here that the healthiest and most mature churches should always be filled with the most immature people because one clear mark of maturity is the ability to reproduce. Where there is new life, there is always immaturity. Churches that are full of only older mature believers are dying churches, not healthy ones.
14   Matthew 28:19.
15   Matthew 16:18.

Jesus-initiated sequence, trying desperately to "build a church" and then praying that God "makes disciples" out of the regular attenders who may show up but don't understand what it is to follow their King.

It is an exhausting process that heavily weighs down leaders with a job they were never intended or empowered to succeed in with "churches" full of people who have no intention of surrendering anything other than some fragment of their Sunday mornings. This also creates an alarming yet accepted norm among attenders: presence at meetings and provision for the meetings to continue have become acceptable replacements for Christ preeminently evidencing Himself in their every word and deed.[16] The expectation is for them to show up, shut up, and pay up instead of read it through, pray it in, live it out, and pass it on.[17]

The above is further exasperated when the "work of the church" is reserved for staff, the spiritual "elite," or the super saint—the chosen few instead of *all* the chosen.[18] When it becomes acceptable

---

16   This is another reason why so many children grow up to abandon the Church. They never saw their parents commit, so they themselves were never convinced it was worth committing to. To be reminded by biting satire, see: http://babylonbee.com/news/after-12-years-of-quarterly-church-attendance-parents-shocked-by-daughters-lack-of-faith/.

17   Ezra is a great example of the kind of "priest" we should all be (Ezra 7:10). He sets his heart on devotion to God, studies the Word, obeys the Word, and *then* passes the Word on to others.

18   For the last thirty years, I have been talking about the need for—and pursuing with anyone who will jump in with me—a second Reformation. This one is not about getting the Word of God away from the "clergy" and into the hands of the people, but rather getting the *work* of God away from the "paid" and returned to all the people.

for a few leaders or paid staff members to be faithful while others are called merely to be present, the Church is presently broken.

This rings true for the leaders and the attenders because God intended a deep, rich, transformative experience for *all* the members of His body—not just the pastors or a select few. He intends this for you! For too long and in too many places, much of the modern church membership model has been based on leaders making "The Deal" with "members." And while the result may be bigger churches, it has not necessarily been more biblical ones. Size isn't the issue—substance is. If something is biblical, then I pray it increases until it is as big as the earth; but if something is unbiblical, growth is not going to lead to anything but bigger problems.

A. W. Tozer had it right when he said, "Religion has accepted the monstrous heresy that noise, size, activity and bluster make a man dear to God."[19]

The Unchurched, De-Churched, Dead-Churched, and Unmoved

While everyone will suffer when there is a perverted version of God's bride, there are four groups of people worth highlighting who specifically suffer from (or settle for) "The Deal." The first group is the Unchurched.

The Unchurched are those who have never been exposed to the grace of Jesus expressed in authentic, biblical community. If you're in this group, I also theorize that most of the time, you have

---

19   Tozer, *Pursuit of God*, chap. 6.

not been truly exposed to the actual gospel of grace in the first place, because all too often, your concept of God is tantamount to a judgmental tyrant who hates you and would love nothing more than to destroy you with fire ... not to mention that He precedes this eternal consequence by sentencing you to regularly attend average weekly meetings made up of largely uninspired, bored adults.

The next group, the De-Churched, are those who have previously been in a church environment but left it for some reason. Those who quantify these types define the De-Churched as anyone who has not been to a church, religious meeting, or faith-based gathering in the last six months, with allowable exceptions for weddings, funerals, and holidays. If you are one of the De-Churched, you used to be in a church, but you found it largely irrelevant to your life, probably because the version you saw was irrelevant, so it's hard to blame you.

If you are either Unchurched or De-Churched, my greatest passion is to call you to know the true Savior by coming to know the true Church. Is it because the Church gains something from your attendance? No, what we gain is the joy of knowing that you, like us, have been reconciled to our Father who loves you and has been seeking you for your welfare. What I gain is your joy—and I know that *your* joy brings *great* joy to my Father.

The Church is not here to tell you that we're better than you. In fact, the Church of Jesus Christ is the only organization I know of that has as its only requirement to join the need to acknowledge that you are flawed beyond repair. If you run into a gathering of people who are convinced they are better than you, you have not run into the Church. The Church is a group of weary and heavy-laden people who have come to find rest[20] in the work Someone else has done to save them from striving to do something they could never do on their own, even if they constantly tried.[21]

We are also broken people who are being led back to life. We are sinners who loved to do what we wanted and hated to follow His commands, but we've realized the futility of that way of thinking and living and have been saved despite ourselves.[22] It is not a stretch to say that we have been among the living dead. But God has resurrected our lives! We want you to know Him before you face the suffering that we faced, or after having already gone through it, we want you to be restored as we are being restored. Like Mary Magdalene[23] or the woman who suffered for many years from a condition that separated her from life and community,[24] you are invited to come and see.

Then there are the Dead-Churched. These are people who are involved in a church under a leadership that is not leading. Rather than naming one, let me describe them all from a biblical standpoint, and then you can spot, name, and stop supporting or attending them yourself.[25] Biblically, a dead church is any church that, in word or deed, does not shepherd God's people the way

---

20   Matthew 11:28.

21   John 6:44; 6:28–29.

22   Titus 3:5.

23   Luke 8:2.

24   Luke 8:43–48.

25   When people ask me how to choose a church, I always send them this: http://realtruthrealquick.com/how-do-i-choose-a-church/.

God says His people should be shepherded. These churches are led by "leaders" who have PhDs in making "The Deal."

Sadly, the dead church is not a new phenomenon. The faithful J. Gresham Machen[26] spoke out against the compromising church in the early 1900s, as did Luther centuries before, as did Jesus[27] against dead religion two thousand years earlier. Dead churches go by the name "Christian," but they are really a different religion altogether.

A dead church might look like they take seriously the things of God, but they only hold "to a form of godliness *while* denying its power. *You would be wise* to avoid such *churches* as these."[28] They might even support sound doctrinal statements, but the way they shepherd their people, failing to care for and correct one another, is anything but sound. They are led by "springs without water,"[29] "hidden reefs ... clouds without water ... wandering stars."[30] Dead churches aspire to things they do not actually pursue.

Someone once said that the problem with the American Church is that they talk about a God without wrath who brings men without sin into a kingdom without judgment through the ministrations of a Christ without a cross.[31] I would add that they give lip service to a book to which they should instead surrender their lives. Any one of these things makes a dead church—and like

---

26 J. Gresham Machen, *Christianity and Liberalism* (Grand Rapids, MI: Wm. B. Eerdmans, 2009).
27 Matthew 23:27–28.
28 2 Timothy 3:5.
29 2 Peter 2:17.
30 Jude 12–13.
31 H. Richard Niebuhr, *The Kingdom of God in America* (1938).

the prophet Malachi, I hope they are either resurrected to life or that someone shuts their doors.[32]

If you find some place where you can view God's Word any way you want and be a member—for instance, one that defines prosperity, health, and success differently than God does—yours is a dead church. If the way your church resolves conflict is not consistent with Scripture, or if the way they admonish you to use your gifts and steward your life is not consistent with Scripture, it is a dead church. If your church chooses political correctness over theological purity, it is a dangerous, dead church. If your church is flexible where the Bible is not flexible or dogmatic where the Bible is not dogmatic, it is a dangerous, degrading, dead church. If your church is not clear on the necessity of faith in Christ alone as the means of salvation, it is a dangerous, degrading, decaying, dead church.

If they have a Watermark[33] Way, a Methodist Method, a Presbyterian Polity, a Catholic Conviction, a Pentecostal Practice, or a Baptist Belief that is inconsistent with God's Word, speak up or get out. It is a dead and dangerous church.

It has been well said that there are two great mission fields in the world today: those who would never step inside a church and, increasingly, those who are there every weekend. I count it as a conversion if people leave a dead church and follow Jesus as His Word says they will when grace and truth genuinely take root in their hearts.

---

32 Malachi 1:10.
33 Watermark is the name of the church of which I am a part.

The last group affected by "The Deal" are the Unmoved. If you fall into this category, more than likely you are underneath good leadership, yet for whatever reason, grace has not yet fully made its way into your heart. The Unmoved are those who are nominally involved with Christ or His purposes. If you say you know Jesus Christ but are not a member of His body, fitted and joined together as the Scripture intends, you should not (as I should have made painfully clear by now) consider yourself a regular attender … you are, by definition, an irregular believer.

At Watermark, when I address the Unmoved, I say something like, "I'm not here to tell you that you're going to hell, but I am here to tell you that you are not pursuing heaven and Christ along with us." Why would I say this? Is it because I want to offend them? Of course not. It is because I am going to give an account.[34]

When we first started Watermark, many friends told me I was crazy if I thought people would put up with this kind of biblical commitment to doing life together. They thought I was naive to think people would stay at Watermark when they could simply drive another two minutes to another one of the hundreds of churches around town that would not ask so much of them.

My response? I said, "Good, let their blood be on someone else's hands."[35] We were not concerned about the size of the church we were starting; we were concerned about the significance of the responsibility we were facing. This passage from Ezekiel describes the hearts of the Unmoved:

---

34 Hebrews 13:17.
35 Ezekiel 33.

"And they come to you as people come, and they sit before you as my people, and they hear what you say but they will not do it; for with lustful talk in their mouths they act; their heart is set on their gain. And behold, you are to them like one who sings lustful songs with a beautiful voice and plays well on an instrument, for they hear what you say, but they will not do it."[36]

If you are one of the Unmoved who come to church and listen—and even invite others to come with you—but who refuse to move yourself to personally commit, I am moved to spur you on all I can. If you're stirred to come but never stirred to follow, I want "to stir you up by way of reminder"[37] that where you are right now in your life *is not* where God wants you to be. If you are around truth but remain largely indifferent to it, you have no small problem. The term "enlightened orthodox pagan" comes to mind again.

Beware, lest you become so slowly indoctrinated with a mild enough form of the faith that you become inoculated against the real thing.[38]

The truth is, we do everything we can to compel our unmoved friends to come to be with us as we gather to sing and share about the goodness of our King with all the creativity, relevance, and excellence we can muster. But if all we are to them is a sensual song, and all they are doing is just singing along without the melody of truth

---

36 Ezekiel 33:31–32 ESV.
37 2 Peter 1:13.
38 "We have inoculated the world with a mild form of Christianity so that it is now proof against the real thing" (*Gandhi—Portrayal of a Friend*, by the Christian missionary to India, E. Stanley Jones).

informing their hearts, then we warn them, as God did in Ezekiel: there are truths in these songs to which they will be held accountable. We remind them that they would be wise to tune their hearts to hear His grace in the tunes we sing. We warn them that God's truth is not to be selectively embraced or picked through to find the parts they like—it is to be seriously considered and fully embraced.[39]

Because I am a pastor, you might find it interesting that I actually do want to entertain people. But it is important that you understand why and that you don't confuse entertainment, the etymology of which simply means "to hold one's attention," with amusement, which generally means "not to think." It is precisely because I want them to think that I want to hold their attention; that way, they can know what they should think about. But the Unmoved are prone to exalt the entertainment above the mission by saying, "That was hilarious. You are so fun to listen to. Great building! Really cool vibe! Kind people! Great coffee! Amazing parking team! Time flies by when I'm there … I love it!"

If this is you, then beware that you are not just tuning in to catch a song you like. Be careful that you don't treat God's Word like one of your Pandora channels, dismissing songs and lyrics you don't like and constantly fine-tuning the divine song to your own preferences. Beware of letting your spiritual experience be merely a sensual song by which you may be entertained but not by which you are moved.

---

39   For a satirical and tragically humorous example of this see, http://babylonbee.com/news/
      im-ready-to-completely-surrender-about-10-of-my-life-to-god/.

I call Unmoved friends to come and see—to engage with Jesus fully. Don't be an irregular believer—a diluted person who professes one thing but pursues the self instead. Don't be the fool who heard the Word but didn't act on it.[40] Come, taste and see what a relationship with the Father—whose grace toward you is immeasurably full—is really like.

We tell the Unmoved—along with everyone else—the truth about God's desire for them to become fully devoted disciples. Why? Because if I "pay close attention to myself and to my teaching; and persevere in these things, I will ensure salvation both for myself and for those who hear me."[41] Thousands more will "come and see" if we become a Church who makes disciples, not as we try to grow churches, but as we set ourselves to grow in grace. When we all become the people the Lord created us to be, we can all invite others to come and see.

Until then, "we proclaim Him, admonishing every man and teaching every man with all wisdom, so that we may present every man complete in Christ. For this purpose also I labor, striving according to His power, which mightily works within me."[42]

---

40   Matthew 7:24–27.
41   1 Timothy 4:16.
42   Colossians 1:28–29.

Chapter 10

Zero Members

We take seriously the charge to "shepherd the flock of God"[1] among us by not treating church membership the same way we would if we were charged with leading a health club or a golf course. Our goal is not to maximize the number of people who call our club home. Nor are we trying to keep out those who are not members. What we are trying to do is make sure those who want to join themselves to Christ understand the implications of that union. Biblically, being a member of *a* church should be exactly the same experience as being a member of *the* Church. Local church membership should be synonymous with being a devoted disciple.

Devoted disciples don't just sign up, pay their dues, and coast along.

You may be thinking, *Membership? Really? In my church (or in my mental impressions of church from my past experiences), membership is more about who gets to vote on the new pastor, the deacons, the*

---

1   1 Peter 5:2.

coming budget, or the change in carpet color. I would never consider it to be something actually integral to my growth as a disciple.

And *that*, my friend, is the problem.

The Church is Jesus's body, and just like your body, His body has "members"—limbs, organs, and the like. Imagine if the vital organs—the members—of your body were as unhealthy, unresponsive, and constantly changing in their functionality and location as the members of most churches. The words "unpleasant" or "unhealthy" come to mind.

Hey, left elbow! Come back, bro … I really need you present and active!

At Watermark and at any church that wants to be biblical, engaging in church membership should be a much bigger deal than simply attending a two-to-four-week class or signing a membership card. And it should mean a lot more than merely having a group of friends with whom you hang out and talk about spiritual things. It should also mean more than regularly going to a place where sermons are preached or even jumping into a Bible study.

Membership in the body of Christ means locking hearts and lives together with other Christ followers under godly, mature, present, give-an-account-for-your-soul, admonish-you-when-you-are-unruly, help-you-when-you-are-weak, encourage-you-when-you-are-fainthearted leadership. It means integrating your life with others for the purpose of doing God's family business[2] as God's chosen children. It

---

2   The word for "fellowship" in the NT is *koinonia*, which contains the ideas of "common" and "shared investment," "doing business," "deeply joined with" or "sharing all things," and "mutually joined to" one another. It is hard to think of a word in biblical or classical Greek that carries with it

means taking your place in God's kingdom of priests[3] and taking your role in His kingdom work seriously.[4]

Jesus said that when we are His, we are part of His family.[5] This means a believer without a church family is an orphan. Similarly, Paul said that when we are Christ's, we are a part of His body[6]—and this means a believer who is not attached to others is a "dismembered" appendage. It doesn't get more brutally graphic than that.

Scripturally, there are so many incredible reasons to approach membership in your local church from this fully devoted paradigm. First of all, Church is a *part* of who we are, identifying individuals as genuine followers of Christ.[7] It is also where God makes *provision* for you—a spiritual family who can support, encourage, and care for you in your walk with Christ.[8] And it provides you the community and accountability necessary to grow and live out in obedience God's design for His people.[9] Thirdly, Church places you under the spiritual *protection* of godly community and godly leaders.[10] And finally, it gives you a *place* to discover and use the gifts that the Lord has entrusted you with for ministry.[11]

---

the idea of a stronger commitment or tie to others. This is not monthly potlucks or casual gatherings. This is an intentional investment in and complete joining to one another.

3   1 Peter 2:9–12.
4   Ephesians 2:10.
5   Mark 3:31–35.
6   1 Corinthians 12:12–20.
7   Ephesians 2:19; Romans 12:5.
8   Galatians 6:1–2; Hebrews 10:24–25; 1 Corinthians 12:26–27.
9   2 Thessalonians 3:14–15; Ephesians 5:21.
10   Hebrews 13:17; Acts 20:28–29; 1 Peter 5:5.
11   1 Corinthians 12:4–27.

A return to the biblical viewpoint of "membership" in Christ's Church is the starting point for moving past the luke-warm, powerless, changeless, ever-shifting, never-confident life that so many Christ followers find themselves in. Going at it alone is not the way to go at it at all.[12] Choosing yourself as an accountability partner is not an option.[13] Simply signing a membership card doesn't change anything but the amount of ink in your pen. But diving into the business of sharing life together with brothers and sisters in Christ—*that* is the first step in walking with Jesus.[14]

At Watermark, we make it clear that we *don't* have a perfect pastor or staff and we are *not* a perfect church. However, we *do* have a perfect mission. That's why we take seriously the opportunity we have to serve our Lord, our world, and each other. These are the foundations on which we endeavor to make disciples. We refuse to let the foundations for how we measure our success be built on the number of people who attend, the size of the buildings we construct, or the amount of money we take in. We believe that our church should measure its success by the size of our love for one another, as well as the consistency

---

12 Proverbs 18:1.
13 For a satirical look at the insanity of this idea, see http://babylonbee.com/news/man-chooses-self-accountability-partner/.
14 Some might say, "No! The first step after belief is to be baptized. Isn't that what Acts 2:37–38 says?" But let me ask you what the purpose of baptism is. It is not for salvation (Titus 3:5), but rather to signify to the body of Christ and to a watching world that you are a part of something greater than yourself. It is a sign that you are Christ's and a part of His people.

with which we yield to the Spirit—which is to say, we measure our success by our ability to be and make disciples.

And that's not by *seating* people weekly but by *sending* people daily to take up their cross and follow Him.

We so seriously desire commitment to becoming fully devoted disciples that we recommit to the process by recommitting to one another every year. That's right, every January, Watermark membership goes back to zero and rebuilds one by one back into a family of committed thousands. You heard me right …

Zero.

At Watermark, there's no such thing as "once a member, always a member" with no questions asked.[15] No, we ask questions because Scripture calls us to encourage one another in love and fellowship better than that. Thus our body asks intentional, biblical, grace-filled questions of one another so that we may "exhort one another every day, as long as it is called 'today,' that none of you may be hardened by the deceitfulness of sin."[16]

Each January, all believers are invited to re-up, and all "irregular believers" are asked to reevaluate their lack of commitment to being a part of something greater than themselves. This is done not to condemn; rather, it allows us to once again covenant with

---

15 We are not talking about salvation here. We are talking about abiding with Christ and walking with others in obedience to Christ. "Once saved, always saved" does not mean "once a member in good standing, always a member in good standing." See http://realtruthrealquick. com/can-christian-lose-salvation/ and http://realtruthrealquick.com/ what-do-i-say-to-my-friend-who-keeps-on-sinning/.

16 Hebrews 3:13 ESV.

everyone who wants to come and see—or come and see again— the fullness of life the grace of Christ has provided for His Church. Why would we desire anything less for them?

Why would you desire anything less for yourself?

3 Bs versus 4 Bs

Our desire to pursue true, biblical membership in the Church is not meant as and doesn't create a judgmental environment where we are always looking over others' shoulders trying to determine whether they are falling in line. On the contrary, it creates an environment where instead of looking *over* each other's shoulders, we are looking *out* for one another, shouldering the weights and struggles of life together.[17] We believe that we all matter to the Chief Shepherd, so we all should matter to one another.[18]

Is this commitment to each other unlike the way the world lives? Yes. Is being *unlike* the world—which lives mostly isolated, insecure, ineffective, self-centered, easily swayed, circumstantially based lives—expected of those who are now in the world but not of it?[19] Yes again.

This kind of familial commitment is mostly foreign to others, yet it is also an offer to them. We should not be surprised when others ridicule us for our commitment to the things of God,[20] nor should we be surprised when the Lord uses our commitment to

17 Galatians 6:1–3.
18 1 Peter 5:1–5.
19 1 Peter 2:11; Philippians 2:15–16.
20 John 15:15–18.

one another to bring others to Him.[21] So even though they may think they *don't like* what is *unlike* them, Jesus uses the lives of fully devoted, "unliked" followers to draw everyone to Himself and to the grace that transforms their lives in ways *unlike* they ever imagined.

That is why we call people to real membership in the body of Christ, not a watered-down, culturally mandated version of it.

You may wonder how we actually determine who is engaging in fully devoted discipleship and who is merely coming as a "regular attender." We certainly don't do it by shining spotlights on people's faults. This is not a prison yard where religious guards cast blinding lights from their ivory guard towers on those living down in the cells and courtyards. The light we shine is not one of checklists, judgment, or condemnation but one that always leads with grace and *then* truth.[22] We call people to live in real community with one another, sharing their struggles and holding each other biblically *accountable* ... because they actually *count*.

They matter to God, so they ought to matter to us.

There is no *committee* who oversees others ... there is *commitment* to one another all throughout the body. And yes, people sometimes make mistakes in this process of shepherding one another, but though we are not a perfect church and though some of the people with whom we pursue Christlikeness are imperfect people, the Lord still perfectly blesses our imperfect attempts to love one another as He loves us.[23] There will undoubtedly be

---

21 1 Peter 2:11–12.
22 Proverbs 3:3–4.
23 John 13:35.

times when community will hurt you, share information they should not share, and spur you on in a way that doesn't seem overly informed by gentleness—days when in their effort to help you remember the goodness of Christ, they forget to do it as Christ would Himself.

But don't let the fact that some will shepherd imperfectly allow you to forsake the fact that you need shepherding. Community and connection can be tough, but the alternative is worse: isolation. And sheep isolated from the shepherd shouldn't expect to live very well, or to live very long, for that matter.

So we endeavor to *maintain the joy* that comes by being *of the same mind*, intent on modeling and *maintaining the same love*, *united in spirit*, and remaining *intent on one purpose*[24] by corporately recommitting to "do business together" as we evaluate how we individually have been about the business of our King.[25] Every year, we ask every member to self-evaluate and then share their evaluation with those they care for, pray for, and live life with in their community groups so they can review, affirm, discuss, and sharpen one another in their walks with Christ.

Who among us doesn't systematically evaluate the money in our bank account? Do we evaluate our health and fitness by seeing a doctor or at least occasionally stepping on a scale? Do we constantly tend to our marriages by celebrating anniversaries, attending marriage conferences, dating our spouses, and daily

---

24 Philippians 2:2.
25 If you would like to see a sample of the questions we ask ourselves, go to http://wordsfromwags.com/assessment-questions-4b.

chasing away the "foxes from our vineyards"?[26] Do we evaluate our cars by having them properly serviced every three to five thousand miles?

Okay, perhaps we don't do all of these (and you're welcome that I didn't even mention flossing your teeth), but we should. And these tasks only service temporal things. How much further should we take an even more serious approach to eternal things?

The evaluation process we use replaces the *3 Bs* with *4 Bs*. We start with what we believe is a strong, biblical picture of faithfulness and spiritual health. Through questions on relevant topics, we individually take an honest, prayerful, noncondemning look at our past year of journeying with Christ.

It all starts with our choice to "Believe in Christ"[27] and the truths the Scripture would have us know and respond to concerning Him. We ask ourselves how we purposed to live and speak in such a way that others could come to a place of belief in the life-giving kindness of the gospel. Did we devote ourselves daily to grow in the grace and knowledge of Jesus Christ? Did our belief show itself in our devotion?

Next, we ask ourselves how we have done in our effort to intentionally "Belong to His Body."[28] Did we pursue each other, live authentically with one another, admonish each other, and counsel each other biblically? How did our entire community do at sharing all of life—from physical needs to spiritual challenges—with one

---

26 Song of Solomon 2:15.
27 John 3:16.
28 Hebrews 10:24–25.

another? Were we about God's business in the way we did business with each other, or was *koinonia*[29] not so common in our living with one another?

We then evaluate how we have purposed to "Be Trained in Truth."[30] How have we each done in the spiritual disciplines like prayer, the reading of Scripture, and daily worship? Do we know how we are uniquely gifted by God to serve other members of the body,[31] and if so, have we grown in our use and development of those gifts? How have we improved in our ability to "give a defense when anyone asks us to give an account for the hope that is within us"?[32]

Finally, we want to "Be Strong in Ministry and Worship."[33] Were we serving faithfully, wholeheartedly participating in external ministry and stewarding our time, talents, and treasure in such a way that the kingdom of Christ was advanced?

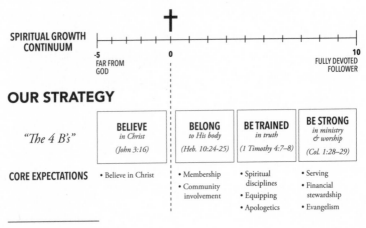

---

29 See footnote on p. 122.
30 1 Timothy 4:7–8.
31 1 Peter 4:10; 1 Corinthians 12:13.
32 1 Peter 3:15.
33 Colossians 1:28–29.

Again, this evaluation is done not from the top down—from the tower of spiritual leadership to the courtyards of spiritual peasantry. No, we do this for one another at *every* level of leadership in the church. I participate in this evaluation along with everyone else.

Together with our community group leaders and elders, we look at the macro data, and from it, we discern areas of theology or truth we need to teach on. We evaluate the strategies we are employing to make disciples, using the data to sharpen our staff and ministry efforts. On an individual level within smaller communities, we look at each other's personal responses so we can encourage and help each other develop plans that can increase our usefulness and fruitfulness as we invest our lives together in the coming months.

We do this because we love Jesus and we love His people—and we know we were made to be more than just Unmoved Christians whose lives look the same today as they did yesterday—and who are anything but compelling examples to "come and see."

Grace, available to us in Christ and His people, is meant to enable us increasingly to reflect the full glory of our King.[34]

Less of the world around us … more of the world above us … for all to come and see.

---

34   2 Corinthians 3:18; Colossians 1:27.

Chapter 11

Better Together

Why Not?

They say confession is good for the soul, and like all truth, this principle rings true first in God's Word.[1] In light of everything I have invited you to come and see so far about Christ's real intentions for you and His Church, I have a confession to make …

In the deepest recesses of my heart, I think if I really loved God as I should, then I really wouldn't need a body—a church experience—like the one I've been describing to you in the pages now continuing to pile up to your left. The "just me and Jesus" heresy makes sense to my small brain and appeals to my selfish flesh. I have this warped idea that if I was serious enough about God, if I understood more about who He is, and if I loved Him as much as I should, then surely I could be faithful to Him on my own.

And I am wrong.

---

1   James 5:16.

The truth is—for me to think that I could walk this faith journey completely on my own is as crazy as thinking I could wholly know God, who is completely beyond my comprehension and ability to grasp or describe Him—without His *Word* to guide me. It is as foolish as thinking I could walk in faithfulness toward Him without the enabling of His *Spirit* who indwells me when I come to believe—the promised Helper who pushes me onward. It is as crazy as thinking I can deny my need to walk with Him in *prayer*—in humble, constant, broken dependence as I constantly turn and return to Him.

No Word? No Spirit? No prayer? And still somehow stumbling into faithfulness? Crazy.

And yet the Word of God, the Spirit of God, and the ability to boldly come before the throne of God in prayer are not the only means of grace the Lord has provided for us to know Him. There is another artery of grace the Lord has given us, and just like the other three, if we choke it off or have it clogged by the plaque of pride, it will be fatal. If you don't believe me, then pay attention to the anatomy book called the Bible, which reveals the spiritual composition of man—not in obscure texts merely suggesting we might need one another, but in large sections that scream of our need for each other.[2]

I implore you not to file this truth away into some mental folder labeled "Stuff I Already Know" or "The Latest Churchianity Buzzwords to Increase Attendance and Giving."

---

2   Although I have already laid a pretty solid foundation with the numerous scriptures I have noted so far, stay tuned for more evidence.

I'm not saying you don't already know this to be true; I'm only asking you if it is true in *your* own life, because if you think you believe something that you don't actually experience, then you either don't really know what it means or you are being actively resistant to it. Evaluate your level of conviction by your consistency of choice. Again, men say what they think, but they believe what they do.

There is no doubt that Jesus repeatedly calls us to more than just a belief in Him. He also expects us to follow Him together. It's hard to make a case that we can go at the idea of faithfulness alone when Jesus said that the world will know He was sent by the Father and that we are disciples saved by His grace *only* if we love and pursue oneness with each other.[3]

Oneness is a pretty strong word that makes it abundantly clear that isolation, separation, and dissension are not at all what Jesus has in mind for His body. We are to be "diligent to preserve the unity of the Spirit in the bond of peace."[4] We are supposed to "reject a factious man after a first and second warning."[5] We are to keep an "eye on those who cause dissensions."[6] We should lay aside "falsehood" and "speak truth each one of you with his neighbor, for we are members of one another."[7]

---

3 John 13:34–35; 17:22–23.
4 Ephesians 4:3.
5 Titus 3:10.
6 Romans 16:17.
7 Ephesians 4:25.

Francis Schaeffer called our love for one another the "final apologetic."[8] Early Christian apologists built their entire case around the observable way the Church cared for each other.[9] It might be easy to make a case against a lot of things related to the family that God created, but the fact that we are to love and live in close relationship with authentic care and concern for each other is not one of them.

It is hard to sum it up any better than Paul did in his letter to the church in Colossae: "So, as those who have been chosen of God, holy and beloved, put on a heart of compassion, kindness, humility, gentleness and patience; bearing with one another, and forgiving each other, whoever has a complaint against anyone; just as the Lord forgave you, so also should you. Beyond all these things put on love, which is the perfect bond of unity. Let the peace of Christ rule in your hearts, to which indeed you were called in one body; and be thankful."[10]

It is not at all an overstatement to say that if we forsake our pursuing of life together, then we are forsaking our calling. Through many notes and emails over the years, I have learned that believers and nonbelievers alike are drawn to find out more

---

8   See *The Mark of a Christian*, by Francis Schaeffer.

9   See the *Apology of Aristides*, where he says, "If one or other of them have bondmen and bondwomen or children, *through love towards them they persuade them to become Christians, and when they have done so, they call them brethren without distinction.*" Also see the *Apology of Tertullian*: "These Christians are very strange people. They meet together in an empty room to worship. They do not have an image. They speak of One by the name of Jesus, who is absent, but who they seem to be expecting at any time. And my, how they love Him and *how they love one another.*"

10 Colossians 3:12–15.

about Jesus when they come and see the way we share our lives together. There is something irresistibly magnetic about communities who live in peace and others-centered service to one another.

Not long ago, I received a note from a woman whose daughter was on our staff. She had invited a friend of hers to come to a wedding celebration where many other members of Watermark were gathered. Her note to me said:

"Watermark has made an everlasting mark on Tucker and Jay ... the body of Christ is alive at Watermark ... David and Julia willingly became His hands and feet as they mentored Tucker and Jay, sacrificing their time to show these two what a Christ-centered marriage looks like. They pointed them to His Word, they guided them in His truth, and they prayed with them. They poured out their love for these two, expecting nothing in return ... I wanted to share with you an email that my friend, Jan, sent to me about the weekend which sums up everything: '... the best part was the depth of love that seemed to be literally poured out on all that were there ... the love of Jesus permeated everything. It wasn't a "contrived" feeling or "make a statement" or "in your face" showy kind of love. It was sincere, sweet, accepting, gentle, kind, joy unspeakable that emanated from your heart and poured out all over everyone there; from the Father to His children from the children back to their Heavenly Father. Thank you for the opportunity to be blessed by all of it.'"

Love in action is *always* a blessing.

Believers who isolate or stay in conflict with others are a barrier to the faith. Being committed to community was never meant to be merely an option that we can add or drop as if we are building out a car to save ourselves trouble or expense. It is not heated seats or a sunroof. It is standard equipment, as necessary to us being who we are as the engine or axle is to a car. Drop community and love from the Christian life, and you are removing what makes it Christian.

Community is not an accessory … it is part and parcel to the function of the car itself. Without it, we won't travel long.

For a church body as large as ours, we know that instead of "come and see," it would be all too easy for "attenders" to "come and hide." Hiding is what we do in isolation, and isolation is the garden in which idiosyncrasies grow. The larger the garden, the more opportunity there is for a great harvest. But the larger the garden, the more difficult it is to keep out the weeds. If we are not careful, a more successful church "size-wise" could inadvertently produce a less successful church "purpose-wise."

It is all too easy to see thousands of people gather and to be impressed with the crowds, forgetting to be diligent about the biblical "one anothers" that must mark God's people. We cannot merely be reminded and encouraged about the transformative grace and truth of Christ only to walk out the doors to live isolated lives, not following through on the one practice that identifies us as Jesus's disciples and verifies His divinity.[11]

---

11   John 13:34–35; John 17:22–23.

But community is not just what *marks* us; it is what God uses to *make* us.

An abundance of verses speak to this truth, some so familiar they roll off our lips. Verses like "As iron sharpens iron, so one man sharpens another"[12] or "A friend loves at all times, and a brother is born for adversity."[13] "Do not forsake your own friend or your father's friend."[14] "Better is a neighbor who is near than a brother who is far away."[15] "Do not forsake our assembling together, as is the habit of some."[16]

But having verses *roll off* your lips doesn't necessarily mean they really *show up* in your life. Over the years, I have seen that the most transformative thing a person can do to respond to grace and experience real transformation is to commit to doing the business of the Godward life with others. The data we have received from our church members' self-evaluations proves that the phrase "life changes happen best in the context of relationships" is not just religious rhetoric but a statistical certainty.

We have seen that members who were practicing the "one anothers" of Scripture experienced radical life transformation. Specifically, year after year individuals who are in community and self-describe as caring for one another, sharpening one another, and serving others are, by percentage, significantly more likely than

---

12 Proverbs 27:17.
13 Proverbs 17:17.
14 Proverbs 27:10a.
15 Proverbs 27:10c.
16 Hebrews 10:25.

those who do not self-describe these ways to be able to do—or to be—all of the following:

82%   More likely to study the Bible five to seven days a week.

177%   More able to consistently apply Scripture to daily circumstances, situations, and struggles in ways that transform their lives.

193%   More likely to describe themselves as consistently content and joyful in all circumstances.

159%   More likely to consistently and effectively communicate with their spouses about both daily challenges and deeper issues.

91%   More likely to love and respect their spouses well by addressing and resolving conflict in a safe, timely, and God-honoring way.

157%   More likely to find contentment in their season of singleness, and maximize this unique time to know and serve God.

117%   More likely to be active in training their children to know and follow Christ.

176%   More likely to yield to the Spirit's leading and to have conversations about spiritually significant things.

172%   More likely to share their story of grace and the gospel with nonbelievers with whom they have relationships.

126%   More likely to handle their financial resources with the mind-set that these resources are God's.

137%   More likely to live under biblical principles related to debt, budgeting, and the use of financial stewardship.

If you're around any faith community, there are two things that will shock you: how *little* some people change and how *much* other people change. The single greatest determining factor of which group you will be a part of is whether you will live in biblical community with others. More people choose to leave our church ultimately to avoid the very thing that is, ironically, the greatest single cause of transformation for those who choose to stay.[17] As the statistics above show, people are radically changed when they humble themselves under God's admonition to let others keep watch over their souls.[18]

It is worth saying again: community is not just what *marks* us; it is what God uses to *make* us.[19]

Watermark has embraced this as a core value from the very beginning. Every biblical church always has. Want proof? Look no further than the very first description of the very first church. Hours past their birth, they were already being described as "continually devoting themselves to the apostles' teaching and to fellowship, to the breaking of bread and to prayer."[20] We have already seen that the word "fellowship" means more than "hanging out." It means taking joint ownership, doing business, or investing together.

But what about the next idea of breaking bread? Notice there is no word separating "fellowship" (*koinonia*) from the idea of breaking bread. This is because the two were never intended to be separate. They are meant to be joined. When we talk about doing

---

17   Proverbs 27:17.
18   Hebrews 13:17.
19   A much more inane example of this is the *Consumer Reports* survey which found that people who went to Weight Watchers meetings were more satisfied with the program and lost more weight than people who used only online or self-management tools.
20   Acts 2:42.

life together, we are talking about choosing companions. Proverbs 13:20 reminds us that "the companion of fools will suffer harm, but he who walks with wise men will prosper."

The word "companion" literally means "bread fellow," or *com* (with) *panis* (bread). It speaks to the regularity with which believers gathered together and is almost certainly a reference to what they gathered around—a table. Meals where they remembered the love and selflessness of their provision, the Bread of Life: Jesus. May I suggest that if you are meeting up with your "business partners" only once a week to remind yourself of God's goodness and to be encouraged to respond to it, you might be a bit spiritually malnourished?

God desires that we come to the table and take the provision of community and life together seriously. It's time to dig in.

To Be Real Community or Not to Be Real Community ... That Is the Question

I am committed to helping and equipping Christ followers to go through life together. I have already shown you and personally experienced that this is where Christ's richest blessings are found. But I want to warn you of an easy mistake to make. It is entirely too easy to make "committed to community" equal with "committed to community groups."

A few years into Watermark's start, I stood up and told our entire church that I, along with the rest of our leadership, was concerned that we were maintaining the appearance of doing life together but were possibly not actually doing it. We knew we had the form, but we were concerned that we were missing the function.[21]

By definition, community does involve groups. So when we addressed this issue, we really didn't make any radical changes in how we were encouraging people to get together. However, we knew that there were people in our body who were in community groups but who really were not immersed in each other's lives.

By merely being in a community group, some were deluding themselves into thinking they were technically doing what God wanted them to do. In the same way that many people are in large, dead churches that are not doing—or calling them to do—what God wants them to do, our church contained lots of little dead churches. Lots of people were regularly attending weekly meetings but were not daily attending to the things of Christ. Deadness happens in all shapes and sizes.

Being in a community group does not necessarily mean you are presently experiencing biblical community.

There are thousands of people who will sit in church this very Sunday wearing rings on their left hands forged from precious

---

21 When I did this, 90 percent of our body was in community groups. Today we have over 1,000 groups of members in community at Watermark. Daily we remind them that being in a group does you no good if your companions (the ones you regularly gather with to remind yourself of the goodness of Christ) are not committed to doing the business of practicing the "one anothers" with you. The goal is always practice, not just presence.

metals—rings whose collective value ranges in the millions of dollars. Yet their marriages are being lived below the relational poverty line. They are isolated from the ones to whom they once vowed to forsake all and everyone else for the purpose of being one flesh together. They may not be actively cheating on one another, but they are not actively pursuing one another. They are missing God's best by not pursuing the oneness that God intends. They may not be committing adultery, but they are not committed to what God wants.

They are more "undivorced" than they are one flesh.

Is the same true for you and me? You may be like so many were in our church—complying with the Bible's call to be in a community but perhaps not really understanding *why* the call is there in the first place. In essence, it's all too easy to forget that the business of doing life together is at the heart of what our business really is. We are our brothers' keepers, and we are in need of our brothers keeping up with us. Our team motto should be "Oneness through the One Anothers." More on the "one anothers" a bit later.

C. S. Lewis said, "A secret master of ceremonies has been at work. Christ, who said to the disciples, 'Ye have not chosen me, but I have chosen you,' can truly say to every group of Christian friends, 'Ye have not chosen one another, but I have chosen you for one another.'"[22]

This even counts if you are one of those, like thousands around the world, who think community groups are just the next fad in

---

22   C. S. Lewis, *The Four Loves* (London: HarperCollins, 1952).

modern Churchianity.[23] Perhaps you feel either sheepishly embarrassed that you haven't involved yourself in a group like this—or maybe you even feel a little rebellious, avoiding and dancing around the responsibility clearly given to us to love one another.

I may not be your pastor, but hear my heart from a biblical leadership standpoint: I do not want you to *just* be in a community group any more than I want you *just* attending church. I want you to be in healthy community. I want you to have "bread-fellows" who daily remind you that if you are in Christ, you have been given "every spiritual blessing in the heavenly places."[24] I want you to experience biblical community. I want this for you because God wants this for you, and what God wants for you is always on the path of life. When or where you gather with a group of friends is not the issue; the fact that you gather regularly and what you do when you are together is. Meeting at night isn't sacrosanct, but meeting regularly and practicing the core disciplines of daily personal devotion, consistent pursuit of one another, authentic sharing, faithful admonishing, biblical counseling, and missional living is.

As we help to equip and establish Christ followers in biblical community, we must keep *the main thing* the main thing. It is a constant battle, and there are constant lies and myths—just like the foolish one I shared at the beginning of the chapter that I am sometimes tempted to believe. But the truth is that community is

---

23 They are not. What you call them may change, but what we are called to never will.

24 Ephesians 1:3.

God's gift to us. He designed us to need it, be blessed by it, and to facilitate it. And yet again and again, I find people resist the provision of this great gift. Why is that?

Over the next chapter, let me share the six main reasons I believe people do not immerse themselves in the lives of others.

Chapter 12

Excuses, Excuses

Reason #1: I Don't Get It (Foolishness and Childishness)

People often avoid godly community because they are either willingly or unwillingly ignorant of the Scriptures. If you read the last chapter, you can't claim ignorance as an excuse anymore. These people already know that Christ calls us to share life with one another, but they don't really care what He says because they don't believe that what God wants is what they should want.

This is *foolishness*, and I wrote the early chapters of this book to try to spare you from this.

Granted, there are many who haven't learned the ways of God's goodness and life yet. They are young in their faith and possibly, like Nebuchadnezzar, they do not yet know that "all His works are true and His ways just, and He is able to humble those who walk in pride."[1]

---

1   Daniel 4:37.

This is *childishness*, and I wrote this book so fewer believers would find themselves needing to learn the danger of living in ignorance the way Nebuchadnezzar did. Experience is a good teacher—but often a very expensive one.

This latter group displays their ignorance because of a lack of information, while the other group is foolish, which means they display rebellion in the midst of information. Both groups suffer from missing out on the provision, but the foolish heaps additional judgment upon themselves for suppressing the truth they have been given.[2]

The God whose image we bear models for us the communal life we were created to thrive in. Relational intimacy is embedded in our created nature and essence. God said, "Let Us make man in Our image, according to Our likeness."[3] One of the things eternally true about God as He has revealed Himself is that He is one, yet this one God exists in three persons: the Father, Son, and Holy Spirit. Those three persons, who are all one God, relate to each other in a mutually submissive, mutually exalting, personally distinct, eternally existing, glorifying way.

Father. Son. Spirit. All distinct. All one. Perfect community.

Community, compassion, love, submission—these attributes are eternally existent in the nature of God. So when God says, "I will make you in My image," He has creatively designed us like Himself—to live in relationship. To deny this relational design is to deny the very divine essence of who we are created to be. People

---

2   Matthew 11:20–24.
3   Genesis 1:26 (ESV).

were designed for each other, and God wants them to enjoy each other—it is not "good for us to be alone"[4] because it is not good for us to live outside of God's perfect will for us.

Being made in the image of God is to be made to dwell in oneness where there is plurality, to express unity where there is diversity. We're not all the same. From Jakarta, Indonesia, to Hereford, Texas, we speak different languages, and we each own a unique story of rebellion against God. Yet each of us is meant to find hope in the same provision—Jesus Christ—and then to walk with Him in obedience. Out of our immense diversity comes a miraculous unity in Him. This is true in the marriage between man and woman, and it is true in the Church. There is a renewal of heart in all who are one with Christ that allows us, whether Jew or Greek, Barbarian or Scythian, male or female, to dwell in peace and oneness with each other.[5]

Authentic, loving community is also our biblical privilege. It is where we live out the "one anothers" of Scripture. I engaged in a study to map out and explore the dozens of times the phrase "one another" is used in the Bible. These "one anothers" show how attractive the real community God has designed us for truly is.

It is where we love one another, care for one another, serve one another, show forbearance to and forgive one another, admonish one another, keep fervent in our love for one another, be hospitable toward one another, employ our gifts in serving one another as good stewards of the manifold grace of God, greet one another,

---

4   Genesis 2:18.
5   Colossians 3:10–11; Galatians 3:28.

be of the same mind toward one another, be kind to one another, and speak to one another in psalms, hymns, and spiritual songs. It's where we build, comfort, pray for, live in peace with, and seek after that which is good for one another, clothe ourselves in humility toward one another, live in subjection to one another, stimulate one another unto love and good deeds, confess sins to one another, live in peace with one another, give preference to one another, honor and encourage one another day after day lest any of us should become hardened by the deceitfulness of sin, and again, love one another just as He commanded us.[6]

Every time I have ever read aloud to a group of people this extensive description of what God intends for His people to enjoy in their relationships with each other, I always ask them, "Who would like this list to describe their relationships?" Do you know how many people have ever said no?

None.

Believer and unbeliever alike are drawn to this description because every one of us would like to be immersed in these kinds of fearless, loving, deeply committed relationships. You and I were made for this.

Biblical community is also our responsibility and charge. We are accountable to model it. John 13:34 captures our King's will

---

6   I invite you to journey through the scriptural map of the "one anothers" yourself: John 13:34–35; 1 Corinthians 12:25; Galatians 5:13; Colossians 3:13; 3:16; 1 Peter 1:22; 4:9, 10; Romans 16:16; 12:16; Ephesians 4:32; 5:19; 2 Corinthians 13:11–12; 1 Thessalonians 5:15; 1 Peter 5:5; Ephesians 5:21; Hebrews 10:24; James 5:16; 1 Thessalonians 5:13; Romans 12:10; Hebrews 3:13; 1 John 3:23.

for us: "A new commandment I give to you, that you love one another: just as I have loved you, you also are to love one another."[7] The mark of being a true disciple of Christ is *not* knowing when He will return or having some map of the future of the earth's history.

The mark of a true follower of Christ is love lived out in real relationships.

Our failure to live in peace and increasing oneness with each another is a primary reason so many people are *not* clamoring to "come and see" the Church. It is also why most of us are completely unwilling to broker all our relational capital to encourage them to do so. They see—and we know they are seeing—something other than compelling love. They don't see what God says they should see if we were really His disciples. They see all manner of backbiting and insecurity. They see convictions of convenience in the way we love people with "acceptable" sin struggles, yet they see us turn our backs on brothers and sisters who are not like us. They see inconsistency between what we say we believe and how we experience and express these beliefs in our relationships with one another.

So they conclude that there is no love here. Instead, they see a society of people who have decided to group themselves together as if to say to the world, "Our issues aren't as bad as your issues, so we're going to be slightly more patient with each other than we are with you." I hope it doesn't surprise you to learn that God has very little tolerance for this.

---

7   John 13:34 ESV.

If hypocrisy bothers you, then Jesus is your man. Never has there been a leader who was so crystal clear in His frustration and outcry against the cruelly superior, out-of-touch-with-his-own-sin individual.[8] It enrages Him when He sees people who "say things and do not do them … [and] tie up heavy burdens and lay them on men's shoulders, but they themselves are unwilling to move them with so much as a finger."[9]

It does not go unnoticed when He sees me love you only because of what you can do for me.[10] Or because of how attractive you are. Or how rich. Or how little you might embarrass me if we're friends. Or how much you might give me if I'm associated with you.

These kinds of relationships run contrary to everything divine. Jesus calls us to love each other as He loves us. So, how does He love? Wholly, fully, sacrificially, unconditionally, perfectly … in other words, rather well. He loves all of us, even when we, like the Pharisees, try to show how good we are by our own good works and efforts to have our "deeds to be noticed by men; for they broaden their phylacteries and lengthen the tassels of their garments."[11]

---

8   See Matthew 23:13–33 for an example. It is also worth mentioning here that it is not hypocritical to say that something is wrong and then to commit that wrong action yourself. That is the human experience. A person is not a hypocrite because he says something is wrong and then does it. He is a hypocrite (meaning literally "under judgment") when he says, "Something is wrong unless I do it."

9   Matthew 23:3–4.

10   Luke 6:31–33.

11   Matthew 23:5.

He loves us in our rebellion. In our addictions. In our abuse. In our bitterness. He loves us through sad childhoods and awkward adolescent years. He sees the pain of our experiences that have left us as we are. Even when we use the abuses done to us as excuses to do more harm to ourselves and others, He loves us. And He demonstrated this love by also dying right there—right where we are.[12]

It is no small thing for us to be called to carry on this kind of love—and with this great privilege comes great responsibility, so we would be wise to "wage war with wise guidance,"[13] the abundance of counsel, and encouragement of others. The truth is, I cannot love others with this "crazy compassionate Jesus" kind of love if I try to do so on my own. No way. There is just too much "me." So unless I have the powerful blessing of God's Word in my life, the enabling presence of God's Spirit in my life, and "day-after-day encouragement" of godly friends in my life, I will not be a man you would want to "come and see," much less than the man God made me to be.

Reason #2: Biased about Being Unbiased (Blindness)

The second reason people avoid immersing themselves in the lives of others is because they think they can discern their own hearts and sort through their own issues without bias, rationalization, or error.

---

12   2 Corinthians 5:21; Romans 5:8.
13   Proverbs 24:6.

Jeremiah begs to differ. "The heart is more deceitful than all else and is desperately sick; who can understand it?"[14]

Many years ago, my wife and I were working our way through a study about resolving conflict in marriage with six or seven of our couple friends. One of our assignments was to take a test to discern what kind of consciences we each had. The test results for one of my closest friends and for my wife both came back with an alarming conclusion: they possessed "seared consciences." The word "seared" in this context is a biblical reference wherein someone's personal conscience has become nonresponsive and numb based on repeated exposure to one's own hypocrisy, bitterness, or rebellious choices.

As conscience tests go, this was *not* good news.[15] However, for years—and even today—it has provided all of us endless fodder for snide remarks and "gentle" reminders. If you think I haven't used this "empirical scientific"[16] data to help me in a few "conversations" with my wife over the years, then you don't know how much Jeremiah had my heart in mind when he was writing his seventeenth chapter.

But the most disturbing part about the whole thing—and what I didn't offer to tell anyone the first time we were sharing our results—is that I knew *exactly* what the self-assessment was looking

---

14 Jeremiah 17:9.

15 1 Timothy 4:2.

16 A short, ten-question self-assessment hardly qualifies as empirical data, but nonetheless it has provided some good ammo these last years. Ironically enough, anyone who knows my bride would challenge the results. Hers is one of the humbler hearts I've ever known, and her complete honesty and effort to challenge herself with her answers really prove the opposite of the results. The verdict is still out on my friend, however (insert smiley-face emoji here).

to establish; so I lied when giving my answers to make myself look like I did not have a seared conscience. What does this say about me? It says that I have a seared conscience about the fact that I have a seared conscience—I could keep a team of psychologists both gainfully employed and equally amused for years![17]

One of my favorite self-reminders, and something I constantly share with others when I am teaching on this topic, is this statement: *there is nothing quite so creative as a person in the midst of self-justification.* I know how creative and self-convincing I can be. Left to myself, I am world class in allowing my heart room to believe that my perspective, informed with all the "genius and goodness contained within me," so "voluminous and noble," is perfectly informed. So I take as much time as necessary to "graciously enlighten" others.

These are not, as you can imagine, my finest moments.

But the truth is, I know myself. I know I am capable of jumping online and impulsively wanting to purchase something I don't need. After a mere few minutes, I know that in isolation I could convince myself that it would be an act of rebellion against the God of the universe for me not to *invest* my Lord's money on a particular purchase.

When there is a new movie out with a scene I've heard could be trouble, I know that, left to myself, I could easily coerce

---

17 Truth be told, after we all laughed that night about the results, I "unseared" my conscience for a moment and shared with them what I had done. In addition to allowing us to laugh again, it served as a good reminder for all of us that self-assessments without broader and loving feedback from trusted friends are not typically the most reliable.

myself into putting trouble before my eyes—because I want to be culturally relevant and "with it" and thus be able to address the topic with my friends. Left alone, I would easily poison my own heart ... all in the name of ministry and relevance, of course.

Left to myself, I am a highly trained master of manipulation, self-rationalization, and justification. I bet if you were honest with yourself, you would admit your own Jedi skills here as well. *Unless, of course, you have a seared conscience.*

God's Word reminds us, "All the ways of a man are clean in his own sight, but the LORD weighs the motives."[18] In other words, we should not be impressed with our level of skill or creativity in the ways we rationalize or justify our own issues—our overspending, overeating, anger, depression, frustration, bitterness, lust, and the like.

So if you avoid biblical community because you instinctively believe you can discern your own tendency to enable yourself through rationalization, you are dodging the truth of the Scriptures. God says that we all have broken souls and seared consciences.[19] There is not a single one of us who, if left to ourselves, will not rationalize and justify some action in our lives that is less than what is best for us and certainly less than best for others.

It is a primary reason we need others in our lives. It is another reason why we cannot afford to choke out the means of grace our Creator has given us to protect us called *life together.*

---

18 Proverbs 16:2.
19 Romans 3:10.

Community is a *means* of grace, which *means* it is not optional.

This really hits home in my life when it comes to "grace in theory" versus "grace in action." I am very capable of quoting a myriad of scriptures about grace and God's loving, forgiving Spirit—which makes it very easy for me to accept God's grace and forgiveness even as I am moving the wrong way. However, it is much more difficult for me to look a brother or a sister in the eye and say, "I did this." When I look them in the eyes, I can see the tangible pain on their faces. Community brings much-needed reality to the cost of extending myself "grace."

There is a biblical principle for this. When I justify wrong actions or attitudes under the umbrella of grace, it grieves the Holy Spirit.[20] The Holy Spirit, who is God, is referred to in Scripture with the pronoun "He." *He* is not an *it.* The Holy Spirit is not an impersonal force I am grieving—He is a divine Person. He feels pain from my actions. We often think that some offenses are theoretical, but they never are. *All* of them are personal. So in terms of community, sometimes it bodes well for me to have to look at a grieved spirit in my wife or in a friend. They put a face to the reality of my actions and help me appropriately grieve that I have grieved my God.

For me to say that I don't need this in my life would be, at the least, blind ignorance and, at the worst, bold foolishness.

---

20   Ephesians 4:17–32 lays out a full foundation of how we are to continue to let grace produce fruits of holiness in the lives we live with one another—in speech, motivation, and forgiveness, to list a few.

Reason #3: I Do What I Do ... It's What I Do (Rebellion and Licentiousness)

The third reason people do not immerse themselves wholeheartedly in biblical community is that they want to do what they want to do with as little accountability or conviction as possible.

This one is pretty simple. It is the attitude that says, "Look, I know what I'm going to do, so why mess around acting like I don't? There's no reason for me to walk all over you in the process or have you make me uncomfortable when I'm around you. So I'd rather not talk to you about this or anything else of real consequence in my life—I'm going to do what I want to do. I'll come to church, but don't think for a second I am going to do this thing you are trying to tell me 'real' churchmen do."

I love the honesty here, but I'm warning you that you are not going to like where this kind of living takes you. Here's the honest truth: isolated living is quarreling against all wisdom.[21]

And quarreling with wisdom is *not* wise.

Reason #4: I Can't Trust You (Fear and Distrust)

Some do not come into biblical community because they are ruled by fear or they are unable to trust other people. People who live in this mind-set are fearful that if they share with others what is

---

21   Proverbs 18:1.

actually going on in their lives or what they are really thinking, people will take this knowledge and use it to exploit them, harm them, embarrass them, and ultimately ruin them.

They choose instead to go through life alone. They decide to continue to walk ahead with blind independence, fearlessly making their own way. They figure it would be better to risk harming their own lives through isolation than to have their lives ruined by the idiocy of others. They make choices and then face whatever may come with the reckless rationalization that whatever may happen is a safer path than seeking counsel and allowing someone else (potentially) to hurt them.

For this person, God's Word invites you to experience real freedom in His love. He says, "There is no fear in love; but perfect love casts out fear."[22] It is worth nothing that the opposite of love is not hate; it is indifference. I am praying this section convinces you that indifference to the love God offers you within grace-informed community will lead you to a place you'll hate.

What is the solution then? You have to love the Truth that pursuing God's will and way, even with imperfect people, is going to be better for you than trying to make your way through life alone. To our own detriment, we often choose to pursue life alone outside of biblical community because we fear what *could* happen more than we trust what the love of God declares to us in His Word.

I know an enemy of yours who loves to recommend this way of thinking.[23]

---

22   1 John 4:18.
23   Genesis 3:4; John 8:44; 1 Peter 5:8.

When you really become aware of the perfect love of God expressed through the grace of Jesus, it changes your willingness to be real with other people. On countless occasions, I have witnessed the love of God miraculously releasing people to be courageous enough to share details of their lives or stories in ways they never dreamed they would be able to do. And the result of sharing—or trusting in God's wisdom that calls His children to live in authentic community with others in His body—produces life-giving freedom and blessing not only in their lives but also in the lives of everyone around them.

I've heard hundreds of people express that, in sharing, they found for the first time what they had always hoped might exist: a group of normal people—full of *not-so-normal* grace—who live authentically with one another and who will readily accept and love them right where they are. This is because those "normal people" have been accepted and have received grace and love themselves— beggars who have found an abundance of bread and are now willing to share it with others who are as hungry as they are. Community is where the radical beauty of grace is most readily seen.

God wants you to experience this kind of love, and it is worth the risk to find it.

True love never lets you do what you want to do without consequence.[24] Real love speaks truth to you as you do what you do, reminding you there are consequences while always creating the avenue for hope and restoration.

Some of us don't trust people because, in the past, we've been around people who haven't fully trusted God themselves.

---

24   1 Corinthians 13:6; Proverbs 23:14; 27:6.

The psalmist actually reinforces the wisdom of not trusting these kinds of people when he says, "Blessed is the man who walks not in the counsel of the wicked, nor stands in the way of sinners, nor sits in the seat of scoffers."[25]

You may not want to be in community because you've been in community before ... with fools. You may have asked them what they think you should do only to receive very unwise counsel from them. Or perhaps they took your information and tried to control or hurt you with it.

But don't throw out truth just because someone else has not been trustworthy. Don't abandon the brand because you ran into someone who operated a franchise poorly. Scripture begs us to be wise about choosing our community. It never promises us it will be easy, painless, or free from problems. Just as my then-five-year-old Ally discovered, the potential for experiencing the love of a real friend in a real relationship is so much better than the superficial acceptance of a fake doll. Scripture *does not* promise us a pain-free experience in real, biblical community, but it *does* promise us we *will* experience pain and problems if we refuse it. We are counseled to do our best to take great care in yoking[26] our lives to others,[27] but we are not given the option to avoid it altogether.

---

25 Psalm 1:1 ESV.
26 A yoke is a wooden crosspiece that is fastened over the necks of two
    animals and then attached to a plow or cart so they can pull it together.
    So to be "yoked" to a person means to live life with them in relationships,
    pursuits, and common values.
27 2 Corinthians 6:14.

So by all means, you must be careful about those with whom you yoke yourself. You must find others walking these paths of grace for themselves. Otherwise, how can they care for you, sharpen you, or speak into the process of your path? Scripturally, if you walk in community with wicked people, you will become more wicked—and probably think that you are right in becoming so. And they will scoff at your efforts to become who God wants you to be.

As you look back, realize your problem may not have been with the idea of community itself but with those whom you were or are in community with. Perhaps you have been "doing business" with those whom you should flee—those who are selfish, self-righteous, or spiritually indignant. Perhaps you are surrounded by people who are not disciples of Jesus. Perhaps these people do not acknowledge their own brokenness, their need for grace, or their own ongoing process of sanctification as they follow Christ *with* you—not *above* you—in humility together.

But in real, Christ-seeking, grace-centered community where the love of God and submission to the truth of His Word is humbly and equally shared with everyone around the table, there is no reason to fear. In this kind of community, the people are far from perfect, but the love is absolutely perfect … because it's the love of a perfect Savior.

Reason #5: There's Just No Time! (Busyness or Laziness)

The next reason people avoid community is because they claim it takes too much time and effort to pull everyone together. There is no denying that life in the modern age brings with it a different level of demand on our schedules. For some of us, our calendars need extra hard drive space just to manage the mayhem. But there are possibly other reasons we just can't seem to "find the time" to get together.

Proverbs 26:13 introduces us to someone like this: "The sluggard says, 'There is a lion in the road! A lion is in the open square!'" Why is this in the Bible? Because God wants us to be educated about the way of the sluggard. Sluggards are people who always make excuses for what they are doing (or not doing, in most cases). A lazy person always has a reason why he is not doing what he should be doing. "You can't expect me to go to work today. A lion may devour me on the way there." While that might have been a *possibility* in the day the proverb was written, it was never a *probability*. But that doesn't keep the lazy man from using it as a plausible excuse.

This reminds me of a farmer who asked his friend if he could borrow some milk. The friend responded, "I don't have any rope."

The farmer was confused. "What? I asked you if I could borrow some milk. You don't need rope to give me any milk."

The friend responded with, "That's right, but when you don't want to do something, one excuse is as good as another."

This is the way we sometimes approach the possibility of living in real community together. "Do you know how hard it is to get everyone together? It's hard to find the right kind of people, you know … I really don't connect well with everyone. Their schedules are different from mine. They are in different life stages than me."

Okay? And? Do you really think you are the only one with reasons not to engage in the divine invitation to full devotion in biblical community?

If you don't want to do community, let's just admit that you don't want to do it. We can stop spouting off about all these other reasons that really aren't the main one. The real reason we don't want to do it is simple: we don't want to do it. Again and again, I run into people at Watermark who are unable to "plug into such a big church." Meanwhile, every day, I also keep running into thousands of others who somehow quickly made it past "the lion" and into the freedom of doing life together with others.

This doesn't mean that the ones who don't persevere in "doing business" with others are horrible people or lazy in every other area of their lives, but it may very well mean that something inside of them is leaning toward laziness in this extremely crucial, God-directed area called biblical community. We may not be sluggards at work or even in our church attendance, but it might mean we need to run at the lions of excuses that are keeping us from pursing living in real community.

Reason #6: But I Already Know Everything, Right? (Arrogance)

This one is very short, sweet, and scary. Some people avoid immersing themselves in the lives of others because they believe they are the compendium of all human wisdom. In other words, they consider themselves to be the personified Library of Congress concerning what is right—they are never wrong.

Scripture speaks a lot about the concept of a fool, who is generally described as someone who rejects God's wisdom and does whatever he wants to do. The harshest words in Scripture are reserved for the fool. Yet the Bible says that there is one person who is *worse* off than a fool: Any guesses?

"Do you see a man who is wise in his own eyes?"

Let me push pause before I finish this proverb.

We have already established that God's wisdom repeatedly calls us to live in community together, so you could read it like this: "Do you see a man who is wise in his own eyes … who doesn't need others because he has it all figured out on his own?"

Now push play: "There is more hope for a fool than for him."[28] *That*, my friend, is scary.

Why is this true? Because after a hundred painful blows, a fool may eventually figure it out. Take a look at Proverbs 17:10. "A rebuke goes deeper into one who has understanding than a hundred blows into a fool." Note what this proverb says. A wise man needs only a rebuke to learn. A fool needs a hundred blows.

But the man who is wise in his own eyes is worse than them both! He won't respond to a rebuke, and even if he takes a hundred blows to the head, he will figure out a way to blame it on injustice, bad luck, or God—*anything* other than himself. He will bloviate his way through the blows and convince himself he is cursed instead of listening to wisdom that calls him to change.

---

28   Proverbs 26:12 (ESV).

How does God feel about this one? Let's take a peek.

"Where there is no guidance the people fall, but in abundance of counselors there is victory.... Without consultation, plans are frustrated, but with many counselors they succeed.... Prepare plans by consultation, and make war by wise guidance.... For by wise guidance you will wage war, and in abundance of counselors there is victory.... *A man's pride will bring him low*, but a humble spirit will obtain honor."[29]

The guy who thinks he is smarter than everyone else is in more trouble than anyone else.

One last word of warning and admonition on seeking counsel in life with others. Too many people who think they are giving heed to an abundance of counsel are actually still living in isolation. To them, seeking an abundance of counsel simply means asking a lot of different friends their opinions.

However, when Scripture says to seek an abundance of counselors, this does not mean that you should call five friends back to back on your phone to convey to them what you want to say and listen to the advice of each in return—all the while keeping the conversations and counselors isolated from one another. When we do this, we are ignoring the human tendency to be inconsistent in the way we share information with different people. And it ignores the reality that, in many cases, what we are really doing is perusing the counseling universe, asking enough people and presenting different levels of information until we find the counsel that we like so we can hide behind it.

---

29   Proverbs 11:14; 15:22; 20:18; 24:6; 29:23 (all).

When you seek input from many different counselors in isolation, you deprive them and yourself of the opportunity to sharpen each other with communal reflection and life perspective. You remain the epicenter—the sole processor and interpreter— of all the information, problematically leaving you as the "most informed," yet consequently *still isolated*, decision maker. This is not the essence of the biblical exhortation to seek an abundance of godly counselors. There is more to community than just communicating with more people.

Much more.

Getting Off the Island

Let me show you, in my own life, why community means more than just listening to many voices. By doing so, it is my hope that you might stop looking for all the reasons not to do this and instead discover all the incredible reasons to commit passionately to this core and often neglected means of grace.[30]

In my life, there are men with whom I personally live in this kind of community. These men, along with the perspective provided by their wives, partner with me in leading our church ... and me. When I need to seek counsel on a leadership issue, I don't call just one of them to tell him what's going on so that he alone can, in turn, give me his advice. If I did this, I would be ignoring

---

30 Next to compromising and/or not paying attention to and humbling itself under the teaching of Scripture, the failure to truly pursue life together as God prescribes is the number one reason the Church in America, and all over the world, is so dysfunctional.

the probability that I would no doubt tell him what I want to tell him in light of my knowledge of his personality, bent, and temperament.

I could even repeat the same process with the others, having unique conversations with each person and hearing each one's feedback based on the way I shared the questions I had with them individually. I know myself—and I know that I would (even if inadvertently) say certain things to persuade each one of them to give me the advice I really want to hear.

If I were to go about community from this angle, I would not be seeking an abundance of counselors. Instead, I would be giving myself the impression that I was heeding the Scripture when I was really only finding a reason to do what I wanted to do. Why? Because even though there may be an "abundance of counselors," there is no *presence of community*. No one would know what everyone else told me except me. And if things come back to bite me later on, I have deniable plausibility—and even the opportunity to shift blame and hide behind what I heard "others" say.

True communication with the people I trust must happen when we all sit down together. We lay all the facts related to the issue on the table in the presence of all. There are gifts in Kyle that do not exist in Dean and Beau. Likewise, Beau's insight on an issue will bring a unique perspective that might sharpen Kyle's bent. Dean will provide insight of his own that helps the rest of us take note of something we never would have seen without him.

When my wife, some friends, and I were praying about starting Watermark, I was blessed to have relationships with an abundance of godly men who were willing to speak into my life and come alongside me as I considered the wisdom either of staying in Dallas where there was a history of service or of accepting an invitation to join others in serving out of state. I asked all of these men to meet with me as a group, not individually. I wanted each of them to hear the whole of my heart, the whole of each other's counsel, and then together—iron sharpening iron—listen to me as I communicated back to them what I understood to be their *collective* wisdom as I sought to discern God's best for me.

In this instance, I was trying to discern whether to join a church start-up in Atlanta or to plant a new one in Dallas. We met and listened to one another. We reflected on biblical principles and practical realities. We prayed. I didn't ask these men to make a decision for me, but I wanted them to give feedback and counsel into my decision-making process. I asked them to speak together into my life, each with their unique perspectives about me, my current situation, and the potential options before me.

I listened, repeated back what I understood to be their perspectives and why, prayed with them, and *then* made the decision with my wife. Interestingly, all of them individually and the group collectively recommended I take my family to Atlanta. Before my wife and I made the decision before the Lord, I asked them together if they thought I would be sinning, unwise, or rebellious if I stayed in Dallas to start what, unbeknownst to us all, would become one of the largest and fastest-growing local churches in America. They all said no, but they did think the Atlanta start-up would be best for me and my family because of the provision already in place, as well as the criticism it would avoid. To them, the one that was the least difficult and avoided the most challenges was in the "Peach City."

The point is, in cases without biblical clarity, wisdom would have you seek an abundance of counsel. But even then, you are still free—*and responsible for*—the choice *you* make. *Community is not sovereign*; only God is. It is the job of community to remind you of God's Word, admonish you when you are ignoring it, help you discern the application of it, and encourage you to live by it. But people are not God. There is a difference between people sharing their counsel with you and people accurately telling you that you are violating the Bible's counsel. The former is to be weighed with humility; the latter is to be obeyed without hesitation.

When people enter our church facility at Watermark, I'm humble and grateful to consistently hear them say, "Your church is beautiful!"

Of course, I know what they mean, but my reply is always the same: "Really, who did you meet?"

They usually return a puzzled expression. "Huh? No, I'm talking about your building."

I smile. "Oh, you like the building! Thank you so much! I was confused because I thought you were talking about the actual Church—you know, the people." I don't do this to willfully confuse them or make them feel small and unspiritual. I am so grateful for their compliments about our facility and their kindness in offering them. I do this because I want to help them see, as we are all attempting to more fully see, that there is something here so much more impressive than a physical structure. I am inviting them to come and see the real Church.

Christ's real Church truly is a beauty. Rightly led and full of humble people, she stands clean and pristinely adorned, even though her many individual parts all came from the ashes of broken, abused, and even ugly individual parts. Most people look for every reason under the sun not to fully enter into all that God calls us to in relationship with one another. They think it too much trouble. Too intrusive. Too beneath their own wisdom. Too messy. Too many ashes.

But what they fail to realize is that Jesus specializes in making beauty come from the ashes[31]—and He invites all those whose hearts are empty or merely half-full, who sit sifting through the silt of their own circumstances, to lift their eyes up and away from their islands of isolation, to come and see a homeland of other broken-being-healed, lost-being-found, dead-being-made-alive people and then become a part of the stunning beauty He is producing in all of them together … His beautiful bride.

Come and see.

---

31   Isaiah 61:3.

Chapter 13

Fight to the Better End

Right smack dab in the middle of all this beauty that Christ intends for us, there is something that most Christians consider to be so ugly that the preferred way to deal with it is to pretend it doesn't exist. But pretending something isn't poisonous doesn't keep us from getting sick when it is mixed into the cocktail of our lives. Still, most choose to deny the opportunity[1] it provides, instead choosing to believe that any presence of it is a sign of some spiritual failure. And while sin is always its cause, it is not always caused by sin.

So what the devil is it?

Conflict.

The truth is, conflict cannot be avoided in real community. It is not only a part of *life*; it is especially a part of life *together*. In fact, as one wise man keenly observed, there is only one place where people gather that is devoid of conflict … and you don't want *that* place to be your address.

---

1   I'll explain this word in a few pages.

"Some misguided Christian leaders feel that they must preserve harmony at any cost, so they do everything possible to reduce friction. They should remember that there is no friction in a machine that has been shut down for the night. Turn off the power, and you will have no problem with moving parts. Also remember that there is a human society where there are no problems—the cemetery. The dead have no differences of opinion. They generate no heat, because they have no energy and no motion. But their penalty is sterility and complete lack of achievement. What then is the conclusion of the matter? That problems are the price of progress, that friction is the concomitant of motion, that a live and expanding church will have a certain quota of difficulties as a result of its life and activity. A Spirit-filled church will invite the anger of the enemy."[2]

There is nothing in the Scripture that suggests we are to deny or avoid conflict. Quite the opposite, actually. Instead of being admonished to avoid it, God's Word tells us that we are to expect it and also how we can handle it. Conflict is not sin, but all sin leads to conflict. How we deal with conflict, not if it exists, is the determinative factor in whether God's Word stands in conflict to us.

God's Word is replete with commands and instructions to remind and help us as we purpose to be "diligent to preserve the unity of the Spirit in the bond of peace."[3] Despite the

---

2   A. W. Tozer, *This World: Playground or Battleground?* (Camp Hill, PA: Christian Publications, 1989), 112–13.

3   Ephesians 4:3.

overwhelming encouragement to lean into our relational troubles, it is shocking how conflict avoidant, which is to say inauthentic, the majority of our relationships are.

People of faith would never doubt the authority of God's Word on matters relating to grace, atonement, the crucifixion, the resurrection, justification, and a whole host of other mysterious and difficult things; yet somehow, we find it hard to believe we should believe what His Word says when it comes to reconciling with one another. Dismissive attitudes abound when words and phrases like "forgiveness," "humility," and a "high call to oneness and reconciliation" are introduced. Somehow, the way Scripture informs us to deal with conflict as we keep growing together in authentic community as the Church seems just too crazy to actually try.

"It'll never work" is a more common response than "Let's get to work."

The irony is, the predominant way most Christ followers function in communication with each other—and specifically in moments of conflict and discomfort—is what is *actually* not working. Sadly, instead of an inseparable, one-minded, otherworldly, effective body of Christ, we bear the fruit of shallow relationships and fractured friendships. Just the rates of divorce and church splits alone effectively and sadly make my case. We talk a lot about our love for and commitment to one another, but we seem to struggle to demonstrate these things when they require forbearance, humility, and selfless communication in moments of awkwardness or conflict.

Simply put, we are *awkward* in our handling of the *awkwardness* between us.

This is taking a toll on people's willingness to come, much less see what Christ intends for them in His Church. The Barna Group found that some of the main reasons people avoid church are the painful experiences they have endured within a local church context. The article noted that among unchurched adults, nearly four out of every ten nonchurchgoing Americans said they avoid churches because of negative past experiences in churches or with church people.[4] People around us are offended because the people within our body are not fully devoted to all that Christ's Word teaches us about dealing with offense.

When we started Watermark, a deep commitment to work through conflict was built into our DNA. The work of my friend Ken Sande at Peacemaker Ministries[5] was exceedingly beneficial in helping us articulate our passion for and plan to maintain the oneness God desires for us. Nothing has been more time consuming, and yet nothing has also borne more spiritual fruit than our efforts to be diligent in this area.

I often say that it feels like I spend 80 percent of my time working through conflict, which is to say, I spend 100 percent of 80 percent of my time making disciples. The other 20 percent of

---

4   "Millions of Unchurched Adults Are Christians Hurt by Churches but Can Be Healed of the Pain," Barna Group, April 12, 2010, www.barna.org/barna-update/faith-spirituality/362-millions-of-unchurched-adults-are-christians-hurt-by-churches-but-can-be-healed-of-the-pain#.V6-HJGWyVEc.

5   Ken's book *The Peacemaker* is still the best book out there on the topic, and I highly recommend it and other resources from Peacemaker.net.

my time, I may or may not be actively about the disciple making I am charged to accomplish in the Great Commission, but I *know* that I am making disciples when I am being obedient to God's Word in the way I lead myself and others to maintain or restore the unity of the Spirit in the midst of conflict.

Working biblically through conflict *is* worship and discipleship.

If you are not motivated by the previous sentence, I don't know what else to write. Conflict is an opportunity to glorify God, serve others, and also grow myself. This means conflict is an opportunity to experience a win-win-win when you face one of the greatest certainties in life: conflict. If you are going to live on earth and if you are going to have relationships with other humans, you are going to have conflict. The only question is this: Will you use it as an opportunity to worship and make disciples, or will you quit?

As a father, I want my kids to grow up to learn how to fight to the *better* end; fighting to the *bitter* end is something I have never had to teach them. It comes quite naturally. The same is true with my faith family—we all know how to fight to the *bitter* end. Isn't that how most friendships end? How marriages end? Isn't that what "irreconcilable differences" are all about? What in the world is a "no-fault divorce"?

Dating relationships. Marriages. Middle and high school friendships. College relationships. Fraternity and sorority relationships. We commit to being friends for a while until it reaches a certain point of being just a little too nasty ... a little bit too bitter. Then we're out of there. Off to something new, to somewhere else with someone "easier to get along with."

This is not the biblical model. This is not Christ's best for us. This doesn't make a great case that we are His disciples,[6] and tragically, it causes others to wonder if Jesus is who He claimed to be.[7] If His grace empowers us to live out what we've covenanted together to be, it should be evident to a watching world. Even as Christ invited us to come and find peace with the Father, we should be able to say to others, "Come and see how to live in peace with one another … even when it gets awkward. Even when it gets messy."

The world should watch our worlds supernaturally unite in the Church.[8] The greatest mystery today is not why the world has not yet attained peace but why the Church hasn't. The real tragedy is not that the world is at war but that so many "Christian" marriages and communities are. It is in the Church that the world should be able to come, learn, and watch people from every tribe, nation, gender, and socioeconomic stratum live in peace with one another. Our collective song should be: "Come and see how to 'beat your swords into plowshares and your spears into pruning hooks.'"[9]

Instead, our song is too often dissonance. We are divided. Our marriages are unhealthy and crumbling. Our relationships are surface level. Our churches are splitting. We are fighting the wrong wars—and we have work to do.

---

6   John 13:34–35.
7   John 17:21.
8   Matthew 5:9; James 3:18.
9   Isaiah 2:4.

The Call to Oneness

When Watermark began, there were only two of us on full-time staff. Within the first few days of our journey, I was glad that we had gone after someone I trusted to keep working with me to keep our friendship growing *better* and not growing *bitter*. We were the best man at each other's weddings. Our families vacationed together. And I cannot tell you how many hours we spent together *working* hard to keep the relationship from becoming bitter … because life around Todd Wagner can become bitter.

You may not know it, but life around you can become the same.

This doesn't *make* you and me bad people—it *proves* we are. Without the grace and leadership of Christ—and the help of others within His body—bitterness is the only possible result in our lives. Stop being surprised by this. Stop pretending. Stop being astounded that relationships take work, because they *all* need work.

I can't tell you how happy *I* was to discover that the difficulties my wife and I were having in marriage were really nothing more than a fulfillment of Scripture.[10] And I can't tell you how happy *she* was when *I* began to get the log out of my own eye and started becoming a leader by humbling myself and fulfilling Scripture's intention for me as God's man in our marriage. Our lives changed when we stopped pretending our relationship was supposed to be perfect and started more perfectly attending to God's revealed way to make relationships work.

---

10 1 Corinthians 7:28b.

God's desire for us in marriage is oneness, not simply that we would be sexually faithful (although that never hurts a marriage) or that we would remain "undivorced."

Likewise, God's desire for His Church is oneness,[11] not solid doctrinal profession (although that never hurts a church) or that they would remain "unsplit."

He wants, expects, and calls us to love one another as recklessly as He loves us.[12] In fact, understanding the depths of God's love for us is the single most important truth any of us can know. Until we see ourselves as valuable and loved, we will be on an endless journey to find meaning and worth. Thankfully, God doesn't hold back in telling us how He feels about us.[13] I love the way my friend Max Lucado says it: "If God had a refrigerator, your picture would be on it. If He had a wallet, your photo would be in it. He sends you flowers every spring and a sunrise every morning … Face it, friend. He is crazy about you!"[14]

Let's remind ourselves of the truths about love. Yes, love is patient and kind. No, it cannot be provoked. If it is true love, it will not take into account a wrong suffered, and it will bear all things. Love never runs out of hope; in fact, it never runs out … period. Love never fails.[15] All these things and "more" are clearly articulated in the "love chapter" of 1 Corinthians 13, but our tendency to leave out the "more" often gives love a bad name.

---

11 Philippians 2:2.
12 John 13:34.
13 Ephesians 2:4–7; 1 John 3:1.
14 Max Lucado, *Just Like Jesus* (Nashville, TN: Thomas Nelson, 1998), 4.
15 1 Corinthians 13:4–7; Matthew 22:37–40.

In addition to love not taking into account a wrong suffered, God's Word makes it clear that love also does not enable or look over anything that dishonors God, anything that damages relationships, anything that hurts other people, or anything that causes a fellow Christ follower's witness to be discredited. Love "does not rejoice in unrighteousness" and "does not seek its own,"[16] which means love is never going to remain silent when there is a need to speak up.[17]

It means "faithful are the wounds of a friend" and "deceitful are the kisses of an enemy."[18] It means that "he who rebukes a man will afterward find more favor than he who flatters with the tongue.[19] It means that we should love people enough to say what needs to be said as winsomely and gently as we can possibly say it, helping them as much as we possibly can."[20]

Our Father could not love us any more than He does. In fact, it is because He is our loving Father that He disciplines us,[21] placing us in a loving family that will speak the truth to us,[22] and commit to admonishing, encouraging, and helping us.[23] Again, Lucado says it better than anyone: "God loves you just the way you are, but He *refuses* to leave you that way. He wants you to be just like Jesus."[24]

---

16 1 Corinthians 13:4–7.
17 Proverbs 24:11–12.
18 Proverbs 27:5–6.
19 Proverbs 28:23.
20 Proverbs 15:2; Ephesians 4:29; Colossians 4:6; Galatians 6:1–2.
21 Hebrews 12:5–6.
22 Ephesians 5:11.
23 1 Thessalonians 5:14.
24 Max Lucado, *In a Gentle Thunder* (Nashville, TN: Thomas Nelson, 1995), 122.

But He also wants us to be *just like Jesus* in the way we love, admonish, encourage, and sharpen one another.

I had another pastor ask me why I thought "his church" wouldn't grow beyond twenty-five or thirty-five people. Doing my best to let Proverbs 15:2 inform my tone, I told him that I didn't know, but I bet if I hung out with him and the church for thirty minutes, I could tell him at least some of the reasons. But the real kicker was this: if he had any real friends in real community in his congregation, *they* could actually tell him these same reasons right now without my thirty-minute observations.

And if they couldn't, I guaranteed him that the people who repeatedly came and left his church certainly could. In other words, there were people who knew what could help him, but either they were unwilling to speak this truth to him in love or he was unwilling to hear it—or more likely, none of them were walking in the kind of biblical community that would allow this kind of conversation to be fruitful instead of destructive.

If God loves you this much, then so should your friends.

There is a reason that there is so much continual dysfunction in God's family. There is a reason why so many people who come to know Christ still find themselves at age twenty-seven, thirty-seven, forty-seven, and *any*-seven as still some of the most angry, bitter, awkward, socially inept, and incompetently life-skilled people in the world. It is because churches are filled with people who would rather sin themselves than confront another person in their sin.

Too many of us are more committed to being *polite* with one another than being *prayerfully committed* to one another. When we don't speak the truth to one another in love, we are choking off a major artery of God's grace, and as a result, people who are supposed to be conformed to the image of the most magnetic, kind, gracious, loving, powerful Personality in history instead remain largely unchanged for years.

To change this, you have to radiate the attitude of David. "Let the righteous smite me in kindness, and reprove me. It is oil upon my head. Do not let my head refuse it."[25]

To change this, the church you go to must be a church full of Nathans who love you enough to say, "You are the man!"[26]

More often than not, it appears to the world that sanctification, which is to be evident in every Christ follower, is the exception and not the rule. When there is no sign of the miracle of God's intervention in our lives, the world rightly observes, "We don't really know who this God is, but He must be unable to radically change people."

I love John Ortberg's descriptions of people he has seen around the church for a long time. Brace yourself because this ain't pretty … and even worse, some of this may look pretty familiar to you.

"Here is an angry guy. Angry with his children, angry with the people he worked with, angry with people he had gone to church his whole life long. He got into fights in the church on a regular basis. His main reason to listen to sermons was not to encounter God or to be broken by God but to see where he might

---

25   Psalm 141:5.
26   2 Samuel 12:7.

point out flaws in the messages. People outside the church would not tolerate him because he was obnoxious but inside the church his obnoxiousness was regarded as zeal for the truth and he was regarded as a spiritual giant.

"She was the most feared person in the church. She was master at guilt and manipulation. She led a Bible study for women but it was clear that they were only welcome if they would do what she would say. She was involved in a lot of people's lives but she didn't love them. The truth is she didn't even like them. Everyone at home knew she called all the shots. So ironically, she was very into a theological system that said her husband was the ruler of the roost. So in her home her husband was boss because she said he was boss! And heaven help him when he didn't boss the way she wanted him to! She submitted him right into the ground. And she was regarded as a spiritual giant.

"He is a Christian leader and author who views himself as a defender of the truth. And he delights in ripping apart other Christians who disagree with any of his doctrinal positions. He caricatures their beliefs, twists their statements, and maligns their motives. He wants to believe bad things about political figures he disagrees with. He wants to believe bad things. He repeats them and spreads them even if he isn't sure they are true. He slanders truth in the name of defending truth and he is thought of as a spiritual leader.

"Her primary language was complain. She complained about her grown children who didn't treat her right, her neighbors, and life in general. At a church where I served many years ago, we weren't reaching non-Christians. They just drove by because our services were quite inaccessible, so we started to do a seeker service. We planned it for over a year and moved quite slowly. I'll never forget when we did the first one. The church, at the last minute, filled up with several hundred people. Most of them had never been to church before. You could tell from little things like the auditorium filled up from the front to the back. But because they were seekers, they weren't very churchy people and she didn't like having them around. Not real long ago at that church, there was a church split and it involved some pretty ugly behavior and the body of Christ was cut in two. And all the seekers were gone. And that church was left stilted and inaccessible to seekers, no pagan sinners likely to wander through those doors. And her comment on that was, 'Isn't it wonderful we got our church back?'"[27]

That's why I wrote this chapter! That's why God put all the verses on which I have based this chapter in His Word. And that's why disobedient, dead churches are the death of *the* Church as God intended it.

Ortberg finishes his observation this way: "Sheldon Van Auken wrote in his book *Severe Mercy*, 'The best argument for Christianity is Christians; their joy, their certainty, their completeness. The best argument against Christianity is Christians. When they are somber, joyless, smug, self-righteous, narrow or oppressive, Christianity dies a thousand deaths.' In his book *The*

---

27   The John Ortberg text in this chapter is taken from my transcription of a talk he gave in 1990 at the Willow Creek Church Leaders Conference. The material is also covered in his *Love beyond Reason* (Grand Rapids, MI: Zondervan, 1998). Used by permission of John Ortberg.

Spirit of the Disciplines, Dallas Willard says, 'How many people are radically and permanently repelled from the way by Christians who are unfeeling, stiff, unapproachable, boring, lifeless, obsessive and dissatisfied? Yet such Christians are everywhere and what they are missing is the wholesome aliveness springing up from a balanced vitality within God's loving rule … Spirituality wrongly understood or pursued is a major source of human misery and rebellion against God.' Spirituality rightly understood is life. Spirituality wrongly understood is death."

Can I get an amen?

Being a believer means getting involved in the lives of others, learning what it means to be a friend to the better end, and learning how to deal with conflict. I am convinced too many of us are stunted in our growth because we never move past "dating" friendships. *Let's spend time together as long as it is new, mysterious, and fun. Let's flirt and distract ourselves with lots of activities. Let's put on our best face as much as we possibly can, and when the force of time finally allows us both to see each other for who we really are, let's move on to some other new, mysterious, easier-to-get-along-with, better person.*

Or maybe say it this way. *Let's "go to church" together and flirt with the idea of Christianity as long as it is fun and we don't take it too seriously. Let's put on the best face we can, and when the force of time or too much proximity makes it hard for us to deny that you are as petty and selfish as I am, we can move on to another church "family" … hopefully one that will have better preaching, music, and coffee.*

Sign the Letter and See the Rhino

We do "life together" until someone speaks truth where we didn't want them to speak it or someone wades into an area we didn't want explored. At that point, we think it is easier to go somewhere else and start all over than to stay and be committed to the awkwardness of humbly addressing our situation—or God forbid, the legitimate issues in our own lives.

Because our Father is serious about transformation in our lives, He calls us to move into transforming relationships with each other. To love until it hurts, and *especially* when it hurts.[28] This is the expectation our Father puts before us in His Word, and this is the example every faithful church should live before the watching world.

The call to full devotion is a call to love and serve one another in committed, covenant relationships. These are *not* relationships of mutual toleration with false peace and faux oneness. These are *not* relationships where we have nearness but no real knowledge of each other or familiarity but no intimacy. These kinds of shallow relationships don't bring about the sanctification, humility, and transformation God intends ... and that we all deeply need.

One of my favorite sayings is "There are only two people who can tell you the truth about yourself: either an enemy who has lost their temper, or a friend who loves you dearly."[29] Nathan loved David dearly.[30] Shimei ... not so much.[31] They both told him the

---

28 1 Corinthians 13:7.
29 A quote from Greek philosopher Antisthenes (444–371 BC).
30 2 Samuel 12.
31 2 Samuel 16:5–7.

truth, but with different, shall we say, "motivations." I have heard what people think of me when they've lost their tempers; having a Shimei around when we are traveling through some of our toughest moments isn't pretty. Having truth hurled at you wrapped in hate isn't the best; it is hard enough to hear it when it is cloaked in love from a Nathan.

Sometimes I'll receive what I'll choose to call "strong feedback" in letters—anonymous ones. I wish I had the discipline never to read a letter when someone doesn't even have the courage to sign it,[32] but sadly, I have glanced at a few over the years, and I honestly can say that the greatest grief the decision has caused me has always had to do more with the fact that I can't go seek understanding, restoration, or reconciliation with a person who hides in the dark.

We need friends who will be real with us and not live in the shadows of anonymity. We need them in the light of authentic, iron-sharpening-iron love. In other words, I want friends who will sign their letters—and who will then live life with me day after day so that if there is any truth to the issues they see in my life, I can grow past them as I move closer to Christ with their encouragement and support. We all need friends like this or we are going to wind up like one of the characters described previously by Ortberg.

One of my favorite *Far Side* cartoons shows a man standing with his physician in the examination room ... but they are not

---

alone. Standing behind the man is a giant rhino with his huge horn going straight into the man's lower back. The caption reads: "Wait a minute here, Mr. Crumbley … maybe it isn't kidney stones after all."

Now maybe Mr. Crumbley never caught a glimpse of the rhino who had gored him in the mirror, but surely his friends must have seen it. That is, unless he went to the *First Church of the Inauthentic and Selfishly Polite* where everyone is so committed to not saying something that might be uncomfortable for someone else to hear that they are forced to continue walking around with large tetrapods protruding from their backs.

What a fitting image of the mockery we have in our so-called "biblical" relationships in the Church. Sometimes I have a rhino following me around, and the whole world can see it, but no one who really cares about me has told me that I have a problem. No wonder the world laughs at us. The proverbial elephant in the room is often that people who "love" each other won't talk about the elephant—or in this case, the rhinoceros—in the room.

It is a blotch on our family name when someone meets a person who claims to have known Christ for years and who has supposedly been in relationships with other Christ followers for years and yet this stranger can tell within fifteen seconds that there is an unaddressed "rhino" problem.

"Iron sharpens iron, so one man sharpens another."[33] Iron is not soft. It does not make a comfortable mattress. There is a reason Solomon did not say, "As cotton sharpens cotton …"

---

33   Proverbs 27:17.

Living in authentic, "I am going to do all I can to serve you" friendship is not typically a painless process. Have you ever heard what it sounds like when a piece of iron repeatedly hits another piece of iron? It's loud. There are sparks. Hunks of metal fall to the ground. If iron had nerves and vocal cords, someone would call the police. The sharpening process is not a painless one.

But real, biblical relationships are not optional if you want to be transformed back toward the glory from which humanity has fallen. Sharpening friendships are necessary if you are going to become the useful tool God wants you to be. Many people like the old saying, "Don't walk ahead of me; I may not follow. Don't walk behind me; I may not lead. But walk beside me and be my friend." It sounds nice—that is, until the friend walking next to you is no longer the man or woman of your dreams holding your hand as you stroll on a moonlit beach, but instead is just another piece of metal crashing hard against your iron will. We need true friends like the slab of marble needed Michelangelo if we are going to become another King David.

If we love each other in Christ, we will faithfully wound one another. And if we are wise, we will actually invite it. As I said earlier, the real David (not the sculpted one) wisely prayed, "Let the righteous smite me in kindness and reprove me; it is oil upon the head; do not let my head refuse it."[34] David's son might have heard his dad's prayer and later turned it into some principled advice for all of us, "He whose ear listens to the life-giving reproof

34   Psalm 141:5.

will dwell among the wise. He who neglects discipline despises himself, but he who listens to reproof acquires understanding."[35] David knew he needed sculpting, and those who want to be God's workmanship need it as well.

The most loving thing we can do is to tell the truth, and the wisest thing we can do is to seek it. Yes, this may feel counterintuitive at times, but doing things that *feel* loving and things that *are* loving are not always the same things—don't be misled by the feeling. This is not always going to be a pretty process, but "a friend loves at all times, and a brother is born for adversity."[36] If we are real friends and real family in Christ, then we will face adversity together. We need friends like blocks of stone and marble need artists. Michelangelo correctly observed, "Every block of stone has a statue inside it, and it is the task of the sculptor to discover it." It is the job of your most Christlike friends to say, "I love you just the way you are, but like our Father, I love you enough to do all I can to not let you stay that way."

But brace yourself—the pain of having friends lash out at you while you are trying to love them by being honest with them is real, and it hurts. Slabs don't slander artists, but the sin that lingers in us can sometimes strike back at friends. Solomon warns us, "A stone is heavy and sand weighty, but the provocation of a fool is heavier than both of them."[37] The good news is that God doesn't want you to bear that weight alone. His Word walks us through

---

35   Proverbs 15:31–32.
36   Proverbs 17:17.
37   Proverbs 27:3.

the process of what we are to do when someone thinks that your willingness to deal with the problem *is* the problem.

Thankfully, a person doesn't have to be an "expert" pastor, leader, or counselor to be this kind of friend. I continually remind my Watermark family that I am no different from them—I am a part of the body of Christ in a kingdom of priests. This isn't my circus, and you didn't pay me to come and watch me perform my Christian act. This is more like a clown school, and we have to all get busy learning to do our part if we are going to be the people God wants us to be.

We are all called to both *have* and *be* the kinds of friends that Christ's way of grace and truth produce. Do you have those kinds of friends? Or better said, is that the kind of Church you desire to be a part of? Here is the great divide. We all want to be sanctified and useful to our Master, but too many fail to allow the chisel of true friendship close enough to sculpt us into the "workman-ship"[38] God intends us to be. Too many "churches" are filled with "Christians" who say to authentic friendships, "No, thank you. I'm happy to come and sing our little songs and take my turn working with kids, but count me out if you want me to change anything more than a kid's diaper. I don't want a brother who is born for adversity[39] … just give me a buddy to cruise through life with. I say we all pretend to be people God has for one another, but I don't want this to get messy. We aren't going to *really* go there."

---

38 Ephesians 2:10.
39 Proverbs 17:17.

God's plan for you includes iron-sharpening relationships where people are so transformed that the world stands in awe at how sharp we are becoming, marveling at how we have been shaped by the grace of God. I'm desperate to have a church body that loves and serves each other as God intends. I am desperate for my kids to have these kinds of friends … and to *be* these kinds of friends.

Most of all. I'm desperately in need of those kinds of friends myself.

Chapter 14

Peace Fakers, Breakers, and Makers

Many people today are brimming with a host of hang-ups and habits that lead to a world of hurt. We worry about everything and obsess over the smallest of things. Coincidentally, the world is full of sadness and sickness in body, mind, and spirit.

There is a better way ... and I want to invite you to come and see a better world. It's not a world where we pretend there is no pain, but it is a world where we courageously face our problems together. It's one where we don't *wander* off alone or *wonder* if we are alone and without anyone who *really* loves us in this world. We don't need a *make-believe* world that we have to carefully construct; we need a *make-it-right* world where we care for one another. There is an obsession in this new world too, but it is an obsession that heals body, mind, and spirit instead of wounding them.

Our world thinks the Church is full of weak men lost in delusion because we claim to know a power that transforms but we lead lives that still need transforming. Could you imagine if instead we were considered aliens[1] not because of our foolish[2] beliefs but because of our crazy commitment to love and stay committed to one another?

God intends for us to be peace*makers,* not peace *fakers* or peace *breakers.*

Peacemakers are wholeheartedly committed to dealing with divisive schisms, destructive gossip, and heartless slander within the body of Christ. Why? Because this is what marks us as children of God. Jesus said as much right from the beginning of His public ministry. "Blessed are the peacemakers, for they shall be called sons of God."[3] His most famous servant later said, "Therefore I, the prisoner of the Lord, implore you to walk in a manner worthy of the calling with which you have been called, with all humility and gentleness, with patience, showing tolerance for one another in love, being *diligent* to preserve the *unity* of the Spirit in the bond of *peace.*"[4]

In his book *Fresh Wind, Fresh Fire,* Jim Cymbala shares how he greets new members to his church. "And now I charge you … that if you ever hear another member speak an unkind word of criticism or slander against anyone—myself, another pastor, an usher, a choir member, or anyone else—you have the authority to stop that person in mid-sentence and say, 'Excuse me—who hurt you? Who ignored you? Who slighted you? Was it *x*? Let's

---

1   1 Peter 1:1; 2:11.
2   1 Corinthians 4:10.
3   Matthew 5:9.
4   Ephesians 4:1–3.

go *get them* right now. He will get on his knees and apologize to you, and then we'll pray together, so God can restore peace to this body. But we will not let you talk critically about people who are not present to defend themselves ...' Members, please understand that I am entirely serious about this. I want you to help restore this kind of thing immediately. And meanwhile, know this: if you are ever the one doing the loose talking, we will confront you."[5]

Can I get an amen?

If you are thinking, *Isn't this a bit much?* I'd say, "We are called to *make much* of anything that threatens the unity and beauty of God's family. God made much of us. After all, it took the death of the Son of God to bring us to a place of peace with God,[6] and it is that peace with God that allows and obligates us[7] to live in peace with one another."[8]

This is serious business and a biblically emphasized job of the leadership of every church. "This is a trustworthy statement; and concerning these things I want you to speak confidently, so that those who have believed God will be careful to engage in good deeds. These things are good and profitable for men ... *Reject a factious man after a first and second warning*, knowing that such a man is perverted and is sinning, being self-condemned."[9]

---

5   Jim Cymbala, *Fresh Wind, Fresh Fire* (Grand Rapids, MI: Zondervan, 1997), 160 (emphasis mine).

6   Romans 5:1.

7   2 Corinthians 5:18–20.

8   Romans 14:19–20.

9   Titus 3:8, 10–11.

Not long ago, I received an encouraging email from a young man who came to trust Christ at Watermark and then grew rapidly in his faith. He sensed that the Lord wanted him to go through formal training routes to deepen his theological understanding, so he enrolled at Dallas Theological Seminary.

"I recently had to write a paper for a class at seminary about what my church's three greatest strengths are. My number one answer was 'our Elders.' Watermark is my first Church home. Three years ago, through a friend's heart for discipleship, I got invited to the family here. I had no idea how incredible the Church could be. My friends in other ministries make comments like 'You understand what I am talking about, you know Church politics,' and I always have to say, 'I really don't know.' I am just one of the hundreds of twenty-somethings at Watermark who have been provided a 'warped' perspective on what Church is like. Alive, authentic, excellent, innovative, without 'politics' or hypocrisy, full of grace and truth. Thank you for allowing me a healthy and biblical perspective on what the Church is. Thank you for the trails blazed through decades of faithfulness. No intention of brown-nosing here, I'm just grateful."

I too have had that other experience. I think back to an earlier time in ministry when I was called into the office of a pastor at another church so he could encourage me *not* to act on what I had just heard other leaders in the church publicly say. This pastor said to me, "I am sure you understand that was just church politics and that it would be foolish to think what they said was wise." I responded that I didn't think church politics was wise, and if he also did not, I would help him get the leaders back together so he could tell them this time that he thought they weren't thinking well about the topic. And I did. It was awkward for him, uncomfortable for both of us, and glorifying to Christ. Amazingly, this same conversation and reply repeated itself two more times before my pastor friend became convinced "church politics" was not something I was willing to be good at.

Does a church without politics sound "warped" to you? Is it "alien" to your experience? If so, we have work to do, and it is my humble hope that you will read and reread these chapters.

This is a never-ending spiritual challenge. As church leaders, we constantly have to shepherd the hearts of our people to speak the truth in love *to* each other. Some of the leaders of our community ministry recently sent me this note: "In our leadership of our community teams, we have to often remind them that we will relentlessly confront statements like 'Well that's just (insert name). He can be kind of insensitive. Or, that's just (insert name). He struggles with anger.' We address it as one of the most unloving things they can say, especially if they have never loved that person enough to tell them face to face. And we are constantly reminding them of the necessity to 'lean into' hard conversations and to directly share with the individual in question their observations and perceptions that they are already sharing with others. We are telling couples that whatever they are talking about on the way home *from* Community Group (that concerns the group or someone in the group) should be something they talk about *in* the group."

This is so difficult to live out because speaking the truth in love can sometimes get you spoken to rather unlovingly. Additionally, in a strange way, it makes us feel better about ourselves when people speak poorly about others to us. We willingly listen to the criticism of others, believing that another person being spoken about negatively somehow makes us better. Scripture warns against this "sweet" addiction of ours: "The words of a whisperer are like dainty morsels, and they go down into the innermost parts of the body."[10]

Yes, this kind of talk, like a French pastry, tastes good going down ... but unlike the pastry, which lands on our hips, the dainty morsel of gossip poisonously lands on our hearts. Sweet-tasting to the lips but deadly to our lives are the words of a gossip. Eventually, the gossip's words weigh us down and begin to shape us into men or women who do not look like our Father desires.

You won't be in good shape for very long if you snack on gossip and slander.

I have had chronic recipients of gossip tell me things like "I don't want to hear all these things about other people, but for some reason, people keep telling them to me! Why is everybody always telling *me* things they don't like about other people?" As graciously as I can, I reply, "There's a reason the bakers of trouble keep coming to your house with dainty morsels of info ... it's because you *eat* them. You're a consistent, reliable customer."

I get it. Dainty morsels are tasty. But if I don't want to look like the guy who lives across the street from the bakery, I better figure out how to stop feasting on the gossip's goods.

---

10   Proverbs 18:8.

This is how I do it. *Any time* and *every time* someone is baking up some sweet story about another person, I stop them midsentence and say, "Before you continue, let me tell you what I am going to do. I am going to help you help this person. It is clear God put them on your heart, so you must want to help them. I understand that tough things happen in friendships and relationships, but you need to tell them what you just told me because it's obviously bothering you or else you wouldn't have brought it up. I'm going to ask you, in the next day or two, to at least make a phone call and tell our friend you just spoke to me and you need to share with them that something that has been weighing on you. If I don't hear from you, then I will help you by calling them, and the two of us will come to you instead."

Let me tell you something: you take this approach one time, and you will find that the "baker" of morsels will not be back at your door selling them anytime soon. I've seen entire churches fail to follow this principle, and the results in the body of Christ are both evident and tragic because "the beginning of strife is like letting out water,"[11] and it creates a flood of insecurity and distrust among God's people.

So why are we to be so passionate about this? Because "a brother offended is more unyielding than a strong city, and quarreling is like the bars of a castle."[12] Before the strong city is built and the castle bars are installed, let's abandon talking *about* one another instead of talking *to* one another. Don't let divisiveness

---

11   Proverbs 17:14.
12   Proverbs 18:19 ESV.

sit in your gut because it will load your soul with calories of arrogance, superiority, and pride ... and those never wear well on any body (pun intended).

When I am dealing with conflict, I am making disciples *and* worshipping well.

When it comes to disunity in the body, Jesus tells us that dealing with it is something we must do *before* we even think about attending to any other religious activity. "Therefore, if you are presenting your offering at the altar and remember your brother has something against you, you leave your offering there before the altar, you go your way. First be reconciled to your brother, and then come and present your offering."[13] This is true if you are the one offending or the one offended.

As many scriptures teach us, pursuing reconciliation and peace with each other is always God's primary definition of worship. We are to leave the "altar" when we need to clean up an altercation in the family. Extreme bias is to be given to the prioritization of moving toward friends and family in the faith when anything threatens the peace and oneness God intends for His people.

Solomon says we are to deal with the careless words and actions that fracture relationships "like a gazelle from the hunter's hand and like a bird from the hand of the fowler."[14] In other words, like our lives depend on it. Paul warns the church in Corinth that their lack of living in unity and peace with one another is the cause of their weakness and sickness, and that going through the motions

---

13 Matthew 5:23–24.
14 Proverbs 6:1–5.

of communing with Christ and one another without truly caring for one another was not only not helping them, it was "eating and drinking judgment on themselves."[15]

It is safe to say that peace faking and peace breaking are not exactly recommended biblical conduct.

Let me insert here the importance of not simply going through the motions when you are finally motivated to move toward your brother. True reconciliation involves true repentance, and true repentance means we do more than simply acknowledge the wrong we have done with an "I'm sorry." It means we own the wrong we have done and the destruction of relationship we have caused as we seek forgiveness.

Seeking and asking for forgiveness with a broken and contrite heart has supernatural power to restore what foolishness has destroyed. Humbly acknowledging that the wrong you have done requires grace and mercy before the trust that has been lost can be restored through a heartfelt "Please forgive me" is divinely powerful for the destruction of fortresses. "Forgive me" is so much more difficult to speak than a flippantly declared "I'm sorry" offered as we keep on charging ahead. When "Sorry!" is our only offering and the relationship continues to be strained, we can say, "Hey, you are the one with the problem! You need to get over it, because after all, I said I was sorry."

Using the words "Will you forgive me?" puts us in a position of humility where we are *asking* for something, not a position of control where we are *declaring* something. If you don't think

---

15   1 Corinthians 11:17–30.

there is a difference between "I'm sorry" and "Will you forgive me?" try the latter the next time you are "sorry" and see how much harder it is to say and how much softer the outcome is after saying it.

Nobody said this would be easy. There is a reason Paul used the words "be diligent" when he exhorted the Ephesians concerning their relationships with one another.[16] A commitment to oneness and unity takes constant attention. Just as weeds naturally grow in a garden, trouble and dissension naturally spring up in human relationships. In church relationships. In life. Conflict is not sin … how you respond to it might be. Be diligent. Be humble. "If possible, so far as it depends on you, be at peace with all men."[17]

The following principles will help you do just that. Whether you're in high school or in college, struggling on a team, have blown it in a dating relationship, or are in a marriage dispute or a business deal that's going south, here are five scriptural principles for how to "do right" when you see wrong being done.

Don't Sweat the Small Stuff … Overlook Minor Offenses

First, make sure you know the difference between something that's merely rubbed you the wrong way and something that obviously isn't right. Don't sweat the small stuff. Overlook minor offenses. "A man's discretion makes him slow to anger, and it is his glory

---

16   Ephesians 4:3.
17   Romans 12:18.

to overlook a transgression."[18] Before I give you a good definition for what are *not* minor offenses, let me give you some practical examples of what are.

If you have ever played pickup basketball, you undoubtedly have met the guy who tends to "over-officiate." You know the guy I'm talking about. He complains about everything. A hand check is a hatchet job. Every loose pivot is a major violation. Every time someone "bodies up" to him, he screams that he has been body checked. And so *our* little game becomes *his* high-court experience until he gets his way. Everyone knows who he is, and everyone just rolls their eyes and rolls him the ball.

When you play basketball with someone who makes every little thing a big thing, it's miserable. But it's a pickup game, so you exercise some self-control and get some exercise. There are lots of annoyances in life, and you don't want to be the over-officious jerk who causes all the eye rolling.

I have had a number of men and women ask me how to apply Solomon's "overlook a minor offense" wisdom to their marriages. They ask, "How do I know when I should sharpen my wife [or husband], and when should I just let something go?"

I liken it to this. Sometimes you eat bad food and the feeling in your stomach immediately lets you know something just isn't exactly right. But you give it a few hours, maybe take a short nap, and soon enough, the feeling passes and everything's okay. In that case, there is no need to call the health department and report your favorite dive. You write it off and just don't sweat it.

---

18   Proverbs 19:11.

But then there are some meals that are just not right … and you know the feeling you have is simply not going to pass. You're going to be sick, miserable, and awkward to be around until it is dealt with. In this case, you don't keep carrying that bad meal with you; you have to get it out because you know if you don't "help it along," it is going to come out in a way that you just can't help yourself. And it won't be pretty.

Offenses are like that. We usually know when something is minor and when something just won't shake off. In the latter case, don't let it sit one day, two days, a week, or a month—to the point that on some other day, something else seemingly minor happens and all of a sudden you find yourself involuntarily projectile vomiting at your spouse as they stand there completely confused. They simply have no idea that what has just happened is a result of something you digested in your relationship hours, or even days, ago. All they know is that they are covered in something that isn't pleasant that has "appeared" to come out of nowhere.

So if you know it's not going to pass, bring it up before it comes up on its own. Yes, there are some small offenses, and it's a glory for you to overlook them. But if it sticks with you after you have prayed about it, then it is time to plan your words carefully,[19] choose the right time and place,[20] seek to understand before you seek to be understood,[21] remind your spouse that your

---

19   Proverbs 12:18; 15:2; 16:23.
20   Proverbs 22:3.
21   Proverbs 18:2, 13.

desire is to help him or her be the man or woman you know they want to be and not to tear them down,[22] remind them of your love and commitment,[23] and trust the Lord.[24]

But enough with the analogies. If you want clear biblical instruction on when we need to speak up, and when it is *not* a glory to overlook something, here you go. Something is always too big to overlook *if* it is dishonoring to God,[25] it has damaged your relationship,[26] it is hurting or might hurt other people,[27] or it is hurting the offender or diminishing their usefulness to God.[28] When any one of these is in play, we cannot play around.

To a wife or husband, I will ask, "Is this threatening the unity God has destined for you to have? Do you feel unwilling to embrace your spouse? To speak well of them? To look forward to physical and emotional oneness with them? If so, then bring it up."

Realize that it may only be a big deal to one of you—in that case, it is still a big deal to the relationship.[29] It's easier to say "Well, it didn't bother me, and you didn't say anything, so we're all good" than it is to live with your spouse in an understanding way[30] and make it your business to know when there is a problem before they bring it up.

---

22 Ephesians 4:29.
23 Song of Solomon 5:10–6:3.
24 Psalm 37:1–4.
25 Galatians 6:1–2; James 5:19–20; Matthew 18:15.
26 Ephesians 4:3; John 17:21.
27 Proverbs 31:8–9; Psalm 82:3–4.
28 Hebrews 10:24–25; 2 Corinthians 6:3.
29 Ephesians 5:28–29.
30 1 Peter 3:7.

We don't need God's Word to know that conflict is a given, but we definitely need Scripture to encourage us that it is an opportunity for good. And while we don't want to invite conflict into our lives or wish its presence in the lives of others, it is an opportunity to glorify God, to serve others, and to grow ourselves.

When you have a conflict with a friend, don't search for new friends; glorify God by leaning in and loving them well through modeling, as much as you are able, what it means to be at peace with all men,[31] and run after them the way the Lord runs after you.[32]

Don't Spread the Big Stuff ... Talk in Private

I touched on this in an earlier section, but it is appropriate to highlight it again here. When we have a problem with or see another person we are in relationship with "dishonoring God," it is not a time to be talking to others. We are called to go and "show him his fault *in private*,"[33] not share it as a prayer request or an interesting *dainty morsel* to others. If you need to talk to someone else, God is the One who stands ready to listen.[34]

---

31 Romans 12:18.
32 Luke 15:20.
33 Matthew 18:15.
34 A case could be made that seeking counsel from a more mature believer as you get ready to "wage war" is also appropriate, especially if you see them as part of the solution to helping you love the brother or sister who is in crisis or with whom you are in conflict.

For anyone serious about living with God's blessing in God's community, we have to stop thinking that getting involved is optional. "Brethren, even if anyone is caught in any trespass, you who are spiritual, restore such a one in a spirit of gentleness; each one looking to yourself, so that you too will not be tempted. Bear one another's burdens, and thereby fulfill the law of Christ."[35]

This is not a suggestion; it is a command. You *must* go if a brother or sister is caught in a trespass. Jesus even tells us how to approach them. "Why do you look at the speck that is in your brother's eye, but do not notice the log that is in your own eye? Or how can you say to your brother, 'Let me take the speck out of your eye,' and behold, the log is in your own eye? You hypocrite, *first* take the log out of your own eye, and *then* you will see clearly to take the speck out of your brother's eye."[36]

In other words, make sure you understand why this conflict really exists. Know your part. How did you contribute to the angst? What could you have done or how could you have responded differently? Did you have an unhealthy need to be validated or understood that further exasperated the conflict? Ask God to show you if there is an overly sensitive or critical spirit in you that is responding disproportionately or inappropriately to the situation. Is there a negative perspective that is providing fertile ground for seeds of dissension to germinate, be fertilized, and grow into unnecessary conflict? It is always a good idea to pray with David, "Search me, O God, and know my heart; try me and know my

---

35   Galatians 6:1–2.
36   Matthew 7:3–5.

anxious thoughts; and see if there be any hurtful way in me, and lead me in the everlasting way."[37]

Jesus admonishes us to take a good look at our own lives and do everything we can to clean our own vision before we rush off to do eye surgery on someone else. Am I overly negative or hypersensitive? Do I need to be validated or celebrated by others? Am I dragging in past hurts and negatively interpreting what I think just happened? If so, then I must ask the Lord and His people to help me get that log out of my own eye so I can see clearly as I try to help others. James adds helpful words: "What is the source of quarrels and conflicts among you? Is not the source your pleasures that wage war in your members? You lust and do not have; so you commit murder. You are envious and cannot obtain; so you fight and quarrel. You do not have because you do not ask. You ask and do not receive, because you ask with wrong motives, so that you may spend *it* on your pleasures."[38]

Of course, the more obvious logs of sinful words and actions need to be dealt with as well. Too often, we're blind to our own sins, and we need an honest friend or an adviser who will help us take an objective look at ourselves before we launch into others' burdens in a spirit of gentleness.

"If your brother sins, go and show him his fault in private; if he listens to you, you have won your brother."[39] Don't carry five years of baggage and sow destruction throughout the community.

---

37   Psalm 139:23–24.
38   James 4:1–3.
39   Matthew 18:15.

If it's a big deal, don't tell your girlfriends and don't tell your three roommates. Tell the person whom you're hurting about. Talk in private.

Don't Stop If You Have Been Stiffed ... Take One or Two Others Along

This one's pretty simple. If going to them in private doesn't work, don't stop the process. "But if he does not listen to you, take one or two more with you, so that by the mouth of two or three witnesses every fact may be confirmed."[40]

I might recommend not taking friends whom you've already briefed on your side of the story. Or if you do take them, make them memorize and meditate on Proverbs 18:17 before they go.[41]

A better way to approach this is to tell the one who has offended you, "I'm going to come back to you one more time because there are still some things I don't think we've resolved. Are there any people you trust and that you would like to have me go talk to and ask to come and sit with us so we can work through this thing? I'll ask them—or you can ask them—to sit and listen with us. And I'm not going to share my story with them until we're all together. But we can't stop now. If you think the problem is my legalism, perspective, or attitude, let's find other believers who

---

40 Matthew 18:16.
41 "The first to plead his case seems just, until another comes and examines him."

can help us figure this out. But I'm not going to stop just because you've stiffed me."

Don't Stop If It Gets Sticky ... Tell It to the Church

If your friend still won't listen after you've taken a few extra people to help, things do start getting a bit stickier. But we are not doing this because it is easy; we are doing it because it is righteous. Let me encourage you: don't stop if it gets sticky. "If he refuses to listen to them, tell it to the church."[42]

It is downright tragic and nearly blasphemous that most people will spend their entire church lives never seeing the process that the Lord gave us in His gospel fleshed out in humility and love in a way that keeps the Church pure and His people holy. When is the last time you've been to a church where somebody was struggling with their flesh and after a brother went to them in private and then two or three moved in and then the elders went to them, and the person was still committed to a certain broken pattern in their life—when is the last time that the leadership around them, in a very humble, godly way, shared it with the wider community of the church?[43]

---

42 Matthew 18:17a.

43 In larger churches like Watermark, we believe the "church" should be defined as those believers connected to the individual under the care and correction of those who know, love, and will continue to minister to and pray for their friend. Obviously, if the person is a leader and known throughout the body, the entire body should be addressed. See 1 Timothy 5:19–22.

Probably never.

Do you want to know why the Church is a powerless creature? Because we don't live the way God wants us to live. So yes, it gets really sticky here, so sticky that most of us choose not to go there. The result is that we are a shadow of who God wants us to be.

This doesn't mean an announcement in your church's bulletin or an all-church meeting to tell everyone, even those who don't really know what's going on in your community. But for those who know you, are in community with you, shepherd you, and lead you, when the private and the group efforts have failed, it's time to bring them in, endeavoring to keep the same spirit of gentleness, unity, and peace throughout the process.

Don't Stop If They Are Stuck in Their Sin ... Treat Them as a Nonbeliever

Not only should we not stop if it gets sticky, but we should not stop if that person gets stuck in sin. "And if he refuses to listen even to the church, let him be to you as a Gentile and a tax collector."[44]

At first glance, this sounds a little extreme because most people wrongly understand this passage to mean you are "writing someone off" for good. As if to say, *"See you later, sinner."* But let me ask you a question: Biblically, how are you called to treat nonbelievers?[45]

---

44   Matthew 18:17b.

45   This no small question, and because a huge percentage of people who profess to know God don't know how to love people who don't profess to know Him nor lovingly deal with others who are living inconsistently with

You love them. You pray for them. You serve them. You seek their best interests. You call them to follow Jesus.

You treat them as people you care about and not projects you are trying to convert. You love them, but you don't expect them to act like, and you don't treat them like, they are part of the body of Christ. You model holiness, goodness, kindness, gentleness, peace, and self-control before them. You keep your behavior excellent before them so that in the day they stand before their soon and coming King, they are not surprised to know who He is and what He expects of them.[46] You are Christ's ambassador to them.[47]

You are called to be *committed* to the *uncommitted*.

Note that Scripture does not say that the person *is* a non-believer at this point. We don't know what they are, but we are called to act biblically, lovingly, and wisely based on what we see.[48] Our job is not to see through others but to see others through … to spur others on to love and good deeds[49] and to encourage them day after day,[50] not definitively announce where they will be one day.

Jesus made it clear in Matthew 13 that He alone will decide how to separate and judge between what is good and bad—the

---

their profession of faith, the Church is not reaching new people and is not shepherding well many who have been around for a long time. It is almost impossible to overstate the tragedy of not knowing how to treat (love) sinners who have never been or who are currently in the Church.

46 1 Peter 2:12.
47 2 Corinthians 5:20.
48 Matthew 7:15–20; Galatians 6:1.
49 Hebrews 10:24–25.
50 Hebrews 3:13.

seeds and tares planted together—at the end of this age.[51] Our job is to admonish, encourage, and help with great patience and instruction and to wait for the great King to come on the day of great harvest. His job is to be the great King and to perfectly winnow at the great harvest. He will do His job, so the question for us after reading these scriptures and this chapter is, will we do ours?

Don't stop, even if they're stuck in sin.

Remember that you cannot guarantee how people will respond to what you do. You are only responsible for being fully devoted to what God calls you to do. In fact, you need to be prepared for unreasonable people—and you need to know that there may even be times that the unreasonable person in question is actually you because we can all become unreasonable when we feel provoked by others. Scripture teaches us that "a stone is heavy and the sand weighty, but the provocation of a fool is heavier than both of them."[52]

Our flesh is constantly provoked and responds in a way that provokes right back until we can't believe how something so small has turned into a hate so great. See the great American example of the Hatfields and McCoys, whose murderous rivalry started as a misunderstanding over a land dispute and an accusation about a pig.[53]

Being provoked does not entitle me to be punitive. I am always responsible for my attitudes and actions. How you act is your

---

51 Matthew 13:24–30; 36–43.
52 Proverbs 27:3.
53 "The Hatfield McCoy Feud," Hatfield McCoy Country, accessed May 10, 2017, http://hatfieldmccoycountry.com/feud/.

responsibility, but how I respond to your actions is mine. I can tell my wife all day long that I love her, but if I demand that she must act a certain way or I will not continue to be loving toward her, then I have a worldly, confused, and failed definition of love.

"He who restrains his words has knowledge, and he who has a cool spirit is a man of understanding. Even a fool, when he keeps silent, is considered wise; when he closes his lips, he is considered prudent."[54] Your words are your words—and your responsibility.

Prayerfully prepare yourself for unreasonable people and difficult situations. "But I say, walk by the Spirit, and you will not carry out the desire of the flesh.… Now the deeds of the flesh are evident, which are … *enmities, strife, jealousy, outbursts of anger, disputes, dissensions, factions* … and things like these … But the fruit of the Spirit is love, joy, peace, patience, kindness, goodness, faithfulness, gentleness, self-control … Now those who belong to Christ Jesus have crucified the flesh with its passions and desires."[55]

The day we forget that loving and responding the way Jesus did is a supernatural act—a walk in the Spirit—is the day we will love and respond in a natural way. If the power of God doesn't allow us to restrain our lips, we will sow enmities, strife, jealousy, outbursts of anger, disputes, and dissensions and create factions instead. It will be anything but *kingdom of God*–like, and there will be nothing to come and see.

It's not your job to get your wife, your friend, your ex-business partner, your husband, your sister, your roommate, your college

---

54 Proverbs 17:27–28.
55 Galatians 5:16–24.

buddy, or your mom to change. You can't—and God doesn't want you to. He wants to be the One who does the changing of lives.[56] What He expects of you is to abide with Him, obey His Word, and as much as it depends on you, be at peace.

Finally, don't buy the lie that we are supposed to end conflict by "meeting in the middle." The problem with meeting in the middle is that most of us are lousy judges of distance. Negotiation and mediation are great, but if relationally we *settle* for anything less than restored trust and oneness, we have fallen short. We are called to never give up pursuing true peace. Keep praying and keep persevering in what is right. That doesn't mean meeting in the middle; it means going the extra mile. In fact, as much as you are able, walk one mile and then walk two … [57]

Blessed *not* are the peace fakers. Blessed *not* are the peace breakers.

Blessed *are* the peace*makers*. They will be called sons of God.[58]

---

56 John 16:8–11.
57 Matthew 5:41.
58 Matthew 5:9.

Chapter 15

Confusing Counsel

Why So Anonymous?

It is a moment that is still vivid to me, though it took place over twenty-five years ago. I had slipped away by myself to grab a late lunch and then stayed in the quiet restaurant to get some extra work done. It was a "help yourself to the buffet" establishment, so I thought I could read and eat for hours. Not long after I was there, a group of people came trickling in and sat across from me in the restaurant. I didn't have to eavesdrop—the way they greeted, inter-acted, and listened to one another was enough to catch my eye.

Their conversations were open. Honest. Vulnerable. They were sharing their deepest, darkest issues with one another, along with their hopes and aspirations for a brighter future. No one was bored. There was no incessant checking of phones or distracted expressions. Everyone was dialed in, intently focused on listening to one another and responding with acceptance, kindness, and honesty.

It was a community of friends whose care for each other and ease of being together was inspiring—a testament to the potential and power of authenticity and trust in real community. I knew right away this *wasn't* a gathering of friends from a church, and yet I also recognized right away a love and care that *was* consistent with God's way—and as it always is, it was inspiring, attractive, and right,[1] everything true community *always* is.

I soon realized I was observing an Alcoholics Anonymous group meeting *after* the main meeting. Many of the regulars had gathered together at a restaurant across the street from their actual gathering place to continue their conversations, encourage each other, and learn more about each other's stories. And it was beautiful. It is always beautiful when you see wisdom's principles practiced, even when it is not operating in a setting that acknowledges the ultimate source of that wisdom.[2]

There was more authenticity, truth sharing, and burden bearing going on in that group of acquaintances than in most churches

---

1   Obviously I could not and was not trying to hear every part of their conversation, so my observation about the "rightness" of their fellowship is not a commentary on what they were sharing but on the obvious love and commitment to one another that was present and evident. If their conversation pushed one another toward a vague higher power, defined however they individually wanted to define it, I obviously would not call that "right," but rather dangerous no matter how loving or well-intentioned they were with each other. Biblical counsel is ultimately a part of all that is right and beautiful.

2   One of the ironies of this story, of course, is that AA was born out of Christian ideals and principles in 1935. "AA sprang from The Oxford Group, a non-denominational movement modeled after first-century Christianity." See Susan Cheever, *My Name Is Bill: Bill Wilson: His Life and the Creation of Alcoholics Anonymous* (New York: Simon & Schuster, 2004), 129.

in America today, which is the reason there are so many church members whose lives are empty, broken, addicted, and lonely. It is why so many have to go outside the church, look for anonymity, or even worse, pay someone to listen and offer wise counsel. It doesn't have to be this way. In fact, it *isn't* this way when the body of Christ behaves like the bride is supposed to.

We shouldn't have to envy the authentic community others are experiencing outside of the Church because God has something even better for us when we engage in truly being fully devoted members of His body.

Before we ever officially started Watermark, my friends and I constantly put these principles to work. We would meet people far from God and simply invite them to join us to go hunting, go to the lake, or simply gather with us over some good food. We believed then what we still know to be true today: if others would simply come and see the fullness of life and genuine joy and friendship that true believers share—without the need for alcohol, strippers, porn, or excess—then Christ would do the rest. This has always been the Lord's design. "Taste and see"[3] the kindness of God's way existed centuries before you could "come and see" the King or His people.

My now close friend and colaborer Jonathan Pokluda recalls very well his experience at one of these weekend getaways at "the lake house." He says, "I spent more than a few years in the dull cycle of working all week and partying on the nights and weekends. Monday through Friday, I'd live for the weekend. We'd start

---

3   Psalm 34:8.

on Thursday to prolong the party. Wash, rinse, repeat. I chased away boredom with the next thrill, but boredom continued to find me.

"One typical Saturday night, I was getting drunk at a bar on Lower Greenville, the then center of Dallas's party scene. There I ran into an old friend I hadn't seen in a while. I asked what she was getting into this weekend, and she unexpectedly responded that she would be visiting a church the next day. 'Great,' I said, 'my church sucks. Pick me up.' Church was a place where I daydreamed for an hour and occasionally asked for forgiveness for the events from the previous night.

"After that first time, I started visiting that church regularly and started to make a few friends there. Soon, one of those friends invited me to join them and a group of other men at a lake house for the weekend. I was used to spending weekends at the lake, but this was different. They weren't there to check out the girls; in fact, this was a guys-only trip, with many of them married and leaving their wives at home. And they weren't there to get drunk; nobody brought any alcohol at all. Some of them were very successful men; the lake house itself was something I could only dream of affording someday. But nobody seemed to care about that; everyone treated everyone else (including me) as equals.

"That night was extraordinary. We had meaningful conversations, not the normal drunken-slurred talk that I was accustomed to. We played cards, and I laughed until I cried. One of the guys was a pastor. But not the normal over-polished, posing kind of pastor I had seen before. He was real and would hold the attention of the other guys there. He wasn't careful with his words, but not in a reckless way. He was just real. We ate, we talked, we played cards, and we laughed.

"That night I couldn't sleep. I couldn't reconcile the joy that I had just experienced when it was so different than my normal weekend activities. It seemed to be a normal time together for these men, but it was so different for me. I couldn't help but wonder if I had been doing life all wrong. I couldn't help but wonder if I had been missing it.

"I was deep in thought all night, in and out of prayer. I left early the next morning, and I called my best friend as soon as I thought he would be awake. I ended up waking him up after he had been partying the night before. As Matt answered the phone in a groggy voice asking me if everything was okay, I told him it had never been better. Although I hadn't slept, I felt great. I didn't feel guilty or have the foggy thinking of a hangover. I told Matt we had been missing out on life."

That was just the beginning for J. P. This incredible young man is now one of my closest friends, as well as the pastor of the Dallas campus and one of our primary communicators here at Watermark. Each week, he shares grace and truth in Christ-centered, biblical community with thousands of young adults and college students from across the Dallas area at The Porch, our weekly young adults gathering.[4] What happened in his life with

---

4   Check out www.theporchdallas.com for more info on this amazing ministry to thousands of twentysomethings.

real people having real fun and real conversations is what God invites everyone to experience within His real Church.

"Come now, and let us reason together."[5] "Taste and see that the LORD is good."[6] "How blessed is the man who finds wisdom … She is a tree of life to those who take hold of her."[7] "The kindness of God leads you to repentance."[8] These are all verses communicating God's expectation that any true encounter with Him or His people is an invitation to Life.

The Christian life is not divinely *imposed* on us; it is divinely *proposed* to us. It is a proposal of love, not an imposition on our lives. This is why the Church is called Christ's bride—she is meant to be beautiful beyond comparison. You see, our love for one another is to be the ongoing, verifying, compelling, irresistible, can't-take-your-eyes-off-of beauty that everyone wishes they could wed.

Sadly, God's glory and goodness toward people are rarely associated with His church. Far too many have to go outside the Church to experience the kind of care and concern—and powerful testimonies—that should be *everywhere* in His Church. Most people can identify with Tozer when he asks why they are a part of their church and just what is it that this church is supposed to be doing. "We have to consider whether we are just going around and around—like a religious merry-go-round. Are we simply holding on to the painted mane of the painted horse,

---

5   Isaiah 1:18a.
6   Psalm 34:8.
7   Proverbs 3:13–18.
8   Romans 2:4.

repeating a trip of very insignificant circles to a pleasing musical accompaniment?"[9]

Most of the watching world sees only a merry-go-round of religious activity with no miraculous sense of awe and no welcoming sense of humility and authenticity. So most people in this world today feel more comfortable sharing the details of their lives with the proverbial local "bartender" than with someone from their local church—if they "regularly attend" a "church" at all.

Our problem isn't a bartender problem, a Twelve Steps group problem, or a counselor problem. Ours is a crisis wrapped up in—and caused by an abandonment of—the Church's post. The problem isn't with the other groups—they are merely doing their best to provide what they can in light of the fact that the Church is not providing what it should. The problem is not with others being available; it is with the shadowy, don't-bring-your-problems-here, high-minded, compromised culture of the American Church that is often too busy with events and programs to invest their lives and energy loving and counseling others within their community who need to be heard, helped, and given hope.

The fact that there is more genuine community at some local bars than in the local church is enough to make me want to belly up to the bar myself.

A lot of people like J. P. are accustomed to these other slurred conversations because that is all they have. What is happening on barstools, often with complete strangers, is simply the process of

---

9   A. W. Tozer, *Tragedy in the Church: The Missing Gifts* (Camp Hill, PA: Christian Publications, 1990), 7–8.

people trying to find some place where the God-given thirst within them—to know and be known—can somehow be satisfied. But talk with strangers—even honest talk—does not quench this thirst. For that matter, even intentional community found in groups like AA, which are doing many good things for many people, cannot fully satisfy what is missing.

God has something planned for us that is deeper and more meaningful than even the best of what this world offers—His Church. And within His Church, God wants us to be tenderhearted toward one another, not to send each other away to someone or somewhere else to be tended to ... to give us the illusion we are loved for a brief moment, or maybe for the evening. God wants our hearts to be open to the hope found in one another, not confined to the hope that someone's isolated office or the local bar might be open for another hour.

The Healthiest People in Any Church

As broken, prideful people, it is easy to stay more focused on how we are perceived than how we really are in practicality. This is especially tragic and true in the Church. No one is in more danger than the person who is committed to creating the appearance that their life is strong and put together when it is actually riddled with sin and surrendered to temptation.

Jesus, in one of His least known and most misunderstood parables, described it this way: "Now when the unclean spirit goes out of a man, it passes through waterless places seeking rest, and does not find it. Then it says, 'I will return to my house from which I came'; and when it comes, it finds it unoccupied, swept, and put in order. Then it goes and takes along with it seven other spirits more wicked than itself, and they go in and live there; and the last state of that man becomes worse than the first. That is the way it will also be with this evil generation."[10]

Translation? As bad as it might be to have your life so ravaged by the storm of sin that everyone in the neighborhood can see it, it is even worse to have pride, self-protection, inauthenticity, and deceit buried deep within the basement of your heart where no one can see the destruction that is so wildly spreading inside. It may seem wise to hide your sickness from others as long as you can, but sickness has a way of eventually making itself known. A tree rotting on the inside may look like a strong tree to those who pass by, but woe to those who are near it when it finally falls. The longer rottenness is hidden, typically, the more spectacular is its revelation.

We often look at those who are facing addiction, despair, marital crisis, and the like as "less strong" in their faith. And while it is possible that a lack of faith or a stubborn inattentiveness to it has created the problem, a humble return to deeply trusting in God's provision and plan can turn around our perception in an instant.

I learned a long time ago that the healthiest people are *not* those who appear to be free from struggles but those who face their "demons" head-on. Pride goes before destruction and a haughty

---

10   Matthew 12:43–45.

spirit before the fall.[11] God is opposed to the proud but gives graces to the humble.[12] Before destruction, the heart of a man is haughty, but humility goes before honor.[13] When pride comes, then comes dishonor, but with the humble is wisdom.[14] Therefore, let him who thinks he stands take heed that he does not fall.[15]

Or to say it as it has become common around my house: if dependence is the goal, then weakness is an advantage.

The healthiest and wisest people I know (according to Scripture) are those who know how vulnerable they are and who refuse to be defined by their struggles, failures, or the guilt and shame that so often accompanies them. At Watermark, let me tell you how this plays out, and how it completely busts the myth about who is healthy and who is not. Every Monday evening, an amazing group of individuals gathers on our campuses for something we call *re:generation*.[16] *Re:Gen*, as it is commonly called, is a Christ-centered discipleship ministry that presents itself as a recovery ministry, inviting anyone in our city to find freedom from struggles, whatever they may be. Codependency, anger, pornography, chemical dependency, eating disorders, depression, abuse, same-sex struggles. Bring it.

Early in this ministry's development, the leadership—many of whom came out of "anonymous" recovery ministries or churches

---

11   Proverbs 16:18.
12   1 Peter 5:5d; James 4:6.
13   Proverbs 18:12.
14   Proverbs 11:2.
15   1 Corinthians 10:12.
16   To learn more about this ministry and how you can serve others in your community with it, visit www.regenerationrecovery.org.

who stigmatized being "poor in spirit" instead of honoring it as the first thing that leads to blessing[17]—was adamant about the idea that we needed to clear the campus thirty minutes before it started so that "these people" could come and be free from the concern that others might see them coming to a ministry where they could deal with their deepest hurts and brokenness. Without outright saying it (or maybe even meaning it), they were insinuating that we needed to segregate the hurting and broken from the "strong" and more qualified believers who were seemingly not struggling (at least not openly) with such "shameful" and "guilt-producing" issues.

I, along with the rest of the elders, felt that it was time we made a strong statement about who we were as God's people. It was time to step on the throat of the perception that being a person desperately in need of God's grace and healing was something to be ashamed of. No, it was something all of us needed to publicly admire. We told our friends leading *Re:Gen* that, if their group was the only place at Watermark where those who were "in distress or discontented"[18] could feel welcome, we needed to shut down every other ministry until each one was as welcoming and authentic as *Re:Gen*.

We needed to let people know that every aspect of our ministry existed for the "weary and heavy-laden."[19] If all Watermark was good for was to reach the unbroken and "un-needy," then we weren't

---

17   Matthew 5:3.
18   1 Samuel 22:2.
19   Matthew 11:28.

being the Church that Jesus had in mind. Finally, I reminded them that I didn't know *anyone* who was unbroken or "un-needy" enough not to need Jesus—and even if they thought they were, I was not interested in providing a place for them. Rather, I was interested in helping them see how desperate they really were.[20]

Why would we clear the campus to reinforce a stigma? Why would we think we needed to cater to an idea that Christ said is the number one barrier keeping people from receiving the help they need from Him?[21] Why would we do anything that would reinforce the idea that it is appropriate for someone to feel shame for acknowledging the kind of heart condition Christ said would lead to blessing?[22] If *re:generation* (or any other place) was going to be the only place where people could be authentic, open, and honest about our brokenness and need, then it should be the only thing we were doing. If we needed to clear the campus of "church people" to reach those who wanted to know more of the grace of Christ, then we needed to sell our campus and go somewhere else with Christ's people.

To communicate the seriousness of this value, I addressed the issue by taking our entire body through the biblical principles of *Re:Gen* in a Sunday morning series. We began to normalize a fearless acknowledgment of sin's power and its devastating grip on all of our lives. A phrase that came out of that series is "The healthiest people at Watermark are here on Monday nights" (at

---

20   Jesus told a story to help the "un-needy" in His day for exactly these reasons. See Luke 18:9–14.
21   Mark 2:17; Matthew 9:12–13.
22   Matthew 5:3–4.

re:generation). I said, "I know there are many people dealing with sin and its struggles all throughout our body, but I *know* you are committed to being healthy if you are coming here on Mondays."

Blessed are the ones who know they are spiritually bankrupt.

While everyone who attended Watermark may not yet have been serious about the hurts, hang-ups, and habits that haunt us all, I made it clear that the courageous and clear-minded people who attended *re:generation* certainly were. Presence in this ministry moved from being a *stigma* to a mark of being *serious* about wanting the freedom that Jesus wants all of us to experience. The people who were going through *Re:Gen* were actually the ones we could assume were committed to being the healthiest people in our church, not the people who should be stigmatized.

If dependence is the goal, then our weakness is a spiritual advantage.[23]

From that moment on, there was no longer a need to clear the campus on Monday; in fact, now the people who didn't come on Monday needed to make clear that the reason they didn't come was because they were already *living* out the truths their "Monday" friends were *learning*.

To this day, our Monday *Re:Gen* crowd is celebrated for their wisdom and courage for coming, not haunted by foolishness and shame for needing to.[24]

---

23 2 Corinthians 12:9.

24 One of the primary reasons "recovery" ministries don't thrive in churches is because they are treated as "recovery ministries" and not as discipleship ministries. Another reason, just as dishonoring to Christ, is that the people who find hope and authentic lives in the recovery ministry cannot find

"Unhealthy" people become heroes of health very quickly when they live in vulnerable, authentic, Christ-centered community with others. It is not the people who hide their hang-ups who get well; it is the ones who hang them out to be addressed, helped, and dealt with in communities of grace.

Grace doesn't care how we come to need it; grace only cares that we come.

And to show that we are serious when we say that the healthiest people at Watermark gather on Monday night and that this isn't something we just say to induce people to come, you should probably know that 70 percent of our pastoral and leadership staff are going through *Re:Gen*. Our best leaders also happen to be our most broken people who have lived in the midst of authenticity, openness, sincerity, and biblical community.

The idea that a desperate need for Jesus to sustain and continually sanctify someone would disqualify them from opportunity in ministry is blasphemous. Not only is the need for Christ a requirement, the idea that anyone is fit for ministry who doesn't readily admit their need for constant grace is ridiculous. Obviously, there are certain instances where a person's recent decisions may temporarily or even permanently disqualify them from serving or leading in specific ministries, both for their safety and the safety or reputation of the mission;[25] however,

---

them anywhere else in the church. Any church that has a sharp diversity in authenticity and dependence on Christ from one ministry to another is not a healthy church.

25 2 Corinthians 6:3.

the idea that only those who don't have or who successfully hide their problems and struggles from others should be qualified to serve is completely unhealthy, unnecessary, unwise—and it is almost certainly an invitation to future troubles.

God calls us to a journey of healing together ... and there's not a single one of us on this journey who is not broken in some way. In need of counsel. In need of abiding in Christ and His provision of grace *every day*. Only when we stop acting as if we have no need for grace or for each other and instead devote ourselves daily to the spiritual disciplines, pursuing each other relationally, living before each other authentically, admonishing one another faithfully, and counseling each other biblically will we see the power of God evidence itself in our minds, relationships, families, marriages, habits, and life together.

This only happens when we fearlessly commit to being real with each other. Confessing our sins to each other. Praying for each other. Forgiving each other. Challenging each other. Offering grace to each other.

James says it like this: "Therefore, confess your sins to one another, and pray for one another so that you may be healed. The effective prayer of a righteous man can accomplish much." Confession to *God* brings forgiveness of sins,[26] but confession to *one another* brings healing.[27]

Biblical churches are made up of communities who counsel each other through their problems, laugh together through life's

---

26 1 John 1:9.
27 James 5:16.

joys, celebrate with one another in God's victories, mourn with each other through life's sufferings, encourage each other through life's challenges, and stay with each other through life's trials.

Nothing anonymous about our struggles ... nothing intoxicating us but His love.

Chapter 16

In Confidence

Most church leaders today keep a list on file of outside experts to call when there is a problem. These experts stand ready to do what the Church was created to do in the first place. Marriage problem? *Call this guy.* Substance abuse problem? *Go over here.* Family problem? *Y'all spend some time with this gal and get it worked out.*

Instead of being a house of prayer, most churches are houses of referral.

The original, and still present expectation for God's presence on earth working in the lives of others sounds like this: they were "proclaiming the gospel of the kingdom, and healing every kind of disease and every kind of sickness. Seeing the people, He felt compassion for them, because they [are] distressed and dispirited like sheep without a shepherd."[1] Yet somehow, churches today see people with problems and feel completely overwhelmed, distressed, and dispirited themselves because they believe they are without the ability or expertise to truly help.

---

1   Matthew 9:35–36.

Jesus's command to His disciples was not "send them away"; it was "bring them to Me."[2]

This "we don't have what we need" mentality has given way to the rise of an entire industry. Despite God's reminders to the Church "that His divine power has granted to us *everything* pertaining to life and godliness, through the true knowledge of Him who called us by His own glory and excellence,"[3] and that He has "blessed us with *every* spiritual blessing in the heavenly places in Christ,"[4] more care and concern are being outsourced to experts than are being experienced by men and women in Christ-centered community.

Let me be clear: I have absolutely *nothing* against the professional counseling community. My concern is not that LPCs[5] are present to help people and provide, in the case of biblical counselors, wise and scripturally informed advice and aid. My concern is that the Church, who has been ordained by God to "know His will and approve the things that are essential, being instructed out of the Law, and who should be confident that they are a guide to the blind, a light to those who are in darkness, a corrector of the foolish, a teacher of the immature, having … the embodiment of knowledge and of the truth,"[6] has become scared and silent. And instead of embodying knowledge and truth, she has abandoned her post and now is forced to hope others can correct, teach, and lead those who are hurting back to health.

---

2   Matthew 14:16–18.
3   2 Peter 1:3.
4   Ephesians 1:3.
5   Licensed professional counselors.
6   Romans 2:17–20.

This has created many problems, not the least of which is that the sufficiency of Christ and His Word have been impugned as churchmen and the world's men alike have no sense that there is anything divine or worth coming to see (or even paying attention to) where God's people are.

Again, my purpose here is not to target or admonish the *counseling profession;*[7] it is to *counsel* and admonish those *professing* to be the Church.

Don't we need to at least consider the possibility that the reason we are so dependent on others to provide counsel for the hurting is that we are not paying attention to the counsel of God's Word? Isn't it tragically true that most churches are full of nondiscipled, nonabiding, overwhelmed, undertrained attenders who are spending more time trying to cover up the pain in their own lives than they are standing ready to help others with healing?

One of the most tragic things I hear church leaders say again and again is that the greatest need in the Church is leader development. This should never be the case in a biblical church. Discipleship *is* leader (and biblical counselor, shepherd, Christlike) development. If disciples of Jesus are not able to care for the spiritual needs of people, we do not have a church problem—we have a Jesus problem. If a church does not have disciples of Jesus, they don't need to call themselves a church. Discipleship is

---

7   So when you forget what I just said, please flip back a few pages and reread the aforementioned statement … read it several times out loud, if you find it necessary.

leadership development. Where there is a "kingdom of priests," there is no problem with helping a flock of people.

To the discipled, abiding Church that is full of an ever-increasing number of faithful believers who follow Him, Jesus has something even more effective than what the world's system offers—and you don't have to have any board-certified, university-recognized, government approval to receive it, and you also don't need that to be a part of offering it to others.

What?

Is this kind of thinking ignorant? Crazy? Dangerous?

Before you answer, let me remind you of what I have *not* said. I have *not* said that people, even lovers of God, don't need counsel.[8] Secondly, I have *not* said that every individual Christian or every local church needs to act as if each and every one of them is the compendium of all wisdom and therefore not in need of seeking out others, even recognized experts, to join them in caring for people. I have *not* said that if you really loved Jesus, you would never need help from those who have dedicated and ordered their lives to study and to recognizing patterns so they can help others deal with problems in the human experience.[9]

I have not said any of this ... not at all.

---

8 I just spent an entire chapter telling you why you are a fool if you think this to be the case.

9 Nothing in God's Word says, as Mary Baker Eddy and her "Christian Scientist" friends wrongly espouse, that we are never in need of seeking medical help when we have issues with our physical health. And nothing in God's Word says we should not widen the circle as much as is necessary to deal with other troubles in the human experience.

Everyone needs counsel. Every day. Almost all the time.[10] This includes those in the Church. In fact, it *especially* includes the Church because the Church is supposed to be made up of individuals who, as a requirement for membership, have acknowledged their helpless state,[11] their deceived and faint hearts,[12] their sick heads,[13] their weak flesh,[14] the corruption of their world, and the existence of an active enemy to their souls.[15] If anyone should know they need encouragement, admonishment, help, and counsel, it ought to be us.

Every Christian ought to be aspiring to be a godly counselor.

Let's start with the fact that Christ Himself, in whose image we were all created[16] and to whose image we are all supposed to be conformed,[17] is the most wonderful of all counselors. Isaiah calls Him as much when he says, "And His name will be called Wonderful Counselor, Mighty God, Eternal Father, Prince of Peace."[18] And it ends with what I have been telling you throughout this entire book—that every believer is called to grow into maturity and be conformed to the image of Christ,[19] which is to say that as we are equipped "for the work of service, to the building up of the body of Christ; until we all attain to the unity of the faith, and of

---

10 Hebrews 3:13; 2 Timothy 4:2.
11 Romans 5:6; Matthew 5:3.
12 Jeremiah 17:9; Matthew 5.
13 Isaiah 1:5.
14 Romans 7:18–23.
15 Ephesians 2:1–3; 1 Peter 5:8.
16 Genesis 1:27–29.
17 Romans 8:29; 1 Corinthians 15:49.
18 Isaiah 9:6.
19 Romans 8:29.

the knowledge of the Son of God, to a mature man, to the measure of the stature which belongs to the fullness of Christ,"[20] we become disciples who are equipped to look, act, and think like Jesus. We become for each other a source of grace, healing, and provision—and *this* creates a sense of awe and divine health in a community. A community full of adequate, equipped-for-every-good-work,[21] compassionate, kind,[22] burden-bearing,[23] wisdom-filled,[24] divine workmanship.[25]

Who wouldn't want to come and see that?

If Jesus is a Wonderful Counselor, then so is His body ... which means, so are *you* as you become more and more like Him through surrender, study, and submission to His Spirit and Scripture.

So the more we become like Christ, the better counselors we will be. Disciple-making churches will raise up counselors. Don't think of this term as people who hang shingles in their offices. Think of people who have Scripture on their tongues and the Spirit of grace in their hearts. Don't think about experts on Freud, Skinner, Jung, or Rogers. Think about men and women of faith who believe in the words of Jesus, hate sin, and walk in righteousness.

I'm talking about a community of people who can, to the deceived, fornicators, idolaters, adulterers, effeminate, homosexuals,

---

20 Ephesians 4:12–13.
21 2 Timothy 3:16–17.
22 Colossians 3:12.
23 Colossians 3:13.
24 Colossians 3:16.
25 Ephesians 2:10.

thieves, covetous, drunkards, revilers, and swindlers say, "Such a person was I, but I have been washed, sanctified, and justified in the name of the Lord Jesus Christ and in the Spirit of our God."[26]

Wouldn't you want to run to a community of healers, lovers, helpers who can speak an "apt answer" and provide a "timely word"?[27] Wouldn't you find wonder, hope, and strength from a people whose "sons were taught of the LORD; and whose well-being was great … who in righteousness were established … who were far from oppression, free from fear and from terror"?[28]

It is *not* a sign of a healthy church that only a few can be what Christ has intended we all become. It is never good for the Church's strategy to be "come and see us so we can send you, without us, to someone else who will see you."

May it cease to be.

We are to be a kingdom of priests that the world—and each of us—can come to. Long gone should be the days of "Come to the professional … come to the senior pastor … come to the expert." It should be said of us, "Come and see 'the holy people, the redeemed of the LORD; a people who are called, "Sought out, a city not forsaken."'"[29]

Again, a pastor's job is to "equip the saints for the work of ministry,"[30] not to do the work of ministry for the saints because the "saints" are not equipped for anything of real consequence or

---

26 All thoughts from 1 Corinthians 6:9–11.
27 Proverbs 15:23.
28 Isaiah 54:13–14.
29 Isaiah 62:12.
30 Ephesians 4:12 (ESV).

substance other than funding the whole operation. Honestly, I can think of very few pastors out there who would disagree with this statement in word, mainly because it is right out of Scripture. But in deed, most of them play into the only narrative about counseling that they've been taught themselves—that counseling is for the professionals and maybe for a few of the pastors, but definitely not for the people.

But we must not forget that we are called to be a kingdom *of* priests,[31] not a kingdom *led by* priests and *legitimized* by secular studies and state-sanctioned professionals. A healthy church will raise up godly counselors and will increasingly be made up of godly counselors—people who care for one another, make time for one another, speak the truth in love[32] to one another, and recognize patterns of sin and human rebellion in one another. People who help each other with grace and truth.

Tragically, the way the state-sanctioned counseling profession is structured today, counselors are bound by law to not speak any more truth to the one seeking or needing counsel, *or to others who can help*, than the one seeking or needing counsel determines they need on their terms and in their time. This protection makes perfect sense if you believe you are seeking counsel from strangers who cannot be implicitly trusted and who are not bound to this higher law: "let everything they do be done in love."[33] But it makes less sense if you are dealing with individuals of good reputation, full of

---

31 1 Peter 2:9.
32 Ephesians 4:15.
33 1 Corinthians 16:14.

the Spirit and wisdom, who are able to teach … people of dignity, not double-tongued, but tested … not new converts or conceited people, not malicious gossips, but people who are dignified, temperate, and *faithful in all things*.[34] People who know the sting of sin and have come to be freed from the bonds of death themselves. People who are also under authority and who live in subjection to others in love.[35] People who, by the grace of God, are committed to be "obedient, to be ready for every good deed, to malign no one, to be peaceable, gentle, showing every consideration for all men."[36]

When you are blessed to be around *these* men and women, you should not only want to receive counsel, but you should also want to humble yourself before them. You want to trust them as they humbly serve you as their faith in God overflows.

Laws are necessary because we do not "love our neighbor as ourselves"[37] and because we "bite and devour one another"[38] instead of living in an abiding relationship with Christ where we are able to live according to Christ's better way and to humble ourselves under godly people, restoring one another in a spirit of gentleness as we depend by faith on God and His Word. In this new community, we can say with David, "Let the righteous smite me in kindness and reprove me; it is oil upon the head; do not let my head refuse it."[39]

---

34   1 Timothy 3:6–11.
35   1 Peter 5:5–6; Ephesians 5:21.
36   Titus 3:1–2.
37   Galatians 5:14.
38   Galatians 5:15.
39   Psalm 141:5.

We should not have to put confidentiality laws on our love for one another in the Church,[40] and while we should be slow to place anyone in positions worthy of our confidence, if we can't find worthy men and women to help us within our church, then maybe we need to start finding another church.[41] Christ calls us to share life with others in godly community—and in His body, we can trust that we are protected and loved in far greater ways than any legal requirement of privacy can afford us.

But can this type of community really exist? If you are willing, come and see.

A Deal I Never Make

Let me walk you through how this practically works its way out in my life. When someone first approaches me asking if I can help them with a situation, they often say, "I am about to tell you something I have never told anyone, and I need you to promise me that you will not tell anyone else what I am about to share with you."

---

40 1 Timothy 1:8–9. However, it is necessary to remember that there are lots of people in "churches," even in leadership, who do not fit the description of godly, mature, wise, and Spirit-led men and women. Proverbs 13:20 is true inside and outside the church. *Be discerning about whom you place confidence in.* Trust those worthy of your confidence, remembering that a trustworthy person lives in subjection to godly authority themselves and never sets themselves up as being above accountability.

41 1 Timothy 5:22; 2 Timothy 2:22.

I know it may not seem to flow with the conventional wisdom of the day, but a promise not to share information is a deal I purpose never to make with anyone.

Etymologically, the word *confidence* originates from the words *con* and *fideo*, which mean literally, "with faith." The modern context of the phrase "keep in confidence" almost exclusively means "not to tell anyone," but that severely shortchanges its original meaning. What it really means is that if you tell me something "in confidence," you are telling me "with faith."

This means that you trust me to do much more than just not tell anyone else what we've talked about. It means you have faith in me that I will *do* the right thing with the information you are sharing—the thing that will be most helpful to you and most glorifying to the God who loves you. This means I won't use your information as a conversation starter at a party or on a date. And it means I won't slide it in inappropriately as a "prayer request." It means I won't use it to slander you, own you, manipulate you, or in any way not serve your best interests as informed by prayer and the Word of God.[42]

Even as you have a responsibility in discerning with whom you should share the information, upon hearing it, I am responsible for what I do with it once it is heard. Instead of just sitting on your information, it is my responsibility before God to, by faith, handle it wisely.

There will be times when wisdom would have me widen the circle and bring other people into the conversation who can

---

42　1 Timothy 4:5.

sharpen and encourage the two of us as we prayerfully discern the most God-honoring course (which will also cause the most human flourishing). In those situations, I am not going to surprise you with what I believe God wants me to do, but I will do it. I will explain who and why others should be included; and these other people will always be individuals who are either part of the problem or a part of the solution. We will communicate and seek to follow the "ancient path"[43] together. But part of me being brought into any situation "in confidence" is my having the freedom and responsibility to handle it according to the faith. Wisdom from the Word of God will dictate my next steps, not permission from the state or from man.[44]

From God's perspective, the healthiest form of counseling is the kind where we don't enable isolationist tendencies or commit to limitations from the outset that keep everyone—from the counselor to the counselee—from responding in a way that is consistent with the life-giving blessing found in obedience to God's Word.

I'm sure you have many questions, the most obvious one being, *How does being in a church make you qualified to dispense dependable counsel, especially when someone is in a significant life crisis?* It doesn't. Being "in a church" doesn't mean very much.[45] There are lots of people in church all the time who are there for cultural

---

43 Jeremiah 6:16–17a.
44 1 Thessalonians 2:3–7.
45 We have all heard the analogies that illustrate the fact that a certain thing's location does not determine its composition, and much less its character. Being in a garage doesn't make someone a car. You may wear fatigues, but that doesn't mean you are a soldier. Sitting in a pew doesn't make you worthy of trust.

reasons, are just beginning their own journey toward faith, or who are so new to the faith that they are not ready to shepherd others' hearts.[46] But being a disciple of Christ who, by God's sanctifying grace, is "no longer a child, tossed here and there by waves and carried about by every wind of doctrine, by the trickery of men, by craftiness in deceitful scheming; but speaking the truth in love, has grown up in all aspects into Him who is the head"[47] makes you more than a little qualified.

I have been immersed in relationships with thousands of God's people for a long time, and I will happily be the first one to tell you that there are many gifted individuals out there who can easily recognize patterns and problems that I have not yet learned to identify. I am certain there are others who, as a result of their past experiences or education, have undoubtedly learned to care for others in crises with much greater insight and empathy than I have at any particular moment.

I am obviously not saying that we do not need people with training or experience. I'm saying quite the opposite—we need *more* people who can counsel, not fewer. But we also do not need counselors operating in isolation from community or God's revealed way. We should never use the waiting, willing, and able "professionals" as our first line of defense. There is never an excuse for a loving Christ follower to "check out" or refuse to walk through difficult situations with others in their community. Walking on the other side of the road or assuming that the person in the ditch near

---

46   1 Timothy 3:10; 5:22.
47   Ephesians 4:14–15.

us is not our responsibility has never been a course of action God celebrates.[48] Getting the right kind of help to have others join you in caring for others might be.

If I don't have what my brother needs, then I am going to be committed to finding the answer anywhere or from anyone I can so that we learn and grow together. That way, both of us will be able to help someone who has a similar issue when we meet it again in the future. What if, instead of referring someone to an "expert" and waiting until they come back recovered or "well," we go *with* them instead? What if, when we don't know what to do, we go with the person we couldn't help to the more learned and experienced to learn *with* them?

As my kids were nearing the driving age and they encountered car batteries that were dead and tires that were flat, I didn't tell them to push an OnStar button, call a wrecker, or wait until an expert could arrive and take care of the issue for them. I walked them through how to deal with the trouble so they could learn for themselves … and also so they would be able to equip and encourage others with the same issues.[49]

---

48 Good Samaritan story anyone? Luke 10:30–37.

49 You might be thinking, *Okay, what if the trouble were with the transmission, the car's electronics? Or what if it had been broadsided and needed extensive help? Did you tell them to go hang out in the auto shop and learn how to do transmission or body work for two weeks?* Of course not. But I did walk them through the process and had them learn what needed to be done and how it was done in order to teach them how to know if the right thing was being done. Even in times where extreme "service" requirements are needed, we should be informed on how to evaluate and understand all the "repairs" that are required, even if we can never actually perform them ourselves.

There are times when a person in my life approaches me and says, "I'm really wrestling with this," and I respond, "I'm not really sure I'm the best guy to deal with that, but I'm committed to learn to be … Let's you and I go and pursue help in this area together." We both *grow* as we both *go* forward in confidence together.

As Jesus's Church, we must break the trend of sending people in crisis off by themselves to "get well." Jesus said, "Do you want to get well? … Then pick up your mat and follow Me."[50] That means we should say, "Do you want to get well? Then let's run to Jesus together."

It is time we stop having people share their problems in "confidence" with strangers who, in turn, help them in complete "confidence" and sign off on their progress and who then send them back to us ready to rejoin a community that has had little or even nothing to do with their journey toward Christ in the meantime.

This is a lose-lose instead of a win-win.

A more biblical way would be for us to "go with them" wherever it is they need to go instead of leaving them to recover in isolation and without the benefit of encouragement from the family God has provided them. In this model, we would choose instead to stick close to them and become equipped along with them so that "we will be able to comfort those who are in any affliction with the comfort with which we ourselves are

---

50   John 5:6–8.

comforted by God."[51] It is not that we are to be overly confident in our own abilities, but we are to be rightly confident that the comfort that comes to any of us from Christ is indeed strong enough to flow through us toward anyone with "any affliction."

Early on in my ministry, the following scenario happened to me constantly—and others like it still happen today. A couple will call me because their marriage is in trouble. When we speak, I ask them a question they are not anticipating: "Who's your community? Who are you walking with as you experience a gospel-informed life together? Have you already shared with those God has provided for you all that you are compelled to share with me?"

They often respond that their issue is too serious for their group of fellow "ordinary" disciples to help with. Infidelity. Anger. Divorce. Substance abuse. Sexual-identity issues. Addiction. Complicated family-of-origin issues. These are things best left to the "experts," or so the prevailing attitude of the day would tell us. But thankfully, we don't need to trust the prevailing attitude of the day. I don't even hesitate to invite others to trust me as I put my confidence in the enduring revelation of God's Word—and that means before they run to me or any other "expert," they should loop in others with whom they are already committed to doing life together. Why share anything with me that they haven't already shared with these other trusted members of their community?

"But we're scared to death of telling this to other people."

---

51   2 Corinthians 1:4.

"Well, let's talk about *that* first," I reply.

If we're the community Christ wants us to be, we should live authentically with one another.[52] We should have the freedom to not be ruled by guilt and shame as we model love for one another.[53] Real love means letting you know who I really am. Authentic living is part of God's prescribed way for us to be really healed.[54] It means trusting that the transformative grace of Christ in you will lead you to accept me for who I am and also to love me enough not to let me stay there. It means I need you and trust you enough to let you spur me on to love and good deeds,[55] helping me break out of patterns in my life that produce real pain and problems.[56]

So again, before I agree to meet with anyone, I always encourage them to go to their community first so that together they may talk, pray, and search God's Word for help. If after exhausting their immediate provision of encouragement and counsel they still have questions or needs, then their entire community meets with me (or the appropriate next person) so we can all seek the heart of God and find wisdom and instruction together. This isn't just how I respond. It is how we all respond.

Whatever we do, we are careful never to walk through the caring process alone.

---

52 1 Timothy 1:5.
53 1 John 4:18.
54 Proverbs 28:13; Psalm 32:3; James 5:16.
55 Hebrews 10:24.
56 Proverbs 25:12; 27:5–7; and Galatians 6:1–2, just to name a few.

So should we talk to counselors?[57] All the time. Should we do it in isolation? I don't see anywhere in God's Word that this is recommended.[58]

What about examples of people seeking Jesus in private? Nicodemus did come to Jesus alone and at night seeking "counsel," but the counsel he sought was related to understanding more about the person of Christ and how to be reconciled to God. He was living in the darkness of not understanding who Christ was and came seeking clarity about the Scriptures. Besides, the very fact that his story is recorded may indicate that other disciples were there when Jesus received him and responded to him.

Jesus was committed to making disciples, and in almost every interaction, we see Him taking at least Peter, James, and John along with Him. We would be wise to do the same. I tell people that Watermark is a training hospital, and because I am committed to training others, "don't be surprised when I have others with me as I meet with or care for you ... and don't be surprised that I ask you to bring others." When we bring others along, it multiplies our time, increases disciples, and allows everyone near to grow.

At minimum, if you feel you must see someone apart (or hopefully in addition to) your church or community, why not ask

---

57 I think by now you know that when I say "counselors" I am talking about others who are Christ-following, humble, committed-to-learning individuals who themselves seek whatever help they need, who live and interact in community, and who refuse to operate in isolation.

58 We do see in Scripture where friends/counselors are to *come to us* alone. That is what friends do for friends when they see trouble brewing in our lives. See chapter 14.

one person from your church to go with you?[59] They can help you hear, help you make sure you don't misinterpret the counsel given to you, and help you as you wrestle each day to apply what you are learning.

Again, if you're not in a community (people of faith with whom you are doing the business of life as you collectively seek God's better way) you can trust with the real stuff you're dealing with, then let's make sure we deal with *that* first. You want a recipe for despair, growing sadness, increasing anxiety, and stress? Then just keep going through life alone, and you'll have it.

I have many friends who are LPCs who not only see the wisdom of involving others in their counseling sessions, they all but insist on it. They, too, know that the source of our hope is in running to Christ, not in managing information in a way that is most comfortable to us. No truly biblical counselor will ever want to counsel you in isolation; they'll want to call you to biblical community. They won't let you hide behind some confidentiality agreement. You'll tell them your information "with faith" so that they can use it well.

You might be scared to death of what you have just read, but I love you enough to tell you the truth: as long as you are scared to death of this idea, you are scared to death to live biblically—and when you don't live biblically, it won't scare you to death ... it will walk you there.[60]

---

59   Or at the very least, when no one can go with you, make the request that the counselor take what you share with them and write a report to send to the people in your smaller, "one anothers"–practicing community. In a loving body of Christ, there should be nothing we hide from our family.
60   Proverbs 14:12.

Don't underestimate what you have to offer others. Don't rob yourself of the joy that God intends for you as a minister of His grace. Be a student of His Word. Stay current on real-time struggles, events, and situations. Counsel biblically. Be unafraid to widen the circle to include others who have faced these issues before. No man has all wisdom for every situation, but people yielded to the Spirit and informed by the Word of God have infinitely more to offer others than they generally have grown to believe with the rise of secularism. Samuel Chadwick rightly observes, "No man is uneducated who knows the Bible and no one is wise who is ignorant of its teachings."[61]

To wrap up this concept, let me share with you an actual email response I sent to a friend from my church. This gentleman who was asking for my time was stumped over a certain biblical passage from a minor prophet in the Old Testament, and he was wisely looking for help, as we all must do from time to time. He presented his "issues" and asked me to give my thoughts. Though in this case the questions were about biblical interpretation and not a request for insight into some personal issue, my response would have remained the same.

Here is what I sent him:

"Will, I have sent my answer to my assistant and asked her to hold it until you send me an email with the best answers that your community/shepherds/friends/partners in ministry have come up with as you all study and reflect on God's Word together. Then, if it is still necessary for me to chime in (because you are all still

---

61   Samuel Chadwick (1860–1932).

unsatisfied with what the Lord showed you *all* as you wrestled with the question), I (or whoever can best serve you) will meet with *all* of you so everyone can benefit together. Wrestling with issues/questions/problems this way is the best because …

It allows you to lead, sharpen, and grow those you are in life with as you model humility, a thirst for God's Word, and a desire to grow in wisdom and an understanding of God's revelation in all things.

It keeps you (or whoever is seeking answers) from being exasperated because you are 'waiting in line' for 'Moses' to speak (Exodus 18).

It keeps 'Moses' from being exhausted while trying to answer everyone's questions (Exodus 18).

It creates a natural forum for community/discipleship and corporate growth.

So you owe me your community's/shepherds'/friends'/partners' in ministry best response (and all the names of the people in your life/community/ministry), and I will then share with all of them my answer. It is done and waiting for you.

Thankful for Jethro,
Todd"

Chapter 17

Changing the Campfire Conversation

I love stories. They fuel me. They motivate me. They are a constant reminder that I serve a living God and that He is still actively engaged in history. They are present evidence that the words of Scripture are true … that the Father is constantly willing to use me and any other willing earthen vessel to partner with Him to make the treasure of His grace[1] available to "anyone who believes."[2]

When you run around on earth with the power of heaven in your life, your world should be full of stories.

Watching God's mercy and kindness daily pour into others' lives is a constant reminder to me that Jesus was serious when He said that His work would continue long after His ascension.[3] His plan was always to continue His raid of hell after he left earth and His plan was always to use His people. It is not a stretch to say that

---

1   2 Corinthians 4:7.
2   John 1:12.
3   John 14:12; Acts 1:8; Colossians 1:25–27.

if you are not around stories of life change and transformation, then perhaps you should ask yourself if you are really running with Jesus. There are people without hope and without God in this world,[4] and there are people like you whom God wants to actually have stories to tell about how God used you to bring the love of God to them.

I love watching people who are convinced of the foolishness of the gospel become fools for Christ's sake.[5] I love continually being able to say with John, "And there are also many other things which Jesus did, which if they were written in detail, I suppose that even the world itself would not contain the books that would be written."[6]

My kids would often ask me, "If you could live during any time in history, what time period would you choose?" After years of hearing my answer of when and why, they learned to insert the caveat: "other than when Jesus was on earth." They know me well.

I always try to describe to them how amazing it would have been to "run" with the other disciples … to gather nightly around the campfire and review the things we would have observed every day as "a great throng of people from all Judea and Jerusalem and the coastal region of Tyre and Sidon, who had come to hear Him and to be healed of their diseases; and those who were troubled with unclean spirits were being cured."[7]

---

4   Ephesians 2:12–13.
5   1 Corinthians 4:10.
6   John 21:25.
7   Luke 6:17–18.

But here's the deal—I don't need to wish I could be around an ancient campfire to experience this … I am getting to do it every week in Dallas.[8]

Today.

Right now.

With softer beds and better transportation.

I am running with Jesus on earth, and you should be too.

When you do, your nightly "campfire" will change just as mine did.

Not long ago, we received a follow-up email from a young man in California who was being asked to join the Elder Team at his church. He had spent some time on the phone with one of our elders, sharpening his understanding of how we lead together and what the Scriptures say about shared leadership. As he was discussing with his pastor and the other leaders of their church what they understood the responsibilities and roles would be if he were to join them, he began to share with them some things he knew about Watermark and the way our team works together. Later he sent this email.

"Thanks again for your time today … very helpful. Very much appreciate your wise counsel during this time. As stated, I have been richly blessed by Watermark; pretty awesome considering that I have no official affiliation other than by proxy through my friends there. Please pass along my encouragement to the team.

---

8   My prayer is you would be able to say this same thing, only ending your sentence differently because you live in a different place. God is at work everywhere there is a willing, grace-informed, yielded heart.

As a reminder: when I 'challenged' my Senior Pastor with my thoughts of what the Elder Board should look like out here, I mentioned Watermark and he said the following: 'Everyone talks about Watermark and no one ever mentions Todd. I mean that is an example of a body that is built around the church (not the pastor). That is exactly the kind of church we want to be.'"

When the Church is what God intends it to be, everyone gets in on the stories.

There is a better than average chance that before you began reading this book, you had never heard my name or rushed onto iTunes to purchase a Watermark worship album. And while it is fine that some churches are known for their well-published pastor or impressive worship products (our worship team is a blessing, and you would be greatly encouraged to learn, use, and sing any of the many songs they have written for the Church), every church should ultimately want to be known—at least if they are the kind of church the Spirit of God plants—by the life changes in the people and the transformation of the city where they serve. Much like in the first century, churches should be famous because Jesus is at work there[9]—not because Peter, John, Paul, or Piper preached there. They should be a place where the Lord adds to their number day by day those who are being saved,[10] not just day by day the number of albums being sold or podcasts being listened to. It is fine if all of those happen, but there is no question which *one* has to be happening if it is Christ's church.

---

9   Acts 8:6–8.
10 Acts 2:47.

The early disciples were not "celebrity" disciples. David was not well known for selling out music festivals that filled up "entire shepherds' fields"—he was known for filling up his heart and his mouth with praise for the King and shepherding well the flock of God around him. Circulating around both the early disciples and the faithful God followers in the Old Testament were constant stories of God's grace working mightily through them.[11] God was being glorified, and God's people were led well, living in peace with one another, and the "place where they had gathered together was shaken, and they were all filled with the Holy Spirit and began to speak the word of God with boldness. And the congregation of those who believed were of one heart and soul; and not one of them claimed that anything belonging to him was his own, but all things were common property to them. And with great power the apostles were giving testimony to the resurrection of the Lord Jesus, and abundant grace was upon them all."[12]

… and it was awesome.

If you ask people their favorite thing about Watermark, you will almost universally hear people say the same thing: we see God working in the lives of His people. You won't see any wheelchairs or crutches attached to the walls, but still the miracles of lives changed are unmistakable. It amazes me that some people are bothered by the stories we share around here. They sometimes say, "There you go again, boasting about _____."

The blank is there for a reason.

---

11   Acts 2:43.
12   Acts 4:31–33.

Depending on what is in that blank, you may be (or *should* be) bothered. If I or anyone else around here boasts about how passionate, creative, funny, winsome, or powerful any of us are … or how powerful a communicator I am, how amazing our facility is, or how talented our creative arts people are, then you should be concerned. But if what is celebrated is Christ powerfully working in and through His people just like He said He would, then you should only be bothered if you are not experiencing the same thing.[13] If you don't have any stories to tell, you have a problem … and if you fill in the blank with anything other than Jesus, then you have a serious problem.

But if I am boasting in what Jesus is doing in the lives of people and someone has a problem with that, then I am not the one with a problem. In fact, if no stories related to life change are present, then Jesus *isn't* and *hasn't been* present either. Jesus is supposed to change lives, His disciples are supposed to be "men who have upset the world,"[14] His church is supposed to overpower the gates of hell, and His presence is supposed to create a sense of amazement.[15]

By this description, have you seen Jesus in your church lately?[16]

---

13 2 Corinthians 10:12–17.

14 Acts 17:6.

15 Luke 4:32, 36; 5:9; 8:25, 56; 9:43; 11:14, just to cite a few.

16 There are parts of the world where devoted followers of Christ labor for a lifetime seeing little spiritual harvest, but in those cases, the faithful, selfless, tireless, gospel-professing, holy, steadfast lives of the devoted followers *are* the story. Faithfulness is not measured by the life change around you as much as the life change within you. That said, radical evidence of the Word of God preached as the reality of the gospel of grace is lived out— that is the normal expectation of the Church at work.

I have. I share this with you because I want you to know that He is alive and He wants to be seen in every life. Every church. *Your* life. *Your* church. Where the body is, the Spirit of Christ is. The Church is the *spiritual* body of Christ[17] that is supposed to be continuing the good that He intends.[18] Working. Delivering. Helping. Healing. And He is not looking for gifted people—He gifts people.[19] He is looking for men and women whose hearts are completely His so He can strongly support them.[20] Bringing glory to God by doing the good work of saving men and women from "lame lives" is why we are here … "for good works, which God prepared beforehand so that we would walk in them."[21]

Recently, I asked a few friends to sit down with me and do something we don't do often enough. And sadly—maybe even blasphemously—I asked them to do something with me that would not take most modern-day church attenders much time to do even if they sat down to do it. We simply took the time to share with one another stories of the amazing things we have seen *Jesus* do *recently* in our midst.

To get ourselves started, we spent some time reading the many miraculous stories of people in the New Testament whose lives were completely changed when they encountered Jesus. Tax collectors. Prostitutes. Pharisees. Lepers. Blind people. Lame people. Deaf people. The broken. The arrogant. The *dead*.

---

17   1 Corinthians 12:12, 27; Ephesians 1:22–23.
18   Colossians 1:24–27.
19   1 Peter 4:10.
20   2 Chronicles 16:9.
21   Ephesians 2:10.

Then we started sharing various stories from the lives of people *we knew*—those whom we had seen the Lord miraculously reach and rescue in our own church community. We sat down to remember what He had done.[22]

Remembering caused us to do what disciples have always been commissioned to do. "Oh give thanks to the LORD, call upon His name; make known His deeds among the peoples. Sing to Him, sing praises to Him; speak of all His wonders."[23] Just as His original disciples had endless stories to share around the campfire each night after any particular day with God on earth, radical transformation is supposed to be something evident and observable in us and in those around us each and every day we are walking with Jesus. Abiding with Him produces a daily, continual call to worship in response to what He is doing.

Consider these words of the psalmist: "It is good to give thanks to the LORD and to sing praises to Your name, O Most High; to declare Your *lovingkindness in the morning* and Your *faithfulness by night*, with the ten-stringed lute and with the harp, with resounding music upon the lyre. For You, O LORD, have made me glad *by what You have done*, I will sing for joy at *the works of Your hands*."[24] If these words are not easily found on your tongue, then it is time to question whether the Truth is dwelling

---

22   Isaiah 12. It is worth your read and worth asking yourself why you and
     God's people around you are or are not experiencing it.
23   Psalm 105:1–2.
24   Psalm 92:1–4.

in your heart[25] or if you know what it is like to see the Spirit regularly work in your midst. Near Christ, uncommon proceedings become commonplace.

The only thing that should surprise us is that we are not continually being surprised by God.[26]

By now, you know me well enough to know that my point here is not to lift up the local expression of Jesus's Church of which I am a part or to write what would be a completely inaccurate narrative about our own perfection as individuals or as an organization … quite the opposite, actually. I am writing to encourage you. To give testimony to the reality of the truth of Scripture, the power of the gospel, the resurrection of Christ, the kindness of God, and the hope of the world. I cannot hide what the apostle John could also not hide: the world-changing realities of what Jesus is still doing in our world, giving testimony to it by sharing what is going on in our community. John saw "His glory,"[27] and God's desire is that the world still sees—and His people still experience—His glory every day.[28] Like John, my long history of seeing Him work, along with my desire for you to know that He wants to work in and through you as well, is the very reason I am writing these words in the first place.[29]

---

25 Not questioning anyone's salvation here. You can do that on your own. I am stating what Jesus said in John 15:5. The word "abide" (gr. *meno*) means "to dwell."
26 Psalm 40:5.
27 John 1:14.
28 Colossians 1:24; Matthew 5:16.
29 John 20:30–31.

The easiest way for me to describe to you all that we have been eyewitnesses to is this: we are like the Gerasenes.[30]

If you remember the story from Mark 5, Jesus arrived on the shore of the Gerasenes only to encounter a man who was a terror to himself and others. "And he had his dwelling among the tombs. And no one was able to bind him anymore, even with a chain; because he had often been bound with shackles and chains, and the chains had been torn apart by him and the shackles broken in pieces, and no one was strong enough to subdue him. Constantly, night and day, he was screaming among the tombs and in the mountains, and gashing himself with stones."[31]

Here you find the perfect picture of any man before the kindness of Christ arrives on his shores. Before Christ, we are all living among the dead (*a man dwelling among the tombs*), defined by rebellion and strife (*with an unclean spirit*), living without restraint and unchecked in our choices because of our seared consciences (*the chains had been torn apart by him and the shackles broken in pieces*), already are or are headed toward being an out-of-control terror to ourselves and our fellow countrymen (*no one was strong enough to subdue him*), separated from friends and family (*living among the tombs and the mountains*), and without hope and without God in this world (*crying out and gashing himself*). This is *not* the guy you want to bump into while taking a leisurely stroll in the countryside. He was as messed up as they come.

---

30   Mark 5:14.
31   Mark 5:3–5.

But he ran into the One who transforms *messes* into *messages* of salvation.

A few moments near Jesus, and the kindness and power of God changed everything—to the point that the man's radical transformation itself scared everyone (*and they came to Jesus and observed the man who had been demon-possessed sitting down, clothed and in his right mind, the very man who had the "legion"; and they became frightened*).

In this particular story, it was actually the pigs who got baptized … and I imagine there were more than a few late nights around the campfire where this day was recounted.

That is a great picture of our community in Dallas—literally overflowing with people who were "dead in their trespasses and sins, walking according to the course of this world, according to the prince of the power of the air, living in the lusts of our flesh, indulging the desires of the flesh and of the mind, and were by nature children of wrath … having no hope and without God in the world."[32] We were menaces to ourselves and to others. "For we also once were foolish ourselves, disobedient, deceived, enslaved to various lusts and pleasures, spending our life in malice and envy, hateful, hating one another."[33] But then the kindness of God appeared and … no more! Now we are clothed and in our right minds—and walking with Jesus.

---

32 Ephesians 2:1–3, 12.
33 Titus 3:3.

So we started by simply creating a list of these "ex-demoniacs" among us—friends who used to live among the dead but were now following Christ with us.

We remembered those who were overstressed. Insomniacs. Bar crawlers. Guys who, not very long ago, were verbally, emotionally, sexually abusive husbands, but who by the kindness of God, just like the man in Mark 5, had been set free. The stories of friends, many of them now leaders in the church, came as quickly as we could share them. While our time overflowed with stories, our hearts were filled with awe.

"How about Lance? Remember? He was an owner of one of the largest party-planning companies for nightclubs in our city. His business and personal energy encouraged the raucous destruction of countless lives in Dallas." But not anymore.

Drug dealers. Drug addicts. Sex addicts. Sex traffickers. Sexually trafficked. Thieves. Alcoholics. Pornographers. Liars. Drunk drivers. Spiritually dead professors. People who claimed they knew God but denied Him by their actions. All radically transformed through a gracious encounter with Christ.

Anorexics. Slaves to body, man, and image. Materialists. Depressed people. Folks riddled by anxiety disorders. Prisoners of fear. Prisoners ... period. Homosexuals. Lesbians. Male prostitutes. Johns. Female prostitutes. Victims of extreme sadness. Muslims. Mormons. Hindus. Jehovah's Witnesses. Atheists.

Now followers of Jesus.

Promiscuous women. Predatory men. Victims of childhood sexual abuse. Perpetrators of sexual abuse. Manipulators of people. Victims of greed. People in massive debt. Cohabitators. Divorcees. Passive husbands. Angry wives. Adulterous men. Unfaithful women. Homeless men. Homeless women. People who were angry, alone, and alienated from society. Incarcerated. Pharisees. Fallen leaders. Fake Christians. Parents who have lost children. Prodigals. Pill poppers. Suicide attempt survivors.[34]

And these are only the stories and lives we could remember in our one sitting. Do these speak to us being somehow especially anointed or gifted? Hardly. No, we are merely a community of people called out of darkness into His marvelous light,[35] now miraculously clothed and in our right minds for no other reason except that Jesus has stepped foot on our shore. We are a group of friends who were saved and who decided to do, by His enabling, what the One who saved us told us to do. "Go home to your people and report to them what great things the Lord has done for you, and how He had mercy on you."[36]

What about you? Do these stories at all resemble your recent church experience? Don't you think you would be experiencing "the life you always wanted" if you were a part of stories like these?

---

34 I know this may sound like a made-up list, but I assure you it is not. There are actual names attached to each of these stories. People living and serving with me in Dallas. This is not whom we hoped the Lord would let us reach. This is just a *sampling* of whom the Lord *has* let us reach, and more than a few are now on our staff.

35 1 Peter 2:9.

36 Mark 5:19.

The Purpose of Miracles and Men

Whether these stories resemble your church experiences or not, they should. Jesus says to you, a member of His spiritual body—that is, one "*who believes*": "Truly, truly … he who believes in Me, the works that I do, he will do also; and greater works than these he will do; because I go to the Father."[37]

In other words, the Lord's expectation is that you, too, would be a healed "demoniac" who is clothed and in your right mind, reporting great things the Lord has done for you. Better still, Jesus ultimately offers a further hope, specifically that you will grow to even lead others to the same grace you have experienced. He wants you to "go home to your people and report to them what great things the Lord has done for you, and how He had mercy on you."[38]

Don't write off this expectation as extreme unless you are also willing to write off God's Word as untrue. If you truly believe that all Jesus has for you is truly "all good," then it is time to run faithfully toward all the goodness He intends for us.

Read it again. "Truly, truly, I say to you, he who believes in Me, the works that I do, he will do also; and greater works than these he will do; because I go to the Father. Whatever you ask in My name, that will I do, so that the Father may be glorified in the Son."[39] These two little verses seem to cause confusion in a lot of circles. So what exactly is Jesus talking about?

---

37 John 14:12.
38 Mark 5:19.
39 John 14:12–13.

The key to clearing up the confusion comes through backing up to the verse just before these two when Jesus told His disciples to "believe Me that I am in the Father and the Father is in Me; otherwise believe because of the works themselves."[40] Can you see it? Jesus's main purpose for all people is that they will "believe" Him.[41] Not just believe a set of truths related to Him, or believe things "about" Him, because belief "about" is not exactly a sign of belief "in." Even the demons have no problem with belief "about."[42]

Lifesaving, world-shaking, eternity-altering belief is *not* found in belief "about" propositional statements or even eternal facts. Jesus desires that we believe Him directly. Believe *in* Him.[43] Belief "in" means believing personally. Fully. It means that we count what He says to be more than just true; we count it also to be trustworthy. It is not that we simply believe the fact that there is a Savior somewhere out there whose job is to save people, but more so that there is a Savior who has actually come near and whose greatest desire is to save *you*. We are not called to accept truth about some theoretical idea or theological reality; rather, we are invited to completely trust *a Person* with our actual lives. Many people who believe "about" are best described as "holding to a form of godliness, although they have denied its power."[44] As Paul says, we should "avoid such men as these."[45]

---

40 John 14:11.
41 John 14:1.
42 James 2:19. We will unpack this concept in greater detail in the pages to come.
43 John 1:12.
44 2 Timothy 3:5a.
45 2 Timothy 3:5b.

Jesus is telling His disciples to believe Him—to trust Him. He knows that sometimes people have trouble simply just trusting Him, so He also tells them that they can find a little extra help by taking note of the miraculous works He had done in their midst.

In John 14, Jesus is making it clear that even the miracles He had performed were not intended to stand on their own apart from the main purpose for which God sent Him—that people every-where might believe Him and subsequently experience the radical, God-initiated transformation that always occurs when people trust Him, moving from death to life.[46] In other words, "Even the mira-cles I have performed are intended to help you believe Me." Don't just be impressed by the miracles, but more so let the Truth they commend to be impressed upon your heart.

You might ask, "How does this distinction about the way Jesus viewed His own miraculous works even matter? And if it does mat-ter, what does this have to do with the works that we, as members of His body, will also do?" I'm glad you asked.

Throughout history, there have been plenty of generally well-meaning believers who have made an entire other religion out of these particular verses, focusing—and even worshipping—miracles and the possibility of miracles. At best, they have innocently mis-taken the main purpose of Jesus's miracles past, present, and future: that all may believe and trust Him as the gracious, all-powerful Savior He is, sent from the Father to rescue us all.

And at worst, they have acted as hucksters, preying on the sick, weak, and desperate for the purpose of exploitation, notoriety, and

---

46   John 5:24.

selfish gain—and certainly not for Christ's clearly stated purpose of providing clarity to His person and then, out of the assurance of His words and authenticating works, inviting all people to become fully devoted disciples, with Him as their Rescuer and Redeemer.

Regardless of the intention, there is danger in interpreting the "greater works" we will do solely in terms of what we tend to think of as "miraculous." I offer this clarification not because I want or need to spiritualize Jesus's words so they can find their fulfillment. No, I believe God is still really doing great works. He is still healing people. He is still delivering people from darkness, and even more, I believe He is still using His disciples to do it.

The miracles today are just as real as the miracles we read about in the New Testament, but even when there was immediate physical healing, Jesus always dealt with sin's eternal grip, not just its present physical effect—its effect on the *soul* more than its effect on the "*skin*."[47] Today's works are greater in scope—that is, in their frequency to be performed by Christ through the hands of many disciples and affecting a greater population in the world today, but they are not typically greater in their spectacular or sudden *physical* nature.

I do believe that God can and does perform physical healings today. So let's keep praying for each other's physical healing, knowing that our God has and can today do whatever He wants. But let's make sure that whether He heals physically or not, we deal

---

47 "Skin" alludes to physical maladies, whether they be lameness or leprosy, which are never our biggest problem. Our soul sickness and separation from God is our biggest problem. I explain and illustrate this more in the coming pages.

with the crippling effect of sin in our lives that we know has always been His focus and should be ours as well.

One of the greatest miracles that anyone can ever see is to encounter the joy, peace, faith, and hope that my friends Joni Eareckson Tada, a quadriplegic, and Nick Vujicic, a friend born with no arms or legs, exhibit while they wait for their physical healing.[48]

Simply from a logical viewpoint, by definition, miracles are not normal. They are not called "normacles." What I mean is that miracles, especially in the sense of divine healing and other such signs and wonders, are not generally daily occurrences, even in Scripture. That is why the miracles Jesus performed stood out so much—they were not normal even for Him, and even throughout His ministry, they did not persist with the same regularity.[49] He performed the majority of His earthly miracles early in His public ministry. The visually spectacular, physically obvious miracles Jesus did (less than forty are actually *recorded* in the Gospels[50]) were not the norm in His day, just as they are not in ours.

Just as there is no debating that Jesus performed incredible signs and wonders in His earthly ministry, there is also no doubt that His signs and wonders were not intended to stand as monuments unto themselves ... things to be solely sought after with no other

---

48 Check out their incredible stories of Christ's faithfulness at joniandfriends.org and lifewithoutlimbs.org.

49 Matthew 12:39; Mark 8:12.

50 A full list of these miracles is found at: www.christianity.com/god/jesus -christ/life-on-earth/the-miracles-of-jesus-christ-11540141.html. This obviously does not account for the innumerable other "signs" and "things which Jesus did" referenced in John 20:30; 21:25.

purpose attached. Like any sign on a street or in a building—even impressive ones—they were put there to point people to something else even more valuable than the sign itself. Miracles are a billboard, an attractive, attention-getting sign. The purpose of the billboard is to make you want not the sign, but what the sign is pointing you to.

So when Jesus tells us we will do even greater works than He did, it does not necessarily equate to us seeing physically blind people physically see, physically deaf people physically hear, wheelchair-bound people run around, or physically dead people physically rise. Yes, God did and *still can* do these things, but we should not be surprised if He doesn't. It was never His intention that we would be *primarily* a movement of physical signs … a bright billboard to be admired but one that never leads people further toward the actual point or product the sign was designed to promote in the first place. In fact, Jesus warns against being an evil and adulterous generation that seeks a sign over seeking understanding who He is.[51]

I am not saying that signs and wonders do not or will not happen today; that would be both foolish and unnecessary. I am only saying that the spectacular, physical manifestations we tend to *typically* think of are not the whole, or even the primary focus, of what Jesus meant by "greater works." This is made especially clear in the several examples where Jesus helped with situational physical maladies and then immediately warned them to believe in Him lest something worse happen to them. What could be worse

---

51   Matthew 12:39–40.

than being lame for thirty-eight years? How about being separated from Christ for eternity?[52]

I do not want to convince you to expect fewer miracles, but I do want to tell you that Jesus says you should expect *more*—and that the more you should expect will involve much more than just miracles of temporal, physical deliverance. I also want to make sure you don't torture yourself by believing the lie that if you just had more faith your every prayer would be answered.[53] To fully see what Jesus was talking about, we have to expand our understanding beyond miracles dealing with situational evil and realize the greater miracles deal with the moral evil in all our lives. Which is greater, a miraculous deliverance of someone from temporal suffering or a miraculous deliverance of someone from eternal judgment and bondage to sin and despair?

We should always consider it a greater usefulness to be part of God's work that delivers someone from being a slave to sin's controlling and eternally condemning effects, even if they continue to have to live in physical and temporal circumstances that are part of a sinful world's condition. Whenever we can, we should do both,[54]

---

52   John 5:1–14.

53   Please take a few minutes and listen to my friend Joni Eareckson Tada, who has been in a wheelchair for fifty years, address the question "If I have enough faith, will God heal me?": http://realtruthrealquick.com/enough-faith-will-god-heal/.

54   1 John 3:17–18 talks about our responsibility to do everything we can to care for the physical and temporal needs of others through the miracle of God's indwelling selfless love actively at work in us. It is not enough to pray for someone's spiritual deliverance when we can also meet someone's physical needs, even as it is especially unloving to address someone's physical needs without offering deliverance from their spiritual poverty.

but if we are only going to be used of God to do one, let it be the miracle of deliverance from eternal judgment. So while we may or may not see any wheelchairs discarded as a result of your ministry, men and women all around us—by the thousands—ought to walk in the newness of life and be evidence of God's "greater works" each and every week.

What's Normal?

For the three years that Jesus engaged in public ministry, His "normal" days were a far cry from what most of us would think of as normal. Let's go back to the crazy story of the demoniac and the "legion" of demons who cowered before Christ, begging Him to allow them to enter a herd of pigs.

Could you imagine Peter telling his wife this story over dinner?

"How was work today?"

"Oh, you know, just another day on the trail. Thomas constantly doubted we were headed in the right direction. Judas kept arguing with the girls about their use of petty cash. I stubbed my toe and used some old fishing words I told Jesus I would try to forget. James and John got in a huge argument again during the staff meeting—mainly about who was going to sit where at the lunch table."

A short pause ensues.

"Oh yeah, I almost forgot. After a trip across the lake that you wouldn't believe, some crazy, naked guy living in a cemetery came charging at Jesus and scared the shawarma out of all of us, so He cast out who-knows-how-many demons from the guy into a bunch of pigs and they ran off the side of a cliff and drowned, causing the entire town to basically riot and demand we take the mission somewhere else. Based on how it smells, I am sure that bacon must taste pretty good, but even so, their reaction seemed a bit extreme to me." An eye roll comes from Peter's wife. He continues, "Pretty typical day, I guess.

"Could you pass the kosher salt, please?"

When we are fully devoted to Christ, our normal days will include a lot of details absent from most people's normal days. And it will be *awesome*. It will be the life you have always wanted, and believe it or not, within Jesus's Church is where you should expect to find it. Gone are the weekly Sunday gatherings with mostly bored adults and the occasional children's dedication. As we have been learning for a while now, Christ calls us not to be irregular believers who simply attend church every Sunday … Christ calls us to head out on the open road with Him and His other disciples to experience a life completely devoid of boredom.

Full devotion to Christ should mean full engagement against the enemy by lovingly engaging those held captive to do His will.[55] Fishers of men don't sit on the shore and talk about fishing; they head off to sea to see what miraculous draught of fish they are going to catch today. In other words, it should be normal that you are sharing your faith, reading God's Word, being informed by Scripture, loving people who are your enemies, forgiving those

---

55   2 Timothy 2:26.

who harm you, giving generously, living sacrificially, teaching the Word of God, making disciples, reconciling with those who are far away from God, caring for those whom the world has forgotten, speaking for those who are oppressed and have no voice, and basically being known as the people who have upset everything in the "inhabited earth."[56] These things should be *normal* for a believer.

And contrary to "normal" belief, this lifestyle and these experiences are not reserved exclusively for pastors, authors, seminary students, or super saints. They should be true for *every* believer. I'm not saying these things are normal for every churchgoer, but they *should be* normal for every Christ follower. If they are not a part of your normal life, it should cause you to pause and ask yourself the question: "Am I a believer '*in*' or a believer 'about'?"

If this feels like dangerous water to wade into, it should. And while I don't want to make you question your salvation, I do want you to evaluate your current station in life. You need to see exactly what Christ is calling you to come and be seen doing in response to what He has come and done. The abundant life is not found in the mundane. It is not found in ritual. It is found in the adventure of an abiding relationship with the living Lord who is still in the business of radically altering everything and anyone that responds to His offer of life. It is worth asking ourselves to consider the reason why the power and usefulness Christ has said will be wildly present in the lives of His followers may not be wildly evident in ours. Shouldn't we at least consider the

56   Acts 17:6.

possibility that the reason the power and adventure are missing is because the presence of a genuine relationship with Him might be missing as well?

Should we simply ignore the words of Jesus that says whoever (i.e., *all*) believes *will* do greater works? Of course not. So if these "greater works" are absent, at the very least we find our lives contradicting Scripture's expectations, and horribly. There is also a possibility that we are deluded in our understanding of what it means to actually believe. We should look deep into our hearts to make sure we are not becoming simply professors of Christ who have never actually possessed an intimate relationship with Him.

We are saved by grace alone,[57] but the Bible is very clear that the grace that saves is never alone. Faith without works is dead faith.[58] That isn't just James's idea; it was Jesus's. In the middle of His last words to His disciples, He all but says, "Look at what I'm doing because it is evidence that what I have been saying can be trusted, and if you trust Me, the evidence of who I am will be made known to others through you."[59]

Anyone can say, "This is what I think about Jesus." But how different it is to be able to say, "If you don't believe what I'm saying, look at my life—at the way I conduct myself sexually, emotionally, relationally, and financially. Come examine the way I steward my time. In fact, you can even look at those moments when I speak

---

57   Ephesians 2:8–9; Titus 3:5–7.
58   James 2:14–17.
59   John 14:10–13.

poorly, fail morally, or live according to the ways of the world. In those moments, watch me confess and repent. Watch me state that my actions were contrary to God."

"You mean, look at what I do when I've done wrongly to prove what I believe rightly about Christ?" Absolutely. Even in our failures we can give glory to God. After all, that is what confession literally means, "to agree." Confession is a public statement that I agree with God that my conduct has been inconsistent with His good will and way.

Too often, out of fear that we might somehow be accused of tampering with the gospel of grace, we're far too hesitant to examine the works that Scripture says will follow the true presence of grace in His disciples. Being a disciple means lovingly calling one another to account when our supposed good *trees* are not bearing good *fruit*.[60] There is much evidence that can be observed from how we live in community with others—*especially* in moments when our works are far from good—that can still fall into the category of "greater works." "Admonishing the unruly, encouraging the faint hearted, and helping the weak"[61] are great works. Confession, transparency, vulnerability, correction, and forgiveness in biblical community are some of the greatest works Jesus's disciples can do.

The reason, then, that we should be careful to make sure the "greater works" Jesus said would be present in our lives are really there is not rooted in a belief that we can secure salvation by them; neither is it to make us feel insecure about salvation if they are absent. Rather, the reason we need to be reminded of these truths

---

60   Matthew 7:16–20.
61   1 Thessalonians 5:14.

is so we might expectantly and faithfully work *out* our salvation in fear and trembling[62] and live *in* the fullness of life that Christ truly intends for those of us who follow Him. He does not want us to be irregular, irrelevant, church-attending believers; He wants us to be fully devoted, transformed disciples whose lives exemplify in word and power the life He lives and the work He does. When full devotion is as normally present as it should be, then the presence of greater works should be normally expected as well.

---

62 Philippians 2:12–13.

Chapter 18

Greater Works

These days, with the increase of media across many forums, it isn't hard to find scores of impressive people. People who look like they just stumbled out of the locker room for the gods on Mount Olympus. People whose social media posts make us wonder why we don't have the spectacular social lives their Instagram accounts say they do. Wealthy. Good looking. Athletic. Successful.

There is a multi-billion-dollar industry today that centers on the lives of the rich and powerful—and more specifically, the steps for "normal" people to spend time with them, learn their secrets, and eventually become as successful as they are. *Let me be your coach. Do these seven easy steps. Let me be your adviser. Here's your pathway to your best life now. Here is how you can unleash the giant within.*

Tragically, more and more people are representing God Himself to be the ultimate guarantor of certain and ever-increasing temporal benefits. *Follow these steps, sow this seed, and you will receive this blessing. Seek this gift. Attend this church and experience this powerful promise. Send your cards and letters to this address. Order this special anointing oil from the Holy Land and receive a whole lot more.*

When anyone tells you that your best life now will look like all the best *this world* now has to offer, you best move on.

Anyone who tells you that life with God means life will always be good and getting better circumstantially should be regarded with circumspection. Even a quick read of Scripture shows you that life with God is not always, or usually for that matter, the quick way to comfort. In the great chapter on faith in Hebrews 11, don't miss that many of the faithful "were tortured, not accepting their release, so that they might obtain a better resurrection; and others experienced mockings and scourgings, yes, also chains and imprisonment. They were stoned, they were sawn in two, they were tempted, they were put to death with the sword; they went about in sheepskins, in goatskins, being destitute, afflicted, ill-treated." They were so faithful that God's Word calls them "men of whom the world was not worthy."[1] Read that again. Faithful men are not men who receive greater and greater net worth, but *men of whom the world is not worthy*.

God is not your pathway to ease; He is the path to life.

The power necessary to experience the greater things is not reserved for only the world's greatest-looking and uniquely qualified people. God never reserved His power or designed a plan where only a few anointed or especially enlightened demigods could disperse their divine insights and share their path to blessing with others. The Lord has not limited and does not secretly dole

---

1   Hebrews 11:35–38.

out a life full of freedom, significance, power, and fulfillment in some hidden place only to be accessed by some *holier-than-thou* medium. In fact, He warns against believing He ever will.[2]

The message of being a fully devoted disciple that I proclaim—the one the Bible proclaims—does not necessarily make for great comfort or convenience, but it does make for great campfire conversations. When you follow Christ, I am not going to tell you that you're never again going to face anxiety. Or that you're going to be completely delivered from the love of self. Or fear of failure. Or that your husband is going to get better looking. Or that your kids are going to get better grades. Or that you are going to lose that stubborn ten pounds of belly fat that you just can't get rid of. Why not?

Because this is earth.

Even though heaven is the eventual home of all who believe, we aren't home yet, and there are a lot of stubborn things we still have to deal with here on this third rock from the sun. The good news is that while you're here on earth, you can—and are expected to—live a life that is fruitful and useful[3] to God and others. The struggle will be real; Jesus promised us as much: "In the world you have tribulation, but take courage; I have overcome the world."[4] You *will* have trouble. It should not surprise you. It doesn't have to overwhelm you.

---

2   Matthew 24:3–5, 10–14, 23–28.
3   2 Peter 1:2–8.
4   John 16:33.

So how are we to overcome? For starters, it is time to stop thinking there's some counselor you can go to, some conference you can attend, some sort of prayer you can pray, or some formula that you can induce that is going to forever CLEP you out of the trouble your trustworthy King told us all to prepare for. To be sure, there will be moments of great joy and laughter, but we must remember these are never the days to grow lazy or to expect ease.

Until our days are done and we reach the harbor of rest fixed for each of us,[5] we are sailing either out of a storm or into a storm. This is true of the world around us. True for the trouble that remains within us. Our battle against fleshly lusts, which wage war against our soul,[6] is a battle in which we must remain vigilant[7] until He completes the good work that He began in us.[8] Tips and techniques—or formulas and fixes—might help you experience a season of successful behavior modification, but on earth, you will never successfully mortify the flesh that motivates the behavior. The Bible has no program to permanently curb the flesh.[9] You must daily crucify it.[10]

Too many of God's people have trusted in false promises or followed poor counsel only to see their faith in the promise of a full, carefree, prosperous life face a slow death. Once this "promise" is broken, people are prone to abandon all their counselors—and

---

5   Job 14:5.
6   1 Peter 2:11.
7   1 Corinthians 16:13; 1 Peter 5:8; 2 Timothy 2:22.
8   Philippians 1:6.
9   Galatians 2:20.
10   Luke 9:23.

tragically, too often the Great Counselor along with them. Do you know why? Because they think they've already tried Him. G. K. Chesterton had it right when he said, "The Christian ideal has not been tried and found wanting; it has been found difficult; and left untried."[11]

Jesus doesn't want you to *try* Him; He wants you to *trust* Him. He doesn't want us to just know about Him; He wants us to abide with Him. Even when Jesus was performing the miraculous, He never offered anything resembling protection from all future temptation or trouble. Nowhere in the New Testament is there an admonition to use an incantation that would free us from ever needing intercession again. Christ's interactions with people— even when He miraculously delivered or healed them—*always* called them to deeper dependence on Him.

Jesus was always compassionate,[12] continually willing to care for those experiencing situational evil and suffering. He was a leader who deeply empathized with people in their pain.[13] But He did not stop with concern merely for their current struggles. He knew that apart from coming to faith in Him, their coming eternal struggles were going to be infinitely worse. That is why He often followed up His care for their situational evil with a warning that they should also trust in Him as their provision for their moral evil.

---

11   This quote by G. K. Chesterton was taken from *What's Wrong with the World*, originally published in 1912.

12   Matthew 9:36.

13   John 11:35.

To the man He had just healed from thirty-eight years of lameness, He said, "Behold, you have become well; do not sin anymore, so that nothing worse happens to you."[14] As I said earlier, what could be worse than four decades of infirmity? How about an eternity of separation from beauty, kindness, rest, friendship, pleasure, love, and peace? If you've ever wanted a good definition of hell, this one should suffice.

If Jesus were standing before us now, I know He would encourage us with words like these: "I know you believe your physical need is your most pressing pain, but it isn't your biggest problem. Don't scoff at God's provision for you available in Me because that will produce a far worse problem for you forever than you will ever face on this earth today. Pay attention to those in My Church and their message of how, through faith in Me, you can have peace with the Father. They are the ones who have My gospel message and who can deliver you from your greatest problem with the greater work I have empowered them to share with you."

When the Church doesn't participate with Christ in the "greater work" of people coming to faith and becoming radically transformed servants of Christ, they naturally look for other "evidences" to "convince" themselves that the Lord is active and alive in the world today. This often results in churches being distracted by or caught up in counterfeit "displays" of the Spirit's activity like claims of "anointing" evidenced by sprinklings of gold dust, wild moments of emotionalism or ecstatic expressiveness, so-called

---

14   John 5:14.

"holy laughter," misuses of the biblical gift of tongues, or other commotions that are, at best, unreliable—and, at worst, deceptive.

Or on the other end of the spectrum from these false evidences of God's power, you will find others who foolishly give themselves over to an obsessive focus on head knowledge, dead rituals, particular doctrines, or other primarily intellectual exercises. People who are always learning but never able to come to the *purpose* of the truth. They may hide behind their discussions and endless debates to keep from ever having to die to themselves. Endless debates about the Truth are their primary defense against having to actually apply it.

The Danish philosopher and theologian Søren Kierkegaard spoke of this danger when he said, "The matter is quite simple. The Bible is very easy to understand. But we Christians are a bunch of scheming swindlers. We pretend to be unable to understand it because we know very well that the minute we understand, we are obliged to act accordingly. Take any words in the New Testament and forget everything except pledging yourself to act accordingly. 'My God,' you will say. 'If I do that my whole life will be ruined. How would I ever get on in the world?' Herein lies the real place of Christian scholarship. Christian scholarship is the Church's prodigious invention to defend itself against the Bible, to ensure that we can continue to be good Christians without the Bible coming too close. Oh, priceless scholarship, what would we do without you? Dreadful it is to fall into the hands of the living God. Yes, it is even dreadful to be alone with the New Testament."[15]

---

15   *Provocations: Spiritual Writings of Kierkegaard* (New York: Plough, 1999).

The works of a church like these do not much resemble the works Christ did on earth, much less the "greater ones" He intends for His people today.

Without a right understanding of what Jesus had in mind when He called us to "greater works," people will move toward *craziness* in the form of increasingly bizarre experiences or become more *comatose* in their obsession with writings and rituals. For centuries, the Church believed that "greater works" were to be primarily associated with so much more than what is passing today as the "power of God" within the signs and wonders movement.

Sadly, over time, as a compromised church leadership began to give more and more attention to forms and ritual rather than faithful practice, there arose a hunger for more of God that opened the door for bored people to seek more evidence that God was there and still making Himself known. Enter pseudospiritual and false evidences of "greater works" in prophetic word, faith healing, and counterfeit revival movements.

Jesus performed (and I am sure still can and is willing to perform) miraculous healings and helpful deliverances from situational evil, but they have never been and are not now His prescribed way to win people or build a kingdom of fully devoted followers of Christ. He Himself warned against sign seeking when He rebuked the crowd with the words, it is a "wicked and adulterous generation that seeks a sign."[16] The primary purpose for everything Christ ever did, and therefore what the Church should be doing, is captured in Peter's words: "The gospel has for this purpose been preached even

---

16   Matthew 12:39.

to those who are dead, that though they are judged in the flesh as men, they may live in the spirit according to the will of God."[17]

This "making of judged-in-the-flesh men alive in the spirit according to the will of God" *is* the greater work. Everything else is, at best, only there to attract people to the potential of Christ's power … and, at worst, it is a distraction from the pure power and will of God.

But alas, there are, if you truly believe Him, greater works *you* are called to do in His name. Jesus is *still* saying, "Greater works I will do through you … if you ask *Me*, I will do it." It is worth taking a little more time to make the case that "greater works" are every true believer's great privilege. We certainly believe John every other time he tells us that believers are promised something.

"But *as many as received Him*, to them He gave the right to become children of God, even to those who believe in His name."[18] Whoever believes in His name has the right to become a child of God.

This "whoever" theme continues throughout the entire book of John. "For God so loved the world, that he gave his only Son, that *whoever* believes in him should not perish but have eternal life.[19] *Whoever* believes in Him is not condemned, but *whoever* does not believe is condemned already, because he has not believed in the name of the only Son of God.[20] *Whoever* believes in the Son has eternal life; *whoever* does not obey the Son shall not see life,

---

17   1 Peter 4:6.
18   John 1:12.
19   John 3:16 (ESV).
20   John 3:18 (ESV).

but the wrath of God remains on him.[21] Truly, truly, I say to you, *whoever* hears my word and believes him who sent me has eternal life. He does not come into judgment, but has passed from death to life.[22] I am the bread of life; *whoever* comes to me shall not hunger, and *whoever* believes in me shall never thirst.[23] Truly, truly, I say to you, *whoever* believes has eternal life.[24] *Whoever* believes in me, as the Scripture has said, 'Out of his heart will flow rivers of living water.'[25] I am the resurrection and the life. *Whoever* believes in me, though he die, yet shall he live …"[26] and "everyone *who believes* in me will not live in darkness."[27]

That's a lot of "whoevers," don't you think? And there is not a single one of them that any true Christian would even try to deny … that is, until we get to John 14:12. Then, for some reason, we tend to think that this *"whoever"* is reserved only for a special few who have somehow all purchased time on various Christian television networks all hours of the day and night.

The "whoevers" we just read explicitly reveal to us that God's gift of grace and power to be pardoned and powerfully used by Him is available to *everyone* who believes, not just a chosen few. We hold all these promises true for *everyone* who believes. Why would the "whoever" in John 14:12 mean something different from what we insist it means everywhere else? Why do we use

---

21 John 3:36.
22 John 5:24.
23 John 6:35.
24 John 6:47.
25 John 7:38.
26 John 11:25.
27 John 12:46.

"blessed scholarship" to make it mean something other than what it should mean?

While we should not expect to always participate in the temporary acts of deliverance from situational evil that Christ sometimes did, we should (must) expect to participate in the greater work that Jesus expects of us. And like every other desire God has for us, when we do, it leads to blessing upon blessing. Others' lives are changed. Jesus is continually glorified, and all of us take part in something that the world wants to come and see again and again. Not only that, but when we live in the midst of the work our Lord has for us, we will never again think of this life as anything but abundant. When we follow Jesus into the world of the rescue and redemption of enslaved souls, our souls become more alive than they have ever been.

When I was a kid in school, the teachers would gather their classes around a screen to watch the launch of the latest space mission.[28] I loved it, even with 250 other classmates all watching the same twenty-four-inch television from twenty-five yards away while sitting on a hard linoleum gym floor. An enormous explosion of reds, oranges, and whites with a cloud of black smoke thrusting the rocket toward the sky and space was all this elementary school boy needed to be all in. Astronauts were our heroes. I had posters of them all over my room.

Want to know what we never did? We never gathered around a screen to watch a satellite circle the earth. Because even though

---

28 I am talking about the Apollo missions, not the later space shuttle missions. And yes, that dates me.

it provides more day-to-day help than an orbiting spaceship, it doesn't grab our attention the way a launch does.

Circumstance-changing, situational miracles draw people like the thrust of a rocket. But it's the ongoing work of a life-changing message of grace that continues to make a difference in our lives and that becomes the greater testimony to God's ever-present power. Launches don't change the world; enduring truth circling through man's every thought and heartbeat changes the world. Our "greater works" are meant to be more than temporary explosions of thrust in the dark sky of this world.

They are meant to continue and remain.

Jesus's greatest work was to provide a way that we could all be reconciled to God,[29] and the purpose of *our* works is to continue to offer the message of reconciliation to others[30] so that other people can also believe in the One who has sent us.

This is the main work we should be doing. It is why we are here. It is the greater work that makes our lives great.

How You Do the Work Matters

While God is using us to do the greater work of reconciling the world to Him, it is worth noting that *how* we do it matters as much to Him as the work itself. Faith matters. Without it you can't please God. Hope is essential. The human soul gets sick without it. The greater work is calling people to faith and watching them

---

29   Romans 5:10.
30   2 Corinthians 5:20.

be renewed with eternal hope, but there is something greater than both of these.[31]

Love.

The ongoing, ever-present, earth-circling mark of a fully devoted disciple is love. Love is the work that remains. The miracle of rebirth launches us into a constant orbit of love. Without love, we are a noisy gong or a clanging cymbal.[32] "If I have the gift of prophecy, and know all mysteries and all knowledge; and if I have all faith, so as to remove mountains, but do not have love, I am nothing. And if I give all my possessions to feed the poor, and if I surrender my body to be burned, but do not have love, it profits me nothing."[33]

You can't say it much stronger than that.

It is the universal language. It can be observed by the naked eye of anyone on earth—and its impact lasts far longer than sudden bursts of flashy productions, emotional outbursts, or the imposing shadow of impressive buildings. The ongoing mark of the miraculous work of God is His love in His Church. It is the mark of a disciple.[34] Next to giving your life for your friend, there is no greater love than to tell others of the One who gave His life for them.[35]

Love should especially be found in the ways we relate to one another in relationships. If our marriages are not defined by a

---

31 1 Corinthians 13:13.
32 1 Corinthians 13:1.
33 1 Corinthians 13:2–3.
34 John 13:34–35.
35 Romans 10:14–17.

constant pursuit of oneness—if they repeatedly end in "irreconcil-able differences" like everyone else's in the world does—then the watching world has a right to doubt whether we know any more about God and His ways than they do. Jesus Himself told us this would be the case.[36]

Recently, I was being interviewed on a radio program when the host made a startling observation. "The Church has been making this big fuss about the redefinition of marriage, but with divorce so rampant even among those who say they are Christians, the Church doesn't seem to be treating marriage like it is defined in the Bible. What do you say to that?"

My response probably shocked him. "I agree with you. By and large the watching world has seen those attending church not tend to their marriages the way God intends. Divorce in the Church is far too common, and in too many churches, pastors are scared to teach on God's design and the permanence of marriage because they don't want to offend anyone who might be there and already be feeling bad about their failed marriage. But our God died for sinners—for people just like us who, left to ourselves, will always ruin relationships because of our selfishness. But if we are people of God, our relationships should no longer be defined by selfishness and failure. Instead, when we face the same issues in our marriages that all natural relationships face, we should respond supernaturally. Instead of rationalizing and justifying our desire to run, we should humble ourselves before one another and pursue reconciliation with our spouses so that we can keep pursuing and

---

36 John 17:20–21.

modeling what God's grace and love look like. That is what He intended, and that is what you should be seeing."

As you would guess, my response surprised him. He said, "If you all did love that way, that would get the world's attention and make a stronger argument about a different view of marriage, but I haven't seen that kind of commitment and love in most church people I know."

He was right. Love should be a "normacle" among those who believe. As Jesus continues to work in our relationships—and as we are willing to be open and honest with each other and with the world about the work He is doing—a funny thing happens: everyone around us will witness the radical, real love of Christ at work. Instead of just telling a story about Jesus, the world is supposed to see His love story played out in and through us.

Anyone with a healthy marriage and an ever-widening circle of authentic relationships around them will forever have a built-in, powerful apologetic to speak of the power of Christ before a curious, watching world. But broken promises? So-called irreconcilable differences? Abandoned children? Not so much.

But brace yourself, because the greatest Lover who ever lived was hated as much as anyone has ever been hated, and He warns us that we should expect the same.[37] Love always rejoices with the truth,[38] and truth sounds like hate to those who hate the truth. We must love, but we must also get ready to endure all things.[39] When

---

37   John 15:18.
38   1 Corinthians 13:6.
39   1 Corinthians 13:7.

the early disciples were willing to let the love of Christ be seen in their words and works, they were not always celebrated. They were arrested.[40] Threatened.[41] Beaten.[42] But they were not unnoticed, and especially in the midst of their sufferings, the "greater works" of Christ were seen … even by their enemies.[43]

The enemies of the early Church were not sure what to make of these men, but they were certain of one thing: the Jesus whom they had crucified was a friend to them and they claimed He was the One behind the great work they were doing.[44] "Now as they observed the confidence of Peter and John and understood that they were uneducated and untrained men, they were amazed, and began to recognize them as having been with Jesus."[45]

Their work of God in them was not evidenced by their religious gatherings. They were not known for their buildings or their worship styles. They were known because of their love for each other and their kindness and concern for the "least of these." They were known as Christians because of the great work of love in them and through them.

It might have been a rocket burst of healing that first thrust them into the public's eye,[46] but it was their boldness in expressing

---

40   Acts 4:1–3; Acts 5:17–18.
41   Acts 4:15–18, 21; 5:12–16.
42   Acts 5:40.
43   Acts 4:21.
44   Acts 5:35–39.
45   Acts 4:13.
46   See Acts 3 for an example of a miraculous intervention in one life leading to a change in thousands.

the source of their power[47]—the same power that enabled them to love one another as if they had one heart and soul, even to the extent that "not one of them claimed that anything belonging to him was his own"[48]—that made the most lasting impression.

Do you get the same impression from your church? The truth is, the sense of awe over the ongoing miracle of selfless love expressed in word and deed should still be the mark of every faithful church today.

Remember our list of "miraculous" life changes we have seen in our community? The real awe comes not from great initial testimonies, but through the testimony of a radically new life that makes amends to those whom they hurt yesterday, lives humbly with others today, and testifies to God's greater way every day.

When former demoniacs are now clothed and in their right minds, sitting at the feet of Jesus, the world pays attention, which is why He told them to "go home to your people and report to them what great things the Lord has done for you, and how He had mercy on you."[49]

Individuals once living "lame" lives are now walking in the truth. Men who were blind to the beauty of God and His way can now see. People who were captive to the ways of this world and the spirit of disobedience are now living moral, redeemed, beautifully free lives.

---

47   Acts 3:12.
48   Acts 4:32.
49   Mark 5:19.

These greater works of Jesus in us and through us make it hard to ignore the reality of how Jesus's love changes everyone's life … just like He said it would.

But you don't have to live in Dallas, Gerasa, or Jerusalem for these "greater works" to be your reality. These works are not done *by* us; they are still done by Jesus *through* His body everywhere His people walk humbly with Him. Since the real work is His to do, our most important work is to fully believe Him and abide with Him.[50] When "we proclaim Him, admonishing every man and teaching every man with all wisdom, so that we may present every man complete in Christ … striving according to His power, which mightily works within us,"[51] we will see "the church throughout all Judea and Galilee and Samaria [enjoy] peace, being built up; and going on in the fear of the Lord and in the comfort of the Holy Spirit, [continuing] to increase."[52]

---

50 John 15:1–5.
51 Colossians 1:28–29.
52 Acts 9:31.

Chapter 19

A Shipwrecked Mission

There is a modern parable written in 1953 worth retelling here.

"On a dangerous sea coast where shipwrecks often occur, there was once a crude little life-saving station. The building was just a hut, and there was only one boat, but the few devoted members kept a constant watch over the sea, and with no thought for themselves, went out day and night tirelessly searching for the lost. Some of those who were saved and various others in the surrounding area wanted to become associated with the station and gave of their time and money and effort for the support of its work. New boats were bought and new crews trained. The little life-saving station grew.

"Some of the members of the life-saving station were unhappy that the building was so crude and poorly equipped. They felt that a more comfortable place should be provided as the first refuge of those saved from the sea. They replaced the emergency cots with beds and put better furniture in the enlarged building.

"Now the life-saving station became a popular gathering place for its members, and they decorated it beautifully because they used it as a sort of club. Fewer members were now interested in going to sea on life-saving missions, so they hired lifeboat crews to do this work. The life-saving motif still prevailed in the club's decorations, and there was a liturgical lifeboat in the room where the club's initiations were held. About this time a large ship wrecked off the coast, and the hired crews brought in boat loads of cold, wet and half-drowned people. They were dirty and sick. The beautiful new club was in chaos. So the property committee immediately had a shower house built outside the club where victims of shipwrecks could be cleaned up before coming inside.

"At the next meeting, there was a split among the club membership. Most of the members wanted to stop the club's life-saving activities as being unpleasant and a hindrance to the normal social life of the club. Some members insisted upon life-saving as their primary purpose and pointed out that they were still called a life-saving station. But they were finally voted down and told that if they wanted to save the lives of all the various kinds of people who were shipwrecked in those waters, they could begin their own life-saving station. So they did.

"As the years went by, the new station experienced the same changes that had occurred in the old. It evolved into a club, and yet another life-saving station was founded. History continued to repeat itself, and if you visit that sea coast today, you will find a number of exclusive clubs along that shore. Shipwrecks are frequent in those waters, but most of the people drown."[1]

---

1   Dr. Theodore Wedel, a canon of the National Cathedral and onetime president of the House of Deputies of the Episcopal Church.

Mission Field or Missionary

"Most of the people drown." Not exactly the Yelp review you're hoping for if you are a lifesaving station. Those last five words say enough to make a watching public decide to sail in a different direction. They certainly did so for me.

It would be tragic and maybe even sadly predictable to take everything we have talked about up to this point and then try to oversimplify the application with a few pithy admonitions. There is nothing pithy or quick about "If anyone wishes to come after Me, he must deny himself, and take up his cross daily and follow Me. For whoever wishes to save his life will lose it, but whoever loses his life for My sake, he is the one who will save it. For what is a man profited if he gains the whole world, and loses or forfeits himself? For whoever is ashamed of Me and My words, the Son of Man will be ashamed of him when He comes in His glory, and the glory of the Father and of the holy angels."[2]

A simple "Get off your *#%[3] and do something for Jesus," while certainly clear, does lack nuance. So let me try and be a bit more eloquent while remaining just as clear.

I have labored in these pages to remind you of the goodness of God Himself, and I have made the case that the inherent beauty and awe that exist in His bride when she is attired in all her intended glory is worth laboring with all our might to reveal and compel others to behold. When the bride is walking in

---

2   Luke 9:23–26.
3   Rear.

faithfulness, she finds it easy to compel others to come and see ... and it becomes her joy to watch them stay. My hope is that your time in these pages has awakened you to something richer and more life giving than anything you have ever known before or even dared to imagine you could be a part of. As I write, I am praying that the result of my words will find us daily surrendering our lives with ever-increasing passion as we join God in the mission He has for us.

This word *mission* is a word we need to reclaim. Sadly we have come to understand *mission* and *missions* as terms exclusively related to distant places or third-world countries. And while it *can* relate to exotic locations, it *must* exist in our everyday ones.

Here is some truth for you. If you know Jesus, your entire life is a long-term mission trip ... and every single week is a short-term mission opportunity.

That means when I'm home, I am on a short-term mission trip in Dallas. Every day. Everywhere I go.

Can you imagine how radically different our lives would be if we were to apply the same mind-sets about foreign mission trips to the mission trip we are on every day? Can you imagine how our cities would change? How our expectations would change? How our communities would change?

Imagine that every day, just as if you were in some exotic foreign land, you lived with a desperation for God's provision, an expectation of God's power, and a sense of being overwhelmed in all the right ways with the same responsibilities David Livingstone, Amy Carmichael, Hudson Taylor, Jim Elliot, and others carried "over there." Imagine that your life was filled with the same courageous engagement with others and prayerful expectation that God is going to use you as part of His plan to rescue, serve, and lead out of darkness the land in which you live.

Is that your mind-set? How have your last seven days of mission been? Have you been on mission? Anything worth reporting to the home office? Ready to give an account of the days and resources used to provide for you as His ambassador? Just imagine how much God has invested in you where you live. How many other missionaries are part of your city—*your* church. How many of your "mission dollars" are being used wisely? Would you support yourself if you were a mission agency?

Living missionally—maintaining a concern for those not yet rescued and caring for those in your land—is almost always the first place a believer's heart begins to grow cold. Somewhere along the way of "doing church," we forget that "being the Church" is being on mission. Jesus came to seek and save the lost,[4] and He has left us here to follow in His steps.[5]

It is not an overstatement to say that every single act of God since the fall of man has been a missionary act. Every word and deed has been and is being done to reconcile people to Him. It is why you are here. It is why you are alive.

So instead of thinking of "mission" in terms of involving foreign lands, exotic places, or expensive trips, try thinking of mission as it truly is meant to be: *life*.

---

4   Luke 19:10.
5   Matthew 16:24; 1 Peter 2:21.

All of it.

Every day.

Everywhere you go.

This moment, right now, is a moment of *your* mission trip.

Life is a mission, and every single one of us is either a mission field or a missionary—there is no other option.

There is a reason that when you were baptized, God didn't instruct others to hold you underwater and send you on to heaven ... There is work to do. The King left you here to represent Him in a foreign land. "Therefore, we are ambassadors for Christ, as though God were making an appeal through us; we beg you on behalf of Christ, be reconciled to God."[6] Christ has not led us this far in these pages and in life—deep into the riches of His grace[7]—for us to keep it to ourselves. He has been and will continue to be committed to conforming us to His image[8] so we can be committed with Him to His work. He has saved us and is always training us to be lifesavers. His expectation that we would join Him[9] should never saddle us with guilt or leave us feeling condemned about our lack of effort in missions, but His love should always compel us to passionately join Him.

We all need to come *to* see, and then continually be reminded, that being truly rooted and grounded in relationship with the living God compels us to become overflowing in our desire and ability to speak of His beauty to others. Just as anyone who truly

---

6   2 Corinthians 5:20.
7   Ephesians 1:7.
8   Romans 8:29.
9   1 Peter 2:21.

knows Jesus is called to live with His people in a way that he or she is fully known and loved, anyone who is fully known and loved by Christ is compelled to do everything possible to make sure others know that Jesus fully loves and has made provision for him or her. Missions is not a program, a campaign, or a motivational initiative.

It is not a guilt-induced trip; and in fact, it is not a trip at all.

It is today. Tomorrow. Every day.

God is love.[10] Love lives on mission to share with others what others need.[11] Jesus came with a mission,[12] and the life we've always wanted is found in being fully engaged on mission with Him.[13]

His Mission

There they stood, looking out across the calm waters they had known so well since they were little boys. These fishermen knew the Sea of Galilee as if it were another member of their families. In fact, a day didn't go by that they didn't sail on it and express thanks for the way it provided food for their families.

But on this day, the waters looked different to them. Something was changing—and not just on the lake. A wind was blowing that would change the world. They were standing beside a rabbi whose reputation was beginning to turn heads and who would soon turn hearts. By those waters in Galilee, Jesus called the first disciples to follow Him into the same adventure that He has been calling disciples

---

10   1 John 4:8.
11   2 Corinthians 8:9; 1 John 3:16–18.
12   Mark 10:43–45.
13   John 21:15–17; Matthew 28:19–20; Acts 1:8.

to ever since. From His initial call to the men He was inviting to follow and know Him, He was making known what following Him would always mean. "Now as Jesus was walking by the Sea of Galilee, He saw two brothers, Simon who was called Peter, and Andrew his brother, casting a net into the sea; for they were fishermen. And He said to them, 'Follow Me, and I will make you fishers of men.'"[14]

You might imagine Jesus saying, "Men, you think it is fun making live fish dead? How about I show you how to make dead men come alive? How about joining Me in rescuing and setting free those captive to everything that holds them in bondage? How about we feed the hungry and heal the sick? How about you come watch Me and then let your relationship with Me change the world?"

Fast-forward three years to find that these same men have moved from curious fishermen to devoted followers … like us, they were not fully mature yet—soon to fail yet again, but they were full of life nonetheless because they had come to know where Life could be found. They were about to be turned loose to flip the world upside down. And like us, they were not called because of their competency, earned value, or accomplishments. They were called because of Christ's sovereign and gracious will—a calling that was supernaturally backed by the miraculous truth that He had chosen them, died for them, had risen, ascended, and had now sent His Spirit to enable them to do the work He left them to do. They had been utterly transformed by their proximity to and deep community with Jesus and one another. Imagine the stories they had to tell … remember the stories they were about to live.

---

14   Matthew 4:18–19.

But Jesus's plan was never that it would be just *their* story; it was always supposed to be *every disciple's* story. Go back and reread the last paragraph starting with "fast-forward three years" and insert "fast-forward to now." Be reminded again of the life God intends for you. Where it says "like us," read yourself into the paragraph and be reminded that "like them" you have a missional mandate to turn the world today upside down.[15] If you will simply believe Jesus as they believed Jesus, you cannot imagine the stories *you* are about to live.

The most pivotal moment in their commissioning is a promise and a commissioning for us as well. Just before they would lay their eyes on Him for the last time, Jesus reminded them, "But you will receive power when the Holy Spirit has come upon you; and you shall be My witnesses both in Jerusalem, and in all Judea and Samaria, and even to the remotest part of the earth."[16]

I say "reminded" because He had said the same thing to them months earlier on the night before[17] He was crucified. Do you see the importance of the idea of mission? It was the very first thing He said when He called them ... and it was the very last thing He said before He went to the grave. It was the very last thing He said to them before His ascension into heaven. Each time, He told them—and then preserved in His Word for us—what He is all about and what we are to be about.

Mission.

---

15 Acts 17:6.
16 Acts 1:8.
17 John 14–16.

This means we are to "not entangle ourselves in the affairs of everyday life in order that we are able to please the One who has enlisted us as a soldier."[18] It means we are to be about seeking and saving the lost.[19] Discipling those who are found. Loving each other by practicing the "one anothers" of Scripture. It means that "since we have so great a cloud of witnesses surrounding us, let us also lay aside every encumbrance and the sin which so easily entangles us, and let us run with endurance the race that is set before us, fixing our eyes on Jesus, the author and perfecter of faith, who for the joy set before Him endured the cross, despising the shame, and has sat down at the right hand of the throne of God."[20]

It means we are His plan A to reach the world … and there is no plan B.[21]

It means there is a lifetime of adventure in front of us where our stories, as a result of our life with Jesus, create a sense of awe.

You were not created to attend a weekly service out of *obligation*; you were created for good works out of God's *proclamation*.[22]

But be ready. If you are serious about the mission, it won't be long before you run up against someone who is offended by your passion and your confident assurance about where life and forgiveness are found.[23]

---

18 2 Timothy 2:4.
19 Luke 19:10.
20 Hebrews 12:1–2.
21 Matthew 5:13–16.
22 Ephesians 2:10.
23 Acts 4:12.

As you live faithfully, preaching the exclusivity of Jesus's offer, it won't be long before someone asks you to justify your belief. "Explain to me, if it is true that there is salvation in no one else, and that there is no other name in heaven by which men must be saved,[24] what happens to those who have never heard of this Jesus you claim to know?"

Let me encourage you to be ready to answer[25] your confused friend who seeks to understand more about God's seeming injustice,[26] but that is not my point here—there is a better one to be made. If you are not being asked this question, or others like it, it might be because you are off mission. Sometime well over one hundred years ago, Charles Spurgeon responded to this question with one of his own. "It is more a question with me whether we—who have the Gospel and fail to give it to those who have not—can be saved."[27]

Ouch.

If your life's activities are not mission related, you should ask yourself how related you are to the Master who puts all of His people on mission.[28]

---

24 Acts 4:12.

25 1 Peter 3:15.

26 To get a short answer to this question, go to http://realtruthrealquick .com/what-happens-to-people-who-have-never-heard-the-gospel/. And check out other questions just like this that I have answered on this same site.

27 "Charles Haddon Spurgeon," Goodreads, accessed May 10, 2017, www.goodreads.com/quotes/805675-someone-asked-will-the-heathen -who-have-never-heard-the.

28 Luke 9:26.

If this is Christ's mission and you are abiding in Him, then you will not have to conjure up excitement or feign emotion. It won't take a pledge card or a tear-jerking video to get you motivated. On the contrary, this mission will simply begin to resonate within you as you grow more and more like Him, even when it requires that you suffer as you live it.[29]

If we know Him and truly love Him, what He loves, we will love. This is why we have to master the Master's life: understanding what is important to Him is what enables us to be about what should be important to us. When we truly know Him, all we truly want to know is how we live for the Truth. Paul says it this way, "Therefore if anyone is in Christ, he is a new creature; the old things passed away; behold, new things have come. Now all these things are from God, who reconciled us to Himself through Christ and gave us the ministry of reconciliation, namely, that God was in Christ reconciling the world to Himself, not counting their trespasses against them, and He has committed to us the word of reconciliation. Therefore, we are ambassadors for Christ, as though God were making an appeal through us; we beg you on behalf of Christ, be reconciled to God."[30]

If "all these things are [indeed] from God," then what an incredible calling and privilege those of us who are called to *work* for Him have been given. We know that ambassadorships are given by sitting presidents to men and women who have supported their candidacy and administration. Look no further than 2 Corinthians 5 to see where they got the idea to do that.

---

29 1 Peter 2:21; 2 Timothy 3:12.
30 2 Corinthians 5:17–20.

Can you imagine being given the privilege to represent the country you love in a place where you would be given every provision necessary to bring grace to its people, including the right to grant them access (a visa) to come and visit—or live—in the greatest nation … in *heaven*? This is the heart of the Father and the desire of *your* Savior: to appoint you and share with you that privilege.

The mission of Christ flows from the passion of Christ—and Jesus's passion is to love and reach those who are far away from Him. What kind of people? Any kind. And don't be surprised that the more corrupt or broken they are, the more desperate your Commander-in-Chief is going to be to reach them. People like a corrupt tax collector named Zacchaeus. Jesus insisted on eating at his house, which not only proved His passion to reach those who are far away but also infuriated the religious leaders—those who were all about attending to all the appearances of God's business[31] and were not fully devoted to God's heart.

"And when they saw it, they all grumbled, 'He has gone in to be the guest of a man who is a sinner.' And Zacchaeus stood and said to the Lord, 'Behold, Lord, the half of my goods I give to the poor. And if I have defrauded anyone of anything, I restore it fourfold.' And Jesus said to him, 'Today salvation has come to this house, since he also is a son of Abraham. For the Son of Man came to seek and to save the lost.'"[32]

If Christ came to seek and save the lost, then we ought to do the same.

---

31   Matthew 15:8.
32   Luke 19:7–10 (ESV).

If He is our Master, then *His* mission should be *our* mission.

But just as you are either a missionary or a mission field, when it comes to your attitude toward those far away from Christ's love, you are either a disciple or a Pharisee … which means you are either attending to religious formalities or you are a real follower committed to attending to the things that your Jesus loves. There is no way to be a fully devoted follower of Jesus without being fully devoted to His deepest mission—the same mission that led Him to die so He could bring you to Him. That mission is now yours … and so is all the Life that comes with it.

More Than Just Words

Those of us who have been in church a long time become very adept at affirming a statement like the previous one … and then completely ignoring it in our daily lives. We agree with it, but we don't own it. We slide it into our minds next to other biblical truths like Eve ate an apple, Noah built a boat, and Samson had poor taste in women. We nod our heads in intellectual approval, and then we move on to other topics.[33]

---

33 Without being able to remember where, I know I have heard (or read) this general concept before. I love its punch and am sorry I cannot remember who first used this kind of language to get a head nod, self-examination, and an "amen" from me. I know creativity is "forgetting where you heard it," but I am thankful to the countless faithful men and women who have gone before me who planted so many of the truths and ideas of this book in me. To all of you whom I have forgotten: thank you, and rejoice in knowing that your King will never forget your faithfulness to Him (Hebrews 6:10).

So before we go on to other topics, let's seriously ask ourselves how we are doing with our ambassadorship. Is the grace we received taking root and blossoming into the fruit of God's love for others? Are we even talking about it? Do our little "embassies," budgets, calendars, and activities make clear we are about the King's business?

For some of us, the idea of being passionate on this mission seems impossible. We feel inadequate to know what to say or how to say it. We don't want to offend, be culturally insensitive, or be judgmental. We are too shy. Too guilty. Too fearful.

It seems impossibly difficult to us, but what's actually impossible is finding a person who is insignificant or unreachable in God's eyes. It doesn't matter who they are or what they've done, they matter to Him—and Jesus says if we are committed to Him, we will be committed to them, no matter what commitment costs us. It starts with regaining perspective on what this life is about. Him. Not us. Not comfort. Not convenience. Not ease.

Him.

It starts with knowing Him and agreeing with Paul, "that the sufferings of this present time are not worthy to be compared with the glory that is to be revealed to us."[34] "For momentary, light affliction is producing for us an eternal weight of glory far beyond all comparison, while we look not at the things which are seen, but at the things which are not seen; for the things which are seen are temporal, but the things which are not seen are eternal."[35] It starts

---

34 Romans 8:18.
35 2 Corinthians 4:17–18.

with the perspective of faith and the hope of a world beyond the one we see every day.[36] And it continues with us seeing those we run into every day as people instead of looking at them like they are projects. It starts with learning their names and telling them ours. Hearing their stories and letting them know how our stories changed when we met Jesus. Initiate, share your story of grace, and invite them to come and see. It is not as hard as we think.

Jesus's passion was so extreme, even His own family struggled with it. When some members of His family heard about all He was saying and doing, "they went out to seize him, for they were saying, 'He is out of his mind.'"[37] In other words, Jesus was so committed to those who didn't know grace—and He gave so generously of Himself toward His mission of reaching them—that even His own family felt uncomfortable. You can almost hear his brothers. "Jesus, You're taking this *way* too seriously. We have always been a religious family careful to keep the customs, but You're taking this too far. You're embarrassing Yourself. You're embarrassing us. We would be willing to stand with You, but You're already beside Yourself!"

When was the last time someone said to you, "You are so convinced of this whole grace-gift-forgiveness-Jesus thing that I think you've lost your mind!" That's what happened to Jesus—and if we love as He loved and walk as He walked, people may talk about us as His kinsmen talked about Him. We should not be considered crazy because we post to Facebook, argue with unbelievers, wear

---

36 Colossians 3:1–2.
37 Mark 3:21 (ESV).

sandwich boards with doomsday messages, or shout horribly into a bullhorn about the end of the earth … that will come when it is supposed to come without us shouting about it to anybody. We also don't have to wait until we are impossibly competent.[38] We have to love like Jesus did with the message of God's goodness, kindness, and grace. Remember, "kindness has converted more sinners than zeal, eloquence, or learning,"[39] and there is nothing kinder than reminding people of the truth because you love them.

You can tell if a man is committed to Jesus by seeing if he is committed to people. To loving them. Speaking the truth to them. Caring for them. Giving his life to them.

"All in" is the mark of a Savior … and "all in" is the mark of a disciple.

Take the Next Step

Life is a long-term mission trip, and each week we have a short-term mission opportunity. We don't need to go abroad to proclaim the grace of Christ. By all means, go if you believe you should, but most often, full devotion and being on mission simply mean taking the next step the Master puts in front of us.

Most of us don't need to cross an ocean as much as we need to cross the ocean of indifference in our hearts.

Just do the next thing in response to who He is and what He has done for you. Yes, at some point, the next thing for you might

---

38 2 Chronicles 16:9; John 15:7.
39 Frederick Faber, Oxford scholar and Anglican priest.

be to travel to some distant land, but it is more likely that there is someone on your street, in your grocery store, next to your cubical, or even in your house to whom, although they are in geographical proximity to you, you remain distant. Being mission minded begins right where we are.

This is why I tell my friends at Watermark all the time that 100 percent of our budget goes to missions. Because we are *always* on mission. Our trips overseas are not "missions" trips—they are merely trips into other lands where we *continue* the mission we live out every day as devoted followers of our King. The tragedy is that too many churches who think of missions as something overseas too often send people *over there* who have not been on mission *over here*.

Instead of taking vacations with a purpose, how about living our lives with one?

Our journey together in these pages has been an exploration of the incredible life Christ truly wants for you as His beloved. It is an invitation. A divine proposal to a better way, not a divinely imposed way. His invitation is to all of us. Not just leaders. Not just for those who have a "call" to evangelism. All of us.

Every one of us who *are* fully devoted disciples *will* share in this mission. We are a kingdom of priests,[40] not attenders of weekly services led by priests.

For all of us, this begins by fully engaging with Christ ourselves. We must decrease and He must increase[41] until His passion

---

40 1 Peter 2:9.
41 John 3:30.

naturally becomes our mission. Here are a few questions to help you evaluate how you might be doing at taking your mission seriously.

Of the people who live in the ten houses closest to you, how many of their names do you know? How many of them can you call on your cell phone? When is the last time you shared a meal with them? Do you know where they are in relationship to the faith? How many people far from God have you initiated a relationship with this week? If God answered every one of your prayers this week, how many people's eternity would be changed as a result? When was the last time that you personally shared your story of grace with someone? When was the last time you personally, clearly presented the gospel to someone? What is worse: someone who lives in a part of the world where they have little or no access to the gospel, or someone on your own street who has access to you but with whom you have never shared the gospel? Pray for the "10/40 window"[42] all you want, but make sure you see the need sitting right outside of your window.

We must be committed to the uncommitted, regularly involved in conversations with those far from God. This means that our churches must stop being professed lifesaving stations that are too comfortable (and "relevant"?) to actually be passionate about loving real people. A. W. Tozer said it well, "The task of the church is twofold: to spread Christianity throughout the world

---

42 The "10/40 Window" is a term coined by Christian missions strategists referring to those regions of the Eastern Hemisphere, plus the European and African part of the Western Hemisphere, located between ten and forty degrees north of the equator.

and to make sure that the Christianity she spreads is the pure New Testament kind … Christianity will always reproduce itself after its kind. A worldly minded, unspiritual church, when she crosses the ocean to give her witness to peoples of other tongues and other cultures, is sure to bring forth on other shores a Christianity much like her own."[43]

As you become more like Christ, you will find that more and more people will approach you, asking you to give an account for the hope that is in you. Why do you love the way you do? Why is it always so important to you to be reconciled to others whom you have offended? Why do you pursue your faithless spouse and your family this way? Why is your commitment to others in your faith community so incredibly strong? How can you live with so much peace when there is so much trouble?

"Job one" is to know Him and love Him. Once you do that, you will love others and your life will be filled with God's "greater works" fleshed out in the "Acts of the apostles *living today.*" You could write this chapter yourself … and others should marvel at *your* mission story. Christ will use you to reach others when the "Good News" is actually "good news" to you. That is, we are told to first "sanctify Christ as Lord in your hearts." Only then will we be able to authentically live out the next part of the verse: "always being ready to make a defense to everyone who asks you to give

---

43   *Evenings with Tozer*, comp. Gerald B. Smith (Chicago: Moody, 1981), Nov. 26.

an account for the hope that is in you, yet with gentleness and reverence."[44]

The mission becomes alive in the Church when we focus on the mission of becoming more like Jesus. When people interacted with Christ, they were astonished and amazed by what they experienced. People wanted to be around Him, longing to hear the next thing He was going to say. They ran and found their friends and were constantly saying, "Come and see!"

This is the life you've always wanted in the place you never thought to look.

Come and get it.

---

44   1 Peter 3:15.

Chapter 20

Go and Be

Here we are. The last chapter. And like others have done with their last words, I hope to stir you up by way of reminder.[1] It may be the ending of our time together in these pages, but my prayer is that it is merely the beginning of something else. I hope you have been either told for the first time or reminded again of the greatness of our God, His incredible love for you, and His desire to do something eternally significant in and through you in His world today.

Not long ago, I was speaking to a group of future leaders at Summit Ministries[2] in Colorado. To buy some time while they were resetting the room before I taught, the young man up front threw out an icebreaker question. He said, "Turn to the people next to you and tell them what your superpower would be if you could have one."

---

1   2 Peter 1:2–14; Philippians 3:1; Jude 5.
2   If you are the parent of a high school or college student, I can't encourage you enough to do whatever you can to have them attend one of their two-week summer conferences. Check out www.summit.org for more info.

Now I have to admit, my eyes rolled when I heard him ask the question, but after about thirty minutes of reminding the group with many of the same things you have just read, I looked out at them and said, "Remember the icebreaker question? Well, do you know who you are? If you do, then this is Sky High[3] and I am about to tell you what your superpower *is*. Flying, invisibility, telekinetic powers, super speed … don't waste your time wishing these small things for yourself. I am telling you that if you understood what I have been telling you, you would know that your superpower, bestowed upon you by divine sovereignty, is the ability to change the world. You have the power to give sight to people who are blind to eternal truth. To allow people who are deaf to life-changing wisdom to finally hear. To free people who have been held captive their entire lifetime by evil and lies. You have the power to give every person who meets you the ability to change their eternal destiny from death and judgment, to life and freedom.

"How about *that* for a superpower?"

But what about you? If you know and walk with Jesus, do you realize these same powers are vested in you? I do because I have seen God do it through my imperfect, broken, yet available and willing life. And He wants to do it with *you*. The verse I most meditated on in my early days of launching into this grand adventure of believing that God wanted to do something great for His name through me was 2 Chronicles 16:9: "For the eyes of the LORD move to and fro throughout the earth that He may *strongly support*

---

3   See www.imdb.com/title/tt0405325. Go ahead; check it out for your next family movie night.

those whose heart is completely His." As I began calling others to join me on mission at Watermark, I would constantly say, "God is going to do something great in this world today, and I believe that if we are willing, He is willing to use us."[4]

What are you waiting for? I hope it isn't tips, techniques on self-help, strategies, or church-growth models—because I have offered you *none* of those here. And you don't need them. Rather, I want to remind you *who* we are doing it for and *why* it's worth it. You don't need to know *who* you are as much as you need to know *whose* you are.

You want to do something great for God? Don't seek to be someone great without total dependence on Him. Follow the way of the man whom Jesus said was the greatest of all men born of a woman[5] (that pretty much covers the gamut, in case you were wondering). "He must increase, but I must decrease."[6]

Don't set out to do something great for God; learn instead to depend on the God who has done something great for you. You might as well depend on Him because without Him, you can't do anything worthwhile anyway.[7]

So let me remind you again of a few things.

Do you feel inadequate? Perfect.

If dependence is the goal, then weakness is an advantage. Remember that it is *His* greater works you are going to be accomplishing, not *yours*.

---

4   1 Timothy 1:12–14; Titus 3:3–4.
5   Matthew 11:11.
6   John 3:30.
7   Hebrews 11:6; John 15:5.

He will do greater works through you—if you ask Him, He will do it. Throughout his gospel, John chose only seven miracles to write about. In fact, he didn't use the word "miracle," but instead he used the word "sign." The word for "sign" in the Greek is used as the root word in "signet," as in *signet* ring. A signet ring had a distinctive, unique, unusual design—one not found everywhere. It was easily recognizable … and it was *only* in the possession of a king.

When a king would finish writing a letter, he would roll it up, drop a little wax on the edge, and then push this unique, easily recognizable, only-in-the-possession-of-the-king signet ring into the hot wax to leave a distinct impression. By this unique sign, everyone who would see it would know that this letter came from the king. It had the mark of the king's personal hand on it.

So in John 14:12, Jesus was in effect saying, "These signs … these unique things that have happened and that are easily recognizable as something only God can do, *you* will also do these things. In fact, you will do even more of these things than I have done." Now I've been around some godly people for the five decades I have been walking on this earth. In all my years, I have never seen water turned to wine. I've never seen wind and waves calmed by a spoken command. I've never seen a person who has been blind from birth receive sight. I've never personally seen someone who is paralyzed from the waist down as the result of an accident stand up, and walk … literally take up their pallet, throw away their wheelchair, and go home.

I believe God can do all of these things and anything else He wants to at any time He wants to.[8] But as we have established in earlier chapters, Jesus's meaning here was not that we would top His signs in kind, but rather in scope. And whatever the attention-grabbing start to any work of God might be, the final and greatest sign is always the miraculously transformed lives that continue through His sustaining, redemptive grace.

Let me give you an example of the greater work Jesus was always after and why we should focus on how someone walks by faith with Him more than whether we can, by faith, make them walk. In John 5 after Jesus had healed the man who had been paralyzed for thirty-eight years, He tracked him down basically to ask him in different words the exact same question He had asked him before He had healed the lame man's legs: "Do you want to get well?"[9]

Can you imagine the healed man's surprise? "I am well! I'm walking for the first time in almost four decades!" But Jesus leaned in, effectively saying, "No, you're not well. You're just not physically lame anymore. You still do have, however, the curse of sin upon you. Do you want to get fully well? Do you want your dead soul revived? Then repent. Quit thinking anything other than Me is your hope for everything … trust in Me continually *so that nothing worse happens to you.*"[10]

---

8   Jeremiah 32:27.
9   This whole story is found in John 5:1–15.
10   John 5:14.

What's worse than being paralyzed for almost forty years? How about being separated from Christ for eternity because you have never come to understand the reason Christ came to earth in the first place? Jesus did not come to give you your best circumstance on earth now;[11] He came to give you life in relationship with Him despite the trouble you will continually face on earth.[12] Even if you never get off your "mat," never come into more money, never get married, or despite your best efforts, never are able to restore your broken marriage, you can have everything Jesus says you need to have peace and fullness of life in Him.[13]

As far as works go, it is *never* your job to do *what* Jesus did. Let's remember, WWJD[14] should not be on your bracelet. It's not your job to die for the sins of the world. That was His job. It is finished. WWJHMD[15] is the bracelet you should wear and the question you should ask. Jesus is saying to us in John 14, "I got this. I will use you if you ask Me to, to do even more amazing things than you have seen Me do. If you ask Me, I will do it."

Think about it: there were about 120 people following Christ at the end of His ministry. We might think the greater works must mean that we will have more people follow us than followed Him, but we should not want people to follow us—we should

---

11   Anybody who tells you that your best life now will be defined with health, wealth, or prosperity is not serving you God's truth … they are setting you up for trouble with God when He doesn't "perform" for you the way they promised.

12   John 14:27; 16:33.

13   2 Peter 1:3; Ephesians 1:3; Psalm 84:11.

14   What Would Jesus Do.

15   What Would Jesus Have Me Do.

want people to follow Jesus. We should not want people to attend our services—we should invite people to join us in tending to the grace message, authentic community, and significant purposes that define a humble, obedient life.

The greater works are His. Our great work is to be fully available to and satisfied in Him. Confused where to start? Let me recommend on your knees. "You can do more than pray after you have prayed, but you cannot do more than pray until you have prayed."[16]

Don't seek to do something great for God. Seek God. His kingdom. His righteousness.[17] Rest in Him[18] as you labor for His glory.[19]

That brings me to the next thing we should be continually reminded of. We are not here for leisure's sake. While it is true that we should rest in His provision, it is also true that we should respond with faithfulness. It is entirely too easy to think like the people on the cruise ship in the video I described in chapter 7. Today's regular attender thinks he needs cushioned seats and entertaining personalities to be happy in church. We need the services to be just the right length—not too short and not too long. We don't want the church to be too big or too small. Too many churches spend too much time trying to get the formula just right instead of forming a body of faithful servants.

---

16   A. J. Gordan, faithful servant to the Burmese people.
17   Matthew 6:33.
18   Matthew 11:28–30.
19   Matthew 5:16; Ephesians 2:10; 1 Peter 2:12.

So much of the "church" world today is obsessed with what "works" to attract a crowd. Too often, "big" is confused with "blessed by God." Crowds of people who gather for religious services don't always equate to large congregations of saints. Too many "church" leaders are obsessed with attracting an audience instead of making disciples. The job of godly leadership is to compel people to come to Christ, not to come to church buildings. The job of pastors is not to get others to come regularly to services, but to help them come to the end of living for themselves on a regular basis.

"Come and see" only works when there is actually something to see—and that something cannot be conjured, faked, or programmed ... It has to have the sign of the King on it. Something easily recognizable as divine. Otherworldly. The bride of Christ ought to have the signet ring of her Bridegroom on her hand and the beauty of the Word of God carried on her lips. This is the only "seeable" thing that will actually change someone's life.

This "bride" who loves one another in *this* kind of way because they are being transformed by *this* kind of Savior ... *this* is what is irresistibly attractive to the wandering eyes of humanity.

When we are grounded in grace and fully devoted to all that following Christ biblically means, we will draw the world with the beauty of His love. We will have the ring of love upon us ... and they will know we are His.[20]

Only the beloved of God have the privilege of calling confused people out of the malaise of dead religion. The Father is calling His people to be a part of something incredible. Not an *audience*

20   John 13:34–35.

of attenders, but an *army* of soldiers who are no longer entangled in the affairs of everyday life.[21] People who no longer merely hear stories of others who are being used greatly by God but who are equipped to participate with God in changing the world.[22]

Anything less than a call to action is simply cutting a deal.

God's Church never cuts deals … especially the one where people's mere presence is the standard by which a leader senses that what they're doing is valuable to God and validated by a watching world. The Lord is calling His Church to be involved in the greatest work in the history of the world. To rescue lives, defeat evil, and bring peace. This is what church—His Church—is really about, and there is no reason you should settle for anything less than the full adventure His grace calls you to.

The Church of Jesus Christ as He intends it is the very hope of the world, but the way many people are "doing church" today is certainly not. God doesn't want the world to come and see what is not His. He hates it and wants to see it shut down. He has said as much before, and we should not think He has an appetite for anything less today.[23] That is why the call of Christ's grace to nothing less than full devotion must ring louder today than ever … we will give an account for anything less.[24] By His grace, we are free and empowered to lead. To initiate. To be people of action. To hate apathy. To reject passivity. To begin assuming this is our time … our moment.

---

21   2 Timothy 2:4.

22   2 Timothy 3:16.

23   Malachi 1:10; Isaiah 1:13; Amos 5:21–24.

24   Hebrews 13:17.

Where we need to get on our knees and ask the people we have not been leading for forgiveness, we should do it. Where we need to call them to something more, we should get after it.

Be awakened and be reminded that you are the servant of the King. He's not angry with you. He wants to quicken your heart. To make you steadfast by His grace, "immovable, always abounding in the work of the Lord, knowing that your toil is not in vain in the Lord."[25]

You have been uniquely placed right where you are by the sovereignty of God. You are His "plan A" right where you are. You are the hope of glory[26] in your family, your church, and your community. If you are ready to kindle afresh the gift of life within you, be humble as you share what you have become convinced of in these pages. Be bold but winsome[27] as you call others to join you, with this fresh reminder or new knowledge of what Christ fully desires His Church—and *every member* in it—to be. Share with others this book or a chapter that has had an impact on you. Pray for them. Pray with them. Look up the scriptures that have shaped the content of all that you have just read. Be like the noble-minded Bereans, who after hearing from Paul, "received the word with great eagerness, examining the Scriptures daily to see whether these things were so."[28] With gentleness and reverence, remind others of the hope you are convinced exists in Christ. If reading this book has been a catalyst for you, I pray that a copy of it may also be a catalyst for them.

---

25 1 Corinthians 15:58.
26 Colossians 1:25–27.
27 Proverbs 15:2; Colossians 4:5–6.
28 Acts 17:11.

Meanwhile and above all else, purpose to live a life that makes others want to come and see what has gotten hold of you. Be able to say for yourself that "the things you have learned and received, heard and seen, practice these things."[29] Whatever anyone else does, *you* live your life in the radical transformation that always follows an encounter with Christ and daily fellowship with His Spirit. *You* repent where you need to. *You* ask their forgiveness for the ways *you* have allowed your heart to get off course. In other words, *you* begin to live your life in a way that demonstrates *you* believe that living for Christ is a life worth living.

Get after it and invite them to come and join you, given what you have come to see.

And this brings us to a new and final thought that I hope will become a constant reminder to you in the future: *a circle.*

Draw a circle around yourself and change everything in it. Inside your newly drawn circle of passionate devotion to Christ, live your faith. Share your faith. Confess your sin. Live out the grace of God in full devotion. When they see you "sanctify Christ as Lord in your hearts, *then* always *be* ready to make a defense to everyone who asks you to give an account for the hope that is in you, yet with gentleness and reverence."[30]

Gentleness and reverence first … *then* passion and perseverance. Do not let others discourage you just because they think you have "lost your senses"[31] as you live faithfully for your King. Live

---

29 Philippians 4:9.
30 1 Peter 3:15.
31 Mark 3:21.

passionately. Radically. Recklessly. And if they respond with "Hey, that's just not the way we're going to do it around here," then you can kindly respond by saying "Peace be with you" as you go and serve your God.

Be God's prophet. Heed the words of the Lord to Jeremiah and stand firm. "Now, gird up your loins and arise, and speak to them all which I command you. Do not be dismayed before them, or I will dismay you before them. Now behold, I have made you today as a fortified city and as a pillar of iron and as walls of bronze against the whole land, to the kings of Judah, to its princes, to its priests, and to the people of the land. 'They will fight against you, but they will not overcome you, for I am with you to deliver you,' declares the LORD."[32]

Be patient and gentle. Everyone may not completely see everything as you are seeing it in the first five minutes after you come to them. Love them well—as one who is full of the grace and truth of Christ. Don't forget that to them, turning around your church may feel like turning around an aircraft carrier … but at least you can now share with them that it isn't as hard and won't take as long as they think.[33] It takes the will of the leadership and the readiness of the crew. It takes commitment.

But it *can* turn. Do what you can to turn it.

As you live in God's grace and in full devotion inside authentic community where you practice the "one anothers" of Scripture before them for an extended amount of time, it is my prayer that

---

32   Jeremiah 1:17–19.
33   See pages 84–85 for a refresher.

Christ will ignite the same mission in their hearts that He has ignited in yours. Trust me, it happens all the time—one person can be used by Christ to ignite the passion of many others.[34] One person willing to draw a circle around themselves and begin living faithfully in devotion to Christ ... and when the circle is changed, be willing to invite others in.

You can be that one person.

When God wants to deliver a people, He raises up a deliverer.[35]

Christ in you can deliver hope and renewal to the land you live in.[36]

Persevere in doing good and do not be discouraged.[37] Do not grow weary, for in due time, you will reap.[38] If there comes a time when it becomes evident that the leadership of a church does not want to change their course from what they've always done, say to them, "I believe you are sovereignly placed here by God. I have sought to live faithfully before you and with you. I love you and I'm going to pray for you and serve you the best I can by calling others to join me in believing and acting like Jesus meant what He said."

Do not be dismayed before them. Speak to them all that He has commanded you. You may hear words like, "We can't turn this ship around here ... we have been sailing like this for a long time and many won't like it." I know that response well. When I started Watermark with a few friends, skeptics and well-meaning friends

---

34 Ezekiel 22:30.
35 Jesus, Moses, Samuel, David ... you.
36 Colossians 1:27.
37 Galatians 6:10.
38 Galatians 6:9.

alike warned me that Dallas was the land of many churches. And they were right. So shortly after Watermark started, *Christianity Today*'s front cover appeared with the image of a ten-gallon cowboy hat. The title read: "A Texas-Sized Faith: How Dallas Has Become the New Capital of Evangelicalism."[39] Even at one of our local seminaries, I've heard a professor say, "Who here wants to plant a church in Dallas? Because I want to go ahead and give you an F ... This is the last city in the world that needs another church!"

I was in this city when this was the prevailing sentiment. We knew this city did not need another church that was capable of gathering large numbers of people ... but it desperately needed people who, by God's grace, would follow Christ with full devotion. I don't know a city anywhere that still doesn't need the same. Including Dallas. So we prayed, and we still pray, that every other church around us would be a thriving, abiding, fully functioning, prevailing church. We knew that despite the huge number of churches in our metroplex of seven million people, there were still many people who were not "attending" to God's business or aware of God's goodness. So we set out to reach them.

But the honest truth was, there were also people who were stuck in churches where they were no longer being called to anything ... where they were merely regularly attenders. Early on, I received a call from another local pastor who told me "tongue in cheek" that I was messing up "The Deal." He said this because people in his church were asking him why they were not experiencing the same

39 See www.christianitytoday.com/ct/2002/may21/new-capital-of -evangelicalism.html.

life change, excitement, and stories of awe that their friends who were at this "new church" were experiencing. I asked him "tongue in cheek" if they were right.

To his great credit, my pastor friend thanked me because we had helped to remind them of what their church also used to be about and what he was committed to getting back to making it about again. He was thankful that we had helped to spur him and other leaders on to love and good deeds. I responded by asking him to constantly challenge and encourage me as I heard in the days to come all the ways the Lord was using him and Christ's church under his care. We prayed and committed to go hard after all the Lord had for us together in this town.

I wish every story ended this way, but it won't. So be hopeful and know that sometimes you may have to keep walking the path you know God has for you, even if your church or other churches won't join you. Your job is to call them to something greater before the Lord assigns them to something worse.[40] Be faithful, and when you think about settling back into something less than your King wants, let your King encourage you with these words: "Blessed are you when people insult you and persecute you, and falsely say all kinds of evil against you because of Me. Rejoice and be glad, for your reward in heaven is great; for in the same way they persecuted the prophets who were before you."[41]

Just think of Jesus. He called Jewish people out of Judaism so they could be true Jews. He also called Romans out of Rome.

---

40   Matthew 10:11–15.
41   Matthew 5:11–12.

He wasn't loved by the Jews. He wasn't loved by the Romans. The world hated Him. The "people of God" hated Him. It should sober us to be ready that a day is coming, and in many places has arrived, where we will need to call people out of this thing they call "church" and into truly following Christ.[42]

As I said in the last chapter, truth sounds like hate to those who hate the truth, so make sure the way you speak the truth is not the problem.[43] Like your King, be full of grace and truth. Both. All the time. Christ's message is loving because it's true and it will be heard because it is delivered with love.

Act like men. Be strong. Let all that you do be done in love.[44]

Speak the truth in love, but don't sit and wait for everyone's approval. Live for an audience of One and go be God's Church. If anyone tries to put a governor on the pure gospel to slow it down, remember that you only have one Governor who is your Lord and King. Serve Him. Fear God and not man.[45]

I wrote this book because it is my prayer that God will awaken the hope of the world—that is, the Church. That is ... you! Great leaders share their passion and their God-given vision with the people around them. Christ is a great leader, and He has told us what He expects of us: full devotion. *Full devotion is normal for a believer*.

If you are a leader in your church (*and you are expected to be*), remember your first love. Hear Christ's invitation to return from

---

42 Matthew 10:34–39; 2 Timothy 3:12.
43 Proverbs 15:2; Colossians 4:5–6.
44 1 Corinthians 16:13–14.
45 Galatians 1:10.

where you have fallen.[46] Commit first to being His servant yourself and second to shepherding well those around you—especially those who think Christ died so they could hang around a building on Sundays as "irregular believers" until they someday fill a hole.

Don't let that be you. When you die, *leave* a hole, don't just fill one. You may need to "grow" your church down to two hundred people … or two people. If it gets down to two, then you and your spouse (or you and your first disciple) need to draw a circle around yourselves and begin to radically pursue full devotion in every part of your own lives—and as you get there, invite others in. Take pains with these things; be absorbed in them, so that your progress will be evident to all.[47] Let no one look down on your youthfulness, but rather in speech, conduct, love, faith, and purity, show yourself an example of those who believe.[48]

If you have known Christ for a while and have been less than "all in" on the mission, a great place to start is to consider asking for forgiveness for being less focused and fruitful than you should have been due to the worries of the world or the desire for other things.[49] If you are a church leader, maybe you need to seek forgiveness for acting as if your church was your business that you were supposed to manage and grow. You may have desired to be *respected* more than *reverent* in all things—to have your church become well funded or well known instead of becoming well fed and faithful.

---

46 Revelation 2:4–5.
47 1 Timothy 4:15.
48 1 Timothy 4:12.
49 Mark 4:13–20.

The Good News for the world is still good news to you: God isn't mad at you. He wants to remind you of who you are: loved by Him with every intention to be used mightily by Him. When you repent, there is no probationary period with God. Only a Father on His toes at the edge of the Ranch of Heaven waiting to run to you when you come to your senses and are ready to get back to the business of doing life with Him.[50]

Be reminded that there are people for whom your Savior died who are expecting you to be His ambassador ... so "pay close attention to yourself and to your teaching; persevere in these things, for as you do this you will ensure salvation both for yourself and for those who hear you."[51] Create an embassy of peace that refugees from every foreign and far-from-God's-grace land can *come* to and *see*, causing them to say, "Give me a visa to whatever blessed place *you* are from!"

Let's go after this together. Join me. Let me say with Paul again, "Be on the alert, stand firm in the faith, act like men, be strong. Let all that you do be done in love."[52]

Finally, remember this. At the very end of the book of John, there is a famous conversation between Jesus and Peter. Jesus has been resurrected. Peter has been humbled. There was a time in his life when he was bold and brash, constantly proclaiming he loved Jesus more than all the other disciples. He was certain he would be faithful to the end, even unto the point of death.[53] But as we now

---

50   Luke 15:20.

51   1 Timothy 4:16.

52   1 Corinthians 16:13–14.

53   Matthew 26:33–35.

know, and as he had just painfully learned, his repeated denial of Christ, even to a small servant girl around the fire, had revealed his fragility and inability to follow Jesus as he thought he could.

The story begins just a few days after Peter's massive failure. "So when they had finished breakfast, Jesus said to Simon Peter, 'Simon, son of John, do you love Me more than these?' He said to Him, 'Yes, Lord; You know that I love You.' He said to him, 'Tend My lambs.'"

While I am by no means a Greek scholar, I do know enough about the language to identify there are two different Greek words for "love" used in this passage by John.

When Jesus asked Peter, "Do you love Me?" He used the Greek word *agapaō,* which is the Greek word for a perfect, covenant-keeping, divine kind of love. In other words, Jesus was asking Peter, "Do you sacrificially, unendingly, unconditionally, wholeheartedly love Me with the perfect love of the Father?" Peter answered yes, but there is a distinction in the Greek word for love with which he responds. It is *phileō,* a human love. It was as if Peter was saying, "I love You the way a man loves. I love You in a way that is moody and inconsistent. I love You as a brother loves, but I am sorry to confess it is not the unconditional, covenant love of God. I'm a fallen man. I'm not who You want me to be. I'm not who *I* want to be. I'm not capable of loving You any more than as a friend who will—and who has—failed You. I love You, but not like I said I would."

But Jesus didn't stop. He asked him again, "Peter, do you unconditionally love [*agapaō* again] me with the perfect, covenant love of God?"

Peter responded again, "I want to, but I know who I am. The kind of love I want to give, I can't and I have never been able to. I *phileō* You—that's all I have."

The first time, Jesus had told Peter to "tend My lambs." In other words, see to it that you do your best to shepherd the flock. This time, Jesus responded similarly, telling Peter to "shepherd My sheep." He was reminding him that the sheep were His and not Peter's. In other words, "Remember … it is My Church and it will never be yours."

Then the question came a third time, but with a major difference … and this is where I want to share with you what I believe Jesus wants us *all* to hear in this text. This time, instead of asking Peter if he loved Him with the perfect, unconditional love of God, He asked, "Peter, do you *phileō* Me?" Jesus didn't use *agapaō* the third time. In other words, He asked, "Are you fond of Me? Are you My friend? Do you love Me like a man wants to love his friend?"

I've heard this explained in many different ways, but let me offer you this possibility as the reason for what happened. Jesus tenderly knelt down next to Peter (and me, since I am so much like Peter) so He could look His broken disciple squarely in the eyes. He basically said, "Peter, look at me. Broken son of Adam, are you loving Me the best you can? I know who you are. I always have.[54] I don't love you because you love Me.[55] I love you because I am the *agapaō* love of the Father. I know you're not perfect … that's why

54   Ephesians 1:4–5.
55   1 John 4:10.

I, the *Son of Man*,[56] told you before I died that I was going places you can't go—to the cross.[57] I died for you. I am redeeming you.[58] I am making you new.[59] Who you are and how you seek to *phileō* Me is enough because *I* am enough."

The truth Christ was saying to Peter then and to you and me today is that there's nothing you can do to love God in a way that would make Him want to love you back. That's why He died in your place. Jesus is saying to all of us, "Look at Me—has your heart been quickened? Have you seen who I am? Can you love Me the best way you can love someone who has done all that you, by the Father's grace, have now come to know that I have done for you? Will you love me the best you can because I first loved you the way only I can?"[60]

Peter again responded with a yes and in effect it was as if Jesus was saying, "Then that's enough … because I *agapaō* you, Peter. I know who you are and that you're imperfect. I know you have made mistakes and that you will make more blunders going forward, but it's enough. Why? Because I *agapaō* you! That's what that cross was all about—the unconditional love of the Father to save men like you. *I don't expect you to be perfect or lead a perfect church. Instead, hold fast to My love and go after the fullness of everything it calls you to.*"

---

56 Daniel 7:13–14.
57 John 14:1–3.
58 1 Peter 3:18.
59 2 Corinthians 5:17.
60 1 John 4:19.

As you come to the end of these pages, I am praying that you see the encouragement Christ wants to give you. He's not expecting perfection, but because of His grace, we can be free to move forward doing the best we can, knowing that our best is not the linchpin holding it all together.

He holds everything together.[61] It is a trustworthy statement worthy of full acceptance—*He* is faithful even when we are faithless.[62] The good work, which *He* began in you, *He* will bring to completion in the day of Christ Jesus.[63]

Ours is to cling to Him and to give Him the glory.

His is to bring us home.

Once that matter was settled and Peter could walk forward knowing that his own perfection or love was not the whole of the matter, Jesus let him know some of what was coming down the road in his life: suffering and ultimately a martyr's death.[64]

These were coming for Peter because a lot of people simply don't like the true, radical Church of Jesus Christ. Maybe you feel this pressure too. Maybe you know that if you call the people around you—and in your church, if you attend one—to be the true, radical Church that Christ intends us all to be, then you won't be welcome in that church very long. Or maybe if you are a pastor, you won't have a job for very long.

Don't you worry about that.

Ours is to cling to Him and to give Him the glory.

---

61 Colossians 1:17.
62 2 Timothy 2:13.
63 Philippians 1:6.
64 John 21:18–19a.

His is to bring us home.

Let's decide right now if Jesus is worth *living* for. It's time to figure out who you are going to serve.[65]

Better to get run out of a dead church than to live with a dead faith.[66]

If you're a church leader, you might as well find out right now if God is really God rather than continuing to believe that His best for you is an underpaying job where you're overworked, under-appreciated, and leading a bunch of uninspired, unregenerated, or Spirit-quenching people who are always learning and never able to come to the knowledge of the Truth.[67] Stop holding to a form of godliness and denying its power.[68] Stop letting those under your care be careless in their response to Christ. "Be on guard for your-selves and for all the flock, among which the Holy Spirit has made you overseers, to shepherd the church of God which He purchased with His own blood."[69]

In Colossians, Paul makes a pretty strange statement about this matter: "Now I rejoice in my sufferings for your sake, and in my flesh I do my share on behalf of His body, which is the church, in filling up what is lacking in Christ's afflictions."[70] What is he talking about? What could possibly be lacking in Christ's afflictions or sufferings? Didn't Jesus suffer enough on the cross?

---

65   Joshua 24:15d.
66   Ephesians 5:14–15.
67   2 Timothy 3:7.
68   2 Timothy 3:5.
69   Acts 20:28.
70   Colossians 1:24.

Yes, He did, but here's what Paul is saying: Jesus is not singularly and incarnationally[71] present on earth today, which means His literal two hands and two feet are not currently working here to reveal His divine nature and servant-hearted love for His people. He's not physically here today to do this ... but guess who is?

His body. His Church. His plan A.

You.

So wherever you are, He wants you to complete what is lacking in Christ's sufferings right where you are. You're going to experience some things you don't want to. People are going to say some things about you that you don't want said. And you may not experience the widespread popularity or fame others may see, so what Jesus says to Peter in the next verses are perfect for you.

Peter knew that John, the disciple writing the gospel in which this story is found, was standing right there with them. "So Peter seeing him said to Jesus, 'Lord, and what about this man?' Jesus said to him, 'If I want him to remain until I come, what is that to you? You follow Me!'"[72]

In other words, "Don't worry about John or what I'm going to do in his life." And He is saying to you, "Don't worry about what I did in Dallas ... what is that to you? If I want someone else's experience to be different from yours, what is that to you? You follow Me with no conditions on what that looks like. Serve Me. Be faithful with what I have given you, and I will be faithful to reward you for your faithfulness, not because of your fame."

---

71   I get to make up at least one word when writing this book.
72   John 21:21–22.

Remember who Jesus is—the King of Kings who loves you and who will be with you to the *better* end.[73] Remember that you are a servant, unable to do anything apart from Him. You are a person desperately in need of God to do everything God wants to do with you, so don't compare what God is doing with you to what He is doing with someone else.

Don't set out to do something great for God; learn to depend on the God who has done something great for you.

Know that when you lie on your bed at night, you can marvel at the mystery and majesty of God because around your campfire, by His grace, you did everything that Christ wanted to do through you that day. Marvel at His kindness. Tell a story. Remember all He has done. Pray that He uses you again tomorrow. Sleep well.

Don't compare … surrender.

Finally (and please read this carefully): don't worry about what God's will is for your life. *Worry instead that you do with your life what is God's will.* In other words, don't worry about the will of God for *your life* … just concern yourself with the will of God.

Don't worry yourself trying to figure out God's will for your church … just concern yourself with God's will. Does He want your church to grow or to split? I don't know. Does He want you to have Sunday school or small groups? I don't know. Does He want you to do contemporary worship or to sing hymns? I don't know. What I do know is that whenever or however we gather as His body, He wants us to concern ourselves with the "one anothers" of

---

73   Jude 24–25.

Scripture as we depend on His Spirit to conform us,[74] His Word to transform us,[75] and His people to encourage us "until we all attain to the unity of the faith, and of the knowledge of the Son of God, to a mature man, to the measure of the stature which belongs to the fullness of Christ."[76]

Paul said it like this: "The things you have learned and received and heard and seen in me, practice these things."[77] If every member of your church read their Bibles, meditated on their Bibles, memorized their Bibles, counseled with their Bibles, shared their faith, confessed their sins, and pursued grace, truth, and community with other people the way *you do* in *your circle*, what kind of church would exist where you live?

The invitation is from Him. The perfect love is from Him. The power to build His Church is from Him. The strength to continue is from Him. The life you've always wanted is with Him.

Come and see … Go and be.

---

74 Romans 8:29.
75 Romans 12:2.
76 Ephesians 4:13.
77 Philippians 4:9.

Acknowledgments

It is of course impossible to mention all the people who have meant and provided so much for me, but it is appropriate to try to acknowledge some nonetheless. I should start by thanking Robert Wolgemuth and eventually Austin Wilson, who stayed after me to get busy and who ultimately introduced me to John Driver without whom the busyness of leading my life, family, and friends at Watermark would have kept me from keeping you busy reading this book. John's gifts, encouragement, and patient drive made this book a reality. Without his "with" there would be nothing to come and read. Additionally, the team at David C Cook took all the risk and provided this author encouragement as they labored to get this book to you. You wouldn't have it without them.

I should go all the way back to John Splinter, Jeff Coggan, Michelle LeCrone, Paul Fraser, and Scott Holley and the many other faithful followers of Christ who first invited a skinny, lonely high school kid to come and see this thing called Young Life, where I for the first time found out there was a living God who cared about me and who knew where the good stuff was. Who knew that kindness and faithfulness to a lost young man in the '70s would have led to a blessing for others four decades later, which it did.

I should thank the myriad of others along the way who were a part of God's kindness and constant grace in my life in the form of friendships, solid fellowship, and the constant fun without shame we have shared together. You know who you are and the Kamps, adventures, conversations, prayers, service, sharpening, and laughter that grace has provided through you to shape and define my life. I have been blessed with more than my share of lifelong friends ... if there has ever been evidence for grace in this world, you each are that to me.

As I said in earlier pages, I never desired to have anything to do with church because I had never seen it lived out in a way that even hinted at the beauty and relevance its Creator intended. That changed when a friend invited me to come and see people on mission at a place called Willow Creek. Bill Hybels, you and yours showed me that a church could be every bit as alive and life changing as any individual or parachurch effort could be. I sat in your lobby one day and wrote in a journal that I was willing and ready to dive into the adventure of being on mission with friends in my town if it could be a blessing to others the way I saw you being a blessing to Northwest Chicago and ultimately the uttermost parts of the earth. Well done, friends. Watermark and Willow could not be more different except for one thing: passion to let others come and see the goodness of the King through the faithfulness of His people, and that one thing is all that matters. Thank you.

A few years after that visit to Chicago, eight families in Dallas began to dream and pray together about what God may want for their city. Dozens joined us quickly, and then God's kindness raised up leaders in the persons of Kyle Thompson, Dean Macfarlan, Brett Johnston, Scott Coy, and eventually Beau Fournet who poured out their lives to join with me in making God's provision for the world tangible and accessible in our corner of the world. From the original eight families, to the dozen more core families, to the amazing staff, to the faithful members who serve with me on the battleship of the local church that I know and love … thank you. Because of you I have not written these pages hoping they could happen somewhere; I wrote them knowing it has by God's grace happened again in the Dallas–Fort Worth metroplex. May the uttermost parts of the earth increasingly be encouraged by Christ in you.

Most of all I am grateful for my sweet wife, Alex, and our kids, Ally/Conner, Kirby, Coop, Landry, Cade, and Camp, who love me, who pray for me, and who love laughing, serving, and seeking faithfulness and avoiding "atomic fireballs" with me. I love you all and love the way God has allowed us to serve together in a way that keeps you always loving the church as much as I do. My greatest joy is for others to come and see the relationships we have and the blessing that you are in my life, because we seek God's best together. This is the love of God, that we keep His commandments and His commandments are not burdensome.

At David C Cook, we equip the local church around
the corner and around the globe to make disciples.
Come see how we are working together—go to
www.davidccook.com. Thank you!